AF837291

Sport Realism

STUDIES IN PHILOSOPHY OF SPORT

Series editor: Shawn E. Klein, Arizona State University

The *Studies in Philosophy of Sport* series encourages scholars from all disciplines to inquire into the nature, importance, and qualities of sport and related activities. The series aims to encourage new voices and methods for the philosophic study of sport while also inspiring established scholars to consider new questions and approaches in this field.

The series encourages scholars new to the philosophy of sport to bring their expertise to this growing field. These new voices bring innovative methods and different questions to the standard issues in the philosophy of sport. Well-trodden topics in the literature will be reexamined with fresh takes and new questions and issues will be explored to advance the field beyond traditional positions.

Titles in Series

Sport Realism: A Law-Inspired Theory of Sport, by Aaron Harper
Surfing and the Philosophy of Sport, by Daniel Brennan
Golf as Meaningful Play: A Philosophical Guide, by W. Thomas Schmid
Defining Sport: Conceptions and Borderlines, edited by Shawn E. Klein

Sport Realism

A Law-Inspired Theory of Sport

Aaron Harper

LEXINGTON BOOKS
Lanham • Boulder • New York • London

Published by Lexington Books
An imprint of The Rowman & Littlefield Publishing Group, Inc.
4501 Forbes Boulevard, Suite 200, Lanham, Maryland 20706
www.rowman.com

86-90 Paul Street, London EC2A 4NE

Copyright © 2022 by The Rowman & Littlefield Publishing Group, Inc.

All rights reserved. No part of this book may be reproduced in any form or by any electronic or mechanical means, including information storage and retrieval systems, without written permission from the publisher, except by a reviewer who may quote passages in a review.

British Library Cataloguing in Publication Information Available

Library of Congress Cataloging-in-Publication Data

Library of Congress Cataloging-in-Publication DataNames: Harper, Aaron, 1982- author.
Title: Sport realism : a law-inspired theory of sport / Aaron Harper.
Description: Lanham, Maryland : Lexington Books, [2022] | Series: Studies in philosophy of sport | Includes bibliographical references. | Summary: "Aaron Harper defends a new theory of sport-sport realism-focusing on sport operations and the decisions made by sports officials like umpires and referees. Sport realism offers an explanation of sport as it is played, along with normative assessment of ethical issues in sport like cheating and rules disputes"-- Provided by publisher.
Identifiers: LCCN 2022026084 (print) | LCCN 2022026085 (ebook) | ISBN 9781666920086 (cloth) | ISBN 9781666920093 (epub)
Subjects: LCSH: Sports officiating. | Sports--Moral and ethical aspects.
Classification: LCC GV735 .H37 2022 (print) | LCC GV735 (ebook) | DDC 796--dc23/eng/20220708
LC record available at https://lccn.loc.gov/2022026084
LC ebook record available at https://lccn.loc.gov/2022026085

Contents

Acknowledgments

As it is for many sons, my relationship with my dad was defined through sports. We were always playing some sport or discussing a local team, and sports provided a common language for us to communicate. My dad was not prone to philosophize about sport, and he was utterly pragmatic in his conception of it. Nonetheless, through him I came to see the experiences, meanings, and relationships that emerge through sport, which surely inspired my own philosophical reflection on sport. Terry Harper passed away in 2020, around the time I was finishing the draft of the manuscript. This book is dedicated to his memory, and at root it probably reflects some of his pragmatist attitude.

I didn't initially set out to write a book, and the progression from idea to book has been lengthy, occasionally frustrating, and thoroughly rewarding. I cannot possibly mention all who supported this project, directly or indirectly, and to whom I am greatly indebted. I am grateful to Eric Schaaf, Krista Thomason, and Steve Criniti, all of whom offered deep and meaningful philosophical conversation on the matters discussed here. They also provided extensive feedback on numerous chapter drafts. I probably asked too much of them, and they always delivered. My basketball games with Eric (especially those with Ty and Chris) and tennis matches with Steve have made their way into the text. I received extensive feedback from an anonymous reviewer that greatly improved the project. Thanks also to Angela Rehbein and Sean Snyder for written comments and feedback. In particular, a question Angela asked me about marathon running led me to refocus some key parts of the book.

I first presented the ideas that would become this book at the 2015 Rockford University Sports Studies Symposium. I'm grateful to Shawn Klein for his insight and encouragement in the years since, without which this book would not exist. Many colleagues have been supportive of and interested in my work, even with most of them not being philosophers themselves. So thanks to Drew Banghart for organizing a forum to share some of this work with the West Liberty University College of Liberal Arts in 2021. Additionally, I received valuable feedback on Chapter 4 from audiences at the 2019 Great Lakes Philosophy Conference and the 2021 North American Society for Social Philosophy annual conference.

Finally, I want to thank Elaine and Marion. Without their love, complete support, and unending patience, I never could have finished this project.

Introduction

Game 6 of the 2019 World Series was a tight affair. Trea Turner came to bat in the seventh inning with his Washington Nationals leading the Houston Astros 3–2 and a runner on first base. Turner tapped the ball toward third base. Pitcher Brad Peacock fielded the ball and hurried a throw to first base. Turner and the ball arrived at the same time, and Turner ran into the glove of Astros first baseman Yuli Gurriel. The ball rolled away, allowing the Nationals' baserunners to advance. However, umpire Sam Holbrook immediately determined that Turner had interfered with Gurriel by running inside the baseline. Therefore, he called Turner out. The umpires discussed the play at length amongst themselves and in consultation with league officials in New York. Since interference is considered by rule a judgment call, umpires could not review it via replay. Following a lengthy delay, the original call of interference was upheld.

Turner ran inside the baseline all the way from home plate to first base, rather than running in the "runner's lane" that comprises the three feet to the right of the baseline. The runner's lane extends for forty-five feet, providing a space for the baserunner intended to prevent interference of this sort. At the moment Turner stretched for the base and the ball arrived, he was in fair territory. After the game, Major League Baseball's chief baseball officer Joe Torre supported the interference call:

> Well, he was called out because he ran, there's a 45-foot restraining line where you're supposed to run as a baserunner in between those lines. He ran to first base. That wasn't the call. The call was that he interfered with Gurriel trying to catch the ball—you notice the glove came off his hand. That's what Sam Holbrook called him out for basically interference.[1]

Meanwhile, Nationals' players, coaches, and fans were incensed at the ruling. Even some on the opposing team were confused. Astros' manager AJ Hinch saw the biggest mistake not with Turner but with his pitcher, commenting, "That one, I wish common sense prevails. Because I actually side with Turner on this one, that I didn't think he was getting in the way of anything. It was an errant throw."[2]

Making sense of the call and subsequent dispute is challenging for a number of reasons. Beyond being a judgment call by definition, the rules themselves require interpretation, such as understanding the nature of interference. And the rules put the baserunner in a difficult position. For Turner, a right-handed batter, the most direct route from the batter's box to first base is to remain in fair territory. The presence of the runner's lane requires him to divert into foul territory, even though the base itself is in fair territory. The baserunner's final stride must enter back into the area of the field that he is supposed to be avoiding at risk of committing interference. Rule 5.09(a)(11) allows that he may do so "in the immediate vicinity of first base for the sole purpose of touching first base."[3] This is no straightforward rule application. Rule changes might be appropriate to address these problems and other complications. Nonetheless, while such changes may be beneficial, they do not contribute to understanding the call made on the field at the time, or what the call ought to have been given the rules in place.

It turns out, fortunately for baseball officials, that the controversial interference call did not affect the outcome. The Nationals went on to win the game 7–2. Still, Michael Baumann of *The Ringer* encapsulates why the confusion was so important to players, writing, "More important than the way the rules are written is how the rules are enforced by umpires, and how their implementation is understood by players. Precedent of enforcement isn't as binding in baseball as common law in the real world, but it informs players' actions just the same."[4] Baumann's statement reminds us that those in the game are especially interested in what call will be made next. I think this perspective has been underappreciated in philosophy of sport, and I will argue for its centrality in conceptualizing sport. More generally, the Turner controversy provokes a number of deeper philosophical questions about sport. Why do some rules require strict enforcement, while others admit of variations or are applied only in certain situations? Is adjudication in sport analogous to the law? How are the rules interpreted? Is sport defined by its written rules, or are the unwritten rules and traditions part of the nature of sport? Can we explain how and why sports are played? And, finally, can we distinguish how a sport is played from how it ought to be played?

The aim of this book is to address these and similar questions by offering a new theory of sport. Theories of sport have been the focus of much philosophy of sport literature in recent years, with new takes on standard definitions and theories. These developments are laudable and thought-provoking, showing that theories can provide meaningful insight into the nature of sport and its moral features. However, I find that these other theories all admit of puzzles and limitations in how they conceive of the activities of sport. Simply put, I find that no current theory offers an entirely satisfactory explanation of the nature of sport or ways to resolve disputes that arise, such as that drawn from Trea Turner's interference. My new theory, which I call sport realism, reconsiders how sport is played and how its decisions are made, keeping in mind that those participating in sports are keenly interested in how disputes are and will be resolved.

JUDGES AND UMPIRES

Sport is often treated as a subset of games, which most scholars and players define in terms of the rules. After all, without rules a game cannot exist. Yet Turner's interference reveals a limitation to this basic definition. Difficult questions are not decided in sport by simply identifying the rules, since there are underlying concerns about the interpretation, application, and enforcement of rules. In sports it is common to have designated individuals like officials, referees, or umpires who are responsible for making these decisions. Of course, games may also have rules officials, and arguably some sports do not. But I think this common difference between sports and other kinds of games is significant for our understanding of sports as activities that people engage in. Common conceptions of sport might be inextricably tied to some idea of an official because the decisions and resolutions define the activity of sport just as much as the originating rules.

To develop a theory of sport from this perspective, I draw from comparable systems and institutions with more well-established theoretical approaches on rules and their adjudication. I am far from the first to make this connection, but I think the association between law and sport has much more to provide. In particular, I find it instructive to examine a surprising context in which the job of sport officials is often invoked—law courts. The baseball umpire has become a familiar analogue to an appellate court judge. Consider the following remarks by John Roberts at his 2005 Supreme Court confirmation hearing:

> Judges and Justices are servants of the law, not the other way around. Judges are like umpires. Umpires don't make the rules, they apply them. The role of an umpire and a judge is critical. They make sure everybody plays by the rules, but it is a limited role. Nobody ever went to a ball game to see the umpire . . . I will remember that it's my job to call balls and strikes, and not to pitch or bat.[5]

Appeals to umpiring have since become commonplace at Supreme Court confirmation hearings. A review of Sonia Sotomayor's confirmation hearing performed by Kristina Moore of *SCOTUSBlog* showed no less than eleven references to balls and strikes and sixteen to umpires in the senators' written statements and oral testimony.[6] Brett Kavanaugh invoked similar language to explain pithily his judicial philosophy: "A good judge must be an umpire, a neutral and impartial arbiter who favors no litigant or policy."[7] Roberts and Kavanaugh embrace the umpire analogy to highlight their understanding of rule application. At Sotomayor's hearing, various Senators took issue with the umpire analogy. Interestingly, they did not dispute what an umpire does, instead suggesting that judges are not like umpires, as when Sheldon Whitehouse stated, "I particularly reject the analogy of a judge to an 'umpire' who merely calls 'balls and strikes.' If judging were that mechanical, we would not need nine Supreme Court Justices."[8]

These characterizations of umpiring fail by offering a limited and likely inaccurate view of how umpires actually act. The standard example of calling a pitch describes a pitch as a strike if it is in the strike zone, and the umpire's call affirms this to be the case. This is not a representative call or decision that sport officials make. Officials are needed because some decisions are hard and require interpretation, discernment, or creativity. In his well-known 1930 book *The Bramble Bush*, legal scholar Karl Llewellyn employs the analogy between judges and umpires to show the humanity of the job. The umpire seeks to ensure that the rules are followed by both sides, but the job is in no way mechanical. The judge may be "partial to one side, or stubborn, or ignorant, or ill tempered."[9] These flaws remind us that the umpire, like the judge, is acting from an assortment of possible reasons and underlying factors.

Though umpires may be misunderstood, the repeated use of the analogy in law suggests an affinity between legal theory and philosophy of sport. In fact, it has long been common for philosophers of law to use sport examples to elucidate legal concepts or to support theoretical claims. H. L. A. Hart, perhaps the most important legal philosopher of the twentieth century, was a particular fan of the sport/law comparison, with one philosopher writing, "It is no exaggeration to say that Hart uses the example of umpired sport (cricket and baseball are his favorites) to illustrate and defend every important aspect of his legal positivist theory."[10] Hart is not alone in his references to sport, and one wonders what examples legal philosophers of the past century would have used without the expansion of sport as a cultural institution.

In the latter half of the twentieth century, philosophy of sport emerged as a discipline in its own right, and it turned the tables on philosophy of law. Legal theories have provided fertile ground as philosophers of all stripes seek theoretical tools and strategies to apply to sport. Similarities between law and sport are manifest; sometimes the rules of sports are even titled laws, as with the International Football Association Board.[11] Patrick Lenta and Simon Beck summarize a number of significant sport/law intersections: both are regulated by rules, including different types of rules that serve to penalize and define jurisdiction and goals, appointed authorities make final authoritative decisions regarding rule application, and each involves the possibility of error, bias, and corruption.[12] The topic continues to garner attention. Two of the most recent philosophical books on sport, by Alva Noë and David Papineau, identify additional similarities. Noë characterizes baseball as a "game of law" due to its focus on determining liability for what happens in a game.[13] Papineau finds that participants of sport and members of civil society have comparable obligations to political authority and the law.[14]

To the above list, I add that with sport and law many individuals question to what extent the rules constitute the institution. Each is comprised of written rules that admit of hard cases to adjudicate. In these hard cases, judges or other officials must do more than apply the rules in a straightforward manner, whether through interpretation, imagination, or some other means. Regardless, both law and sport are rule-governed activities that are, in practice, much more complicated than they first appear. No matter how many rules are written, new cases emerge that provide unexpected challenges to the system. Thus, studying these cases involves exploring the processes by which they are decided. Comparison to law has contributed much to the field of philosophy of sport, though I contend that this legal approach to sport has been most influential for developing broader theories of sport. The dominant philosophical theories of sport amongst philosophers routinely reference comparable legal theories. This includes theories supported by influential philosophers of sport over the last twenty years like John Russell, Robert Simon, Nicholas Dixon, and William Morgan.

I agree that drawing inspiration from legal theory in order to better understand sport is both appropriate and fruitful, and this idea motivates my account of sport in this book. To be clear, this does not mean that legal theories can or should be uncritically adopted or transplanted directly into sport. Russell is surely correct when he writes that the application of legal theories to sport will "fail as general accounts of sport and games as legal systems."[15] The causes of such failure can be summed up with a statement so obvious it may not even need to be said—law and sport are not the same thing. But with a long history of legal theories that aim to clarify the nature of law and guide adjudication in hard cases, philosophers of sport would be imprudent not to consider how advancements in legal theory might spark insights into the nature of sport.

THEORIES OF LAW AND SPORT

I propose to explore insights from legal theory in my development of sport realism. That legal theory is even comparable to theories of sports is a matter of recent historical development in law. Going back through the annals of Western thought, natural lawyers sought a foundation for law in universal moral truths. However, as classical natural law with its reliance on teleology became less influential in subsequent centuries, positive law—human laws created by sovereigns, legislatures, and courts—became the focus of legal studies.[16] Legal scholars today debate the degree to which law consists of and depends upon social facts. Legal positivists, beginning with John Austin in the nineteenth century, argue that the law can and must be studied as it is, independent from what we might think the law ought to be. This is not to say that moral questions have been excluded from legal studies, or that all legal standards derive authority from social criteria. Nevertheless, the law as studied today is effectively embodied in human institutions. On this we find legal discussion parallel to that within philosophy of sport. Values that emerge from and govern sport might prove universal in nature, but the rules by which we play come from no source beyond human beings. The study of both law and sport can be said to examine an organized form of human activity, with the rules, their interpretation, and their application providing a critical component.

Debates concerning legal rules dominated philosophy of law in the mid-twentieth century. On some legal positivist theories, the law was held to consist of rules, with continuing analysis of the kinds of rules in question. Yet others pushed back against legal positivism, arguing that the law must consist of elements beyond the rules. Popular candidates for such features included underlying values or guiding principles. Philosophers of sport began to develop theories of sport in the mid-to-late twentieth century, with some of the same concepts at the heart of the discipline. There we find an analogous debate about the nature of rules. Some hold that sport is exhausted by its rules, with much discussion about the different kinds of rules involved. Others argue that defining sport requires the inclusion of moral principles, unwritten rules, or other traditions that influence the way sport is played. In recent years, these features have been at the center of the philosophical conversation.

The Turner interference call provides a useful case study to differentiate these kinds of philosophical theories, but it also reveals some of their limitations. Those who argue that sports are fully constituted by their rules can point out existing rules sufficient to explain the interference call. The rules describe where the runner should and shouldn't be while running from the batter's box to first base. Although interference is technically a judgment call, this does not mean that the umpire needs to use broad discretion in reaching a decision. Traditionalists might appeal to the unwritten rules to argue that the baserunner won't (or can't) be in the runner's lane the entire time or even on many plays. Thus, the rules are not followed as written. That being said, it also widely accepted that when a runner is on the wrong side of the line and the play goes awry for the defense, the runner is typically the one penalized. A deeper problem for explanations that appeal to rules alone, or rules plus unwritten rules or conventions of sport, is that they may not have much perspective on what the rules or traditions of the sport ought to be. The normative standpoint appears limited.

Theories that locate underlying moral principles often put these in terms of the purpose or skills inherent to the sport. Sometimes this includes appeal to the spirit of the rules. This kind of theory could investigate why the rule is written as is. The underlying principle at work seems to be that fielders should be allowed to make the play to the greatest extent possible. In baseball, the runners move from base to base but do not play an active role in interrupting the defense. However, these claims about purpose and skill are contentious. For example, the runner also needs to be able to get to the base, requiring the runner and first baseman to occupy the same space, and baserunning is a skill of baseball. To resolve the dispute we may need to identify an overriding purpose or conception of excellence, and no clear procedure exists for doing so. Legal theories of this sort can appeal to foundational documents like a constitution, or central values like justice. On these matters sports diverge from legal systems and undercut the analogy between sport and law.

SPORT REALISM

These other theories of sport are all valuable in drawing our attention to important features of sport. Although I find the drawbacks of each, including those mentioned above, reveal that they are incomplete. The focus on the rules or conventions that configure sport limits any moral perspective. Conceiving of sport as structured by implied moral principles adds a normative component, but it may do so at risk of its more basic explanation. In particular, I will explore a conflict between the universality of these theories with the particular details of any specific sport in question. I am skeptical that any currently held theory provides a satisfactory way to bridge the gap. These and other concerns motivate my development of a new theory that better explains the practice of sport and provides resources for its ethical assessment.

I maintain that legal theory provides a useful resource, partly for the above similarities and history. Also, I think that attitudes toward law provide a useful corrective for sport. In general I worry that theories of sport tend to be overly moralized, turning all sport disputes into ethical issues when this may not be the best framework. For example, I will argue that this has happened in philosophical discussions of cheating. There are many instances in sport where I think decisions are a matter of preference or agreement among stakeholders, not moral theory. Also, many theories are overly romantic about sport, attributing selfless or idealistic motivations to situations that may not call for these. Philosophy of law allows us to differentiate legal disputes from moral disputes, recognizing distinct means of adjudication. The legality of an action is distinct from its morality. We see this most clearly when we view sport from the perspective of its participants, for whom questions of how decisions will be made might be more important than how they ought to be made.

Russell remarks that once philosophy of law is applied to the world of sport, there is no reason to stop with only a few instances. He writes, "We might think that there could be a critical legal studies, or a feminist, or maybe even an originalist, theory of law and adjudication in sport."[17] With these examples Russell means to slow the movement from law to sport by warning of the slippery slope ahead. I do not think Russell should be so worried; other theories might illuminate features of sport that have been downplayed or overlooked. To this end, I draw upon elements of American legal realism as I develop a theory I call sport realism. Legal realists hold that the law is found most clearly in the decisions made by legal officials, including judges, because these decisions comprise what the law really means to those individuals it applies to. By comparison, participants of sport look to decisions made by sport officials, broadly construed. Umpires and referees are obviously officials, but in practice a sport official is anyone who resolves disputes and metes out punishments or sanctions. League commissioners, managers, and even other players serve these roles. An adequate theory of sport must acknowledge that decisions made by these various figures define the sporting landscape.

The goal of sport realism is to explain sport as it is actually played in order to provide a more accurate account of sport as an activity. The nature of sport is not fully exhausted by the rules, principles, or traditions of a sport. Decisions made by sport officials are influenced by a wider array of factors and reasons, which the participants of sport anticipate or predict; they modify their actions in light of expected decisions and resolutions. Often patterns can be identified regarding what decision to expect in a given situation. I contend that my theory of sport realism has applicability to sports of all types, including amateur and informal sporting events that lack a traditional official such as a referee or umpire. The main objective of sport realism is to offer the best explanation of how sport is played, although this does not preclude ethical considerations. Sport realism is especially well-suited to analysis of good reasoning in sport, yet it also provides normative guidance for some sport dilemmas.

The attractiveness of sport realism is evident in analysis of Turner's interference. Commentary on the call from players, coaches, and media outlets emphasized confusion about the call when compared to similar situations experienced previously.[18] Turner himself asked, "What else do you do?" in expressing bewilderment at being called out for running in a straight line.[19] In sport, philosophical questions aren't abstract but are pursued for what they mean to those involved. For the participants of a sport, whether professional or pick-up game, there is something at stake. The sport is what will be called; actions will be modified based on expectations of decisions from sport officials. Accordingly, the sport realist explanation requires a deeper investigation into how such calls actually get made. From there, it has the ethical resources to assess possible improvements to both the rules and the officiating of this kind of situation.

CHAPTER SKETCH

To develop my theory of sport realism, I must put it into a broader theoretical context of philosophical accounts of sport. In the first chapter I explore other theories of sport, with particular focus on those inspired by legal theory. I begin with a discussion of formalism and conventionalism, which were the earliest ways that legal theory was applied to sport. Formalism defines sport in terms of its rules, while conventionalism does so in terms of its practices. I find neither approach adequate. Then I turn to the interpretivist theory that has become prominent in philosophy of sport. Interpretivism defines sport in terms of rules and principles, with the latter informed by a conception of sport. I investigate why interpretivism has been the most attractive and compelling theory of sport through its application to numerous real-life situations and philosophical issues in sport. The remainder of this chapter provides an overview of interpretivism in the current literature, including realist and anti-realist formulations. The chapter ends with a discussion of challenges to interpretivism, exploring modified versions of interpretivism that have emerged in recent years.

The second chapter comprises a critique of interpretivism. The chapter is organized around two particularly tricky cases—Michael Pineda's ejection and suspension for pine tar found on his neck in a 2014 Major League Baseball game and Tiger Woods' illegal drop and mistaken scorecard, without disqualification, at the 2013 Masters. Interpretivism claims to serve as the best explanation of sport while also offering normative guidance to sporting dilemmas. While I question both components, the chapter focuses on its explanatory claim. The most significant challenges I explore here pertain to the level at which an interpretation of sport must be provided. Interpretivism holds that hard cases must be adjudicated with reference to principles implied by one's interpretation of sport. However, there is a tension between interpretations made of sport in general and interpretations of a particular sport in a specific context. An interpretation that is too general will often prove unsatisfactory with limited offerings to the specific sport, while an interpretation that is more particular to the sport risks collapsing into conventionalism or relativism. I contend that this problem is evident in the work of many interpretivist defenders. I show that modifications of interpretivism likely give up too many core interpretivist commitments, yet also fail to provide adequate normative guidance given how they incorporate conventions. Finally, I argue that Morgan's revised conventionalism is an insufficient alternative theory, despite some resemblances to my position.

In the third chapter I offer my own theory, sport realism, which aims to best explain sport. I begin with an overview of legal realism to show where I draw from it to illuminate the nature of sport. I argue that a complete theory of sport must include as inputs the sport equivalent of non-legal reasons, like social consequences and pressures, which motivate and influence behavior. I develop a realist theory that is both functionalist and predictivist, capturing sport as it is played with its participants most focused on how dilemmas are likely to be adjudicated in the future. To do so, I broaden the notion of who constitutes an official or referee to include all who arbitrate and penalize actions. Next, I argue that sport realism provides a number of additional virtues that make it preferable to competing theories. Among these are the pursuit of reform and justice in sport and applicability to sports that lack institutional structure. Finally, I work through a number of case studies to demonstrate how sport realism applies in practice to explain and identify patterns in decision-making.

Cheating is a central concept in sport ethics, yet there is a surprising lack of agreement in the literature concerning what precisely constitutes cheating. Generally, cheating is thought to entail intentional rule-breaking aiming at some unfair advantage, but these components all prove elusive, such that some have advocated setting aside the concept of cheating in philosophical sport ethics. In response to these problems, my fourth chapter provides a sport realist account of cheating, illustrating that the theory can provide substantive philosophical or conceptual analysis. Cheating is a subset of dispute in sport. Its necessary features include it being a distinct kind of wrong, which pertains to rule-breaking, that warrants a sanction related to competitive balance. The particular features of cheating are defined in distinct ways in different sports, just as what constitutes a specific crime or legal liability (e.g., negligence) is evaluated differently across jurisdictions in terms of its definition or standards (e.g., subjective or objective test for negligence). Essentially, different sports are akin to different legal systems, so specific applications of cheating vary accordingly. Through this assessment of cheating, I show that its wrongness is not limited to moral evaluation. It might be that cheating is (usually) morally wrong as a form of promise-breaking or lack of respect, but there is another sense in which cheating can be wrong, comparable to legal wrongs.

I argue that the concept of cheating in sport includes some unintentional rule-violations. I conclude the chapter with an examination of strategic fouls, which some have argued are instances of cheating.

If sport realism identifies a kind of wrongness distinct from morality, one might wonder how it provides normative assessment. Moreover, sport realism might appear too relativist or conventionalist to do this work. In the fifth chapter I present two strategies of normative analysis that sport realism supports. The first is rooted in pragmatism. American legal realism emerged alongside pragmatism, and my position is similarly consistent with pragmatist ethics, especially with its interest in innovation and successful action. Second, legal realism has long emphasized practical wisdom as a virtue of the judge. The same should be true for sport officials. I draw on recent work in virtue ethics, particularly the field of virtue jurisprudence, and I explore its applications to sports officiating.

NOTES

1. R. J. Anderson, "World Series: What MLB Rulebook Says about Bizarre Interference Call Against Nationals' Trea Turner," *CBSSports.com*, October 30, 2019, https://www.cbssports.com/mlb/news/world-series-what-mlb-rulebook-says-about-bizarre-interference-call-against-nationals-trea-turner/.

2. Jeff Passan, "Houston Astros' AJ Hinch Sides with Washington Nationals' Trea Turner on Controversial Game 6 Call," *ESPN.com*, October 30, 2019, https://www.espn.com/mlb/story/_/id/27968971/houston-astros-aj-hinch-sides-washington-nationals-trea-turner-controversial-game-6-call.

3. Office of the Commissioner of Baseball, *Official Baseball Rules*, Major League Baseball 2019 Edition, https://content.mlb.com/documents/2/2/4/305750224/2019_Official_Baseball_Rules_FINAL_.pdf.

4. Michael Baumann, "The Trea Turner Interference Call Didn't Sway Game 6—but It Will Go Down As the Defining, Bewildering Image of the 2019 World Series," *The Ringer*, October 30, 2019, https://www.theringer.com/mlb-playoffs/2019/10/30/20939580/washington-nationals-houston-astros-world-series-trea-turner-interference-call.

5. Senate Committee on the Judiciary, *Confirmation Hearing on the Nomination of John G. Roberts, Jr. to be Chief Justice of the United States*, 109th Cong., 1st sess., 2005, 55–56 (statement of John G. Roberts, Nominee to be Chief Justice of the United States).

6. Kristina Moore, "Box Score: Calling 'Balls and Strikes' at Sotomayor's Confirmation Hearing," *SCOTUSBlog*, July 13, 2009, https://www.scotusblog.com/2009/07/box-score-calling-balls-and-strikes-at-sotomayors-confirmation-hearing/.

7. Senate Committee on the Judiciary, *Confirmation Hearing on the Nomination of Hon. Brett M. Kavanaugh to be an Associate Justice of the Supreme Court of the United States*, 115th Cong., 2nd sess., 2018, 110 (statement of Hon. Brett M.

Kavanaugh, Nominee to serve as an Associate Justice of the Supreme Court of the United States).

8. Senate Committee on the Judiciary, *Confirmation Hearing on the Nomination of Hon. Sonia Sotomayor to be an Associate Justice of the Supreme Court of the United States*, 111th Cong., 1st sess., 2009, 36 (statement of Hon. Sheldon Whitehouse, U.S. Senator from the state of Rhode Island).

9. Karl N. Llewellyn, *The Bramble Bush* (Oxford: Oxford University Press, [1930] 2008), 15.

10. J.S. Russell, "Limitations of the Sport-Law Comparison," *Journal of the Philosophy of Sport* 38, no. 2 (2011): 254.

11. Mitchell Berman makes the same point, with additional examples, in "Why Sport Illuminates Law (and Vice Versa)," *New York Law School Law Review* 63, no. 2 (2019): 237.

12. Patrick Lenta and Simon Beck, "A Sporting Dilemma and Its Jurisprudence," *Journal of the Philosophy of Sport* 33, no. 2 (2006): 125–126.

13. Alva Noë, *Infinite Baseball* (Oxford: Oxford University Press, 2019), 51.

14. David Papineau, *Knowing the Score* (New York: Basic Books, 2017), 58–62.

15. Russell, "Sport-Law," 255.

16. A teleological conception of nature is one that interprets the universe as having an inherent order, design, or goal. Natural law theorists often connect this to a conception of human nature and the identification of some human good or purpose to be achieved, in part, through the law.

17. Russell, "Sport-Law," 255.

18. For examples of responses from other players and members of the baseball community on Twitter, see Nick Schwartz, "World Series: MLB Players, Fans Rage Over Controversial Interference Call," *USA Today*, October 29, 2019, https://ftw.usatoday.com/2019/10/world-series-interference-call-reaction.

19. Passan, "AJ Hinch."

Chapter 1

Interpretivism

Eliud Kipchoge of Kenya holds the official world record in the marathon. In 2018 Kipchoge covered the 26.2 miles of the Berlin Marathon in 2:01:39. His time was an incredible one minute and eighteen seconds faster than the previous record time. Yet Kipchoge's world record time is not actually his fastest marathon. In 2019 Kipchoge broke the fabled two-hour marathon barrier with a time of 1:59:40 at the INEOS 1:59 Challenge. This event was designed to support the achievement of the sub-2:00 marathon. Organizers chose a six-mile stretch in Vienna, Austria, for being flat and near sea level. Kipchoge ran behind a rotating team of pacemakers who kept the correct pace for him and also blocked the wind. A cyclist rode alongside to provide his preferred drink, as needed. The day was chosen from within a specified period to have the best possible weather conditions. Kipchoge wore a prototype shoe that is now under an indefinite ban for providing an unfair advantage.[1] And he did not compete against any other runners in the event.[2]

Kipchoge's 1:59:40 is not recognized by World Athletics (formerly known as IAAF), the international governing body for track and field. Due to the atypical equipment and support, along with the lack of competition, World Athletics considered the INEOS 1:59 Challenge to be more of an exhibition rather than an official marathon. Others evaluate the run differently. For example, *Guinness World Records* credits Kipchoge with the world records of "fastest marathon distance (male)" and "first sub-2-hour marathon distance."[3] Moreover, there is a history of track and field events being organized for the purpose of breaking records. This history includes various attempts made at the four-minute mile, which is perhaps the athletic achievement most comparable to Kipchoge's effort. Roger Bannister had a 1953 attempt at the mile record, which resulted in a British record of 4:02.0, disqualified by the British Amateur Athletic Board on grounds that it wasn't a genuine competition.[4] His record-breaking 3:59.4 mile in 1954 had its own skeptics who contested its legitimacy. John Bale and P. David Howe describe the event as "a race only in name" that relied on pacemakers in an unconventional manner.[5] So the level of organization behind Kipchoge's sub-2:00 marathon was unprecedented, but from another perspective it might just show what is possible when resources are dedicated to the pursuit of a specific athletic accomplishment.

Running as fast as Kipchoge did is an impressive physical achievement under any conditions. Yet most seem to agree with the distinction accepted by World Athletics: Kipchoge ran a marathon distance but not a marathon. Determining whether Kipchoge's sub-2:00 should count as a record and what our attitude should be toward the INEOS 1:59 Challenge both require a definition of sport because the distinction between marathon and marathon distance is essentially philosophical in nature. We expect consistency and clarity in how these distinctions are made and justified. A theory of sport should help us define sport and shed light on the adjudication of disputes like this within sport. This is important not only for deciding past and present cases, but also for athletes making decisions about future endeavors. For instance, if we think of sport as merely a physical activity or event, then Kipchoge's run meets this elementary understanding. However, this does not match current practices, and few accept such a minimal conception of sport. Most definitions of sport entail reference to structure or organization in order to differentiate sport from just any physical movement. To assess Kipchoge's run, we must appeal to elements like the rules, purpose, traditions, or some other sense of the nature of the sport.

In later chapters I will develop and defend sport realism, a new theory of sport. The successes and limitations of other theories, including their influences from legal theory, provide the context for sport realism. Accordingly, in this chapter I explore some of the most influential theories in the philosophy of sport landscape. I begin with formalist and conventionalist theories. Then I spend the majority of the chapter working through interpretivist theories of sport. Interpretivism has become the dominant theory in philosophy of sport, with numerous types of it now recognized. Interpretivism advances definitions of sport beyond rules and traditions, resulting in a theory that aims to bring together explanatory and normative features in a compelling manner.

LAW AND SPORT

Formalism and Conventionalism

The philosophical study of sports as it exists today is greatly indebted to the work of Bernard Suits. According to Suits, games are created when a relatively straightforward goal must be achieved in an inefficient manner.[6] Sports may comprise a subset of games.[7] For instance, the aim of golf is to get a ball into a hole. This straightforward state of affairs is known as the pre-lusory goal. But in golf, maneuvering a ball into a hole must be done using only clubs and following numerous other rules and limitations, completed on a course that includes obstacles. So winning the game, also called the lusory goal, can only be attained through the game's terminology and legitimate actions. The rules that define winning, losing, and the permissible moves within the game are known as the activity's constitutive rules. Without these rules the sport would cease to exist as an activity with a clear structure. So in a world without the constitutive rules of golf, a person could still hit a small ball toward a hole, and perhaps one might do so as a form of play. But this activity would not count as golf, and there would be no way to win.

If Suits is right about the nature of sport, then rules are the critical feature around which any theory of sport should be organized. Many theories follow the Suitsian strategy to define sports in terms of their aims and constitutive rules. Formalism is the umbrella term for the view that sports can be defined completely in terms of these formal structures. Formalism captures the intuition that since sports and other games are invented by humans, they must consist entirely of the rules that govern them. These rules are perhaps the only concrete features of sport.

Formalism in sport parallels two distinct positions in the philosophy of law—legal positivism and legal formalism. Legal positivism is a claim about the nature of law, which holds that law is separate from morality or what the law ought to be. It opposes the idea that the law exists apart from the human creation of law. For many legal positivists, law amounts to nothing other than a system of rules. These rules include both rules that govern conduct and rules that determine how the laws themselves may be changed. Legal formalism, on the other hand, is a position on adjudication.[8] Legal formalists hold that the law is a gapless system of rules, meaning that judicial decisions should be made through the straightforward application of rules.[9] A judge decides a case by identifying the relevant rule and established facts, then determining the outcome through logical inference. Formalism as a theory of sport has more in common with legal positivism than legal formalism because the former attempts to capture the nature of law while the latter primarily addresses rule interpretation. There are philosophers of sport who defend the sport equivalent of legal formalism, claiming that officials are to directly apply the rules as written. However, my focus will be on formalism as a theory of sport, not as a philosophy of officiating.[10]

Critics of formalism argue that relying on formal structures or constitutive rules ignores crucial features that define sport. A competing view, known as conventionalism, defines sports in terms of their conventions or social practices.[11] In an early defense of conventionalism, Fred D'Agostino characterizes these practices as the "ethos" of a sport. He argues that the application of rules by officials and players often differs from the way the rules are written, as if they have agreed to ignore certain rules in some contexts. He offers the example of basketball fouls, where fouls are not always called by the letter of the law, and sometimes such rule violations are disregarded by players and referees. The fact that rules are ignored or interpreted differently at various points does no damage to the game itself, since neither team gains any advantage. Rather, D'Agostino insists that we must understand sports as an "unofficial *system* of conventions which determines how the official rules of the game will be applied in various concrete circumstances."[12] D'Agostino concludes from this that a sport is defined jointly by its formal rules and ethos. However, some have taken the implication of conventionalism to be that the formal features of a sport are secondary and not part of the basic definition, since ethos would seem to trump the rules in any specific case.[13]

CHALLENGES

Both formalism and conventionalism offer plausible accounts of the nature of sport based on some key feature of it. However, each has been challenged from numerous directions. Most scholars accept that a theory of sport needs to have explanatory power along with some normative component. That is, a theory should help us make decisions, resolve dilemmas, or otherwise address difficult issues in sport.[14] Yet both formalism and conventionalism face serious questions regarding their ability to provide adequate normative guidance. Formalists encounter this challenge in two dimensions. First, the formalist in sport may not have the resources to deal with difficult cases without relying on an interpretation of the rules that goes beyond what is written. Robert Simon, Cesar Torres, and Peter Hager argue that many such cases are related to sportsmanship.[15] Consider an incident at the 2006 Olympics in Torino. Canadian cross-country skier Sara Renner had her ski pole snap in the middle of a relay. Norwegian coach Bjornar Hakensmoen gave one of his ski poles to Renner. The Canadians ended up finishing second in the race, while the Norwegians finished fourth and missed the medal stand. The question here goes beyond mere conformity to the rules, giving the formalist little say about whether Hakensmoen's action was allowable or appropriate.

Formalism encounters a second normative issue in that its analysis begins only once the rules are established. The formalist defines a game in terms of its constitutive rules but takes no perspective on the rules themselves. For instance, golf's 2010 PGA Championship was hosted at Whistling Straits, which employed a unique local rule. The course has over one thousand sand areas, which for the purposes of the PGA Championship were considered bunkers. Dustin Johnson grounded his club on the 18th hole, as he assumed his ball had settled into a waste area rather than a bunker. The resulting two stroke penalty knocked him out of the playoff. Although the rule was posted in the locker room, many players and officials criticized the local rule for being unfair or impracticable given the challenge of determining which areas of trampled-down dirt were considered bunkers. Formalism seems to have no clear resources for evaluating this local rule, and it offers no direction concerning a possible rule change.

The unique rule at Whistling Straits also highlights that formalism typically requires institutional structure. Some governing body is needed to create and change the rules of sport. Many formalists, including Suits, believe that institutions are an essential component of sport. Institutions include formal associations and administrative bodies. They work toward the codification of rules and establishment of norms, imposing organization and regulatory patterns on previously informal activities.[16] Such a requirement limits the field of study, since many physical activities that appear to be sports lack organization or institutions of this sort, including pick-up basketball at the local gym or individual sports like mountaineering. Law might seem similarly institutional in that we associate laws with various regulatory institutions, although exceptions might be made to this framework.[17] For current purposes, the problem is that institutions do not resolve the question of normativity. Institutions may explain how rule changes are made or offer their own criteria, but they do not provide the formalist with sufficient resources for analyzing whether proposed rule changes are good or bad in a moral sense.[18]

Conventionalism defines sports in terms of how they are played in practice, not through the written rules alone. But it has a parallel difficulty in evaluating what ought to be done. The "hack-a-Shaq" strategy in the National Basketball Association (NBA) provides one such example. Some teams choose to foul poor free throw shooters in order to disrupt the opposing offense, or to motivate the opponent to remove a key player from the game. Some have criticized this strategy on grounds that it makes the game of basketball unenjoyable and virtually unwatchable. In recent years, various rule changes have been made in order to reduce opportunities to intentionally foul poor free throw shooters throughout the game. However, the conventionalist describes only the current practices of the sport, which does not appear to make room for an evaluation of the wider appropriateness of the "hack-a-Shaq" strategy, including whether it should be adopted in other leagues.

The conventionalist can provide normative evaluation through internal criticism. Bogdan Ciomaga proposes that a critic "could argue that the community has drifted away from its original values and needs to return to its roots."[19] I agree that this normative strategy is available to the conventionalist, but only to limited effectiveness. Internal criticism as Ciomaga outlines depends entirely on the originating conditions of the activity. If these initial values are themselves flawed, internal criticism will be ineffective, or even harmful. Additionally, the strategy of internal criticism is available to any theory of sport, so it offers no unique reason to prefer conventionalism. The theory itself does not offer compelling resources for any further critique or moral assessment.[20]

Normative issues for both formalism and conventionalism leap out as their greatest challenge, although we also have reason to wonder if either offers a satisfactory explanation of sport. A successful theory explains sport by providing an accurate description that makes sense of the activity. I argue that a theory's explanatory power also entails that it should be reasonably predictive concerning future developments, responses, and interpretations. That is, explaining sport entails understanding how possible circumstances are likely to be dealt with, or how problems will be addressed. Both formalism and conventionalism encounter limitations in explaining or predicting various kinds of situations. To put it most simply, the emergence of these two opposing views reveals the flaw in the other. If formalists hold that sport consists solely of rules, then those who break the rules seem to not be playing the game at all. This conclusion is unpalatable.[21] Additionally, it is evident that the rulebook does not always explicate a decision or interpretation. We routinely accept that an understanding of sport requires a conception of the spirit of the rules and a look at how they are applied in practice. Meanwhile, conventionalists have difficulty placing the significance of the rules in the first place. We often find rules that are applied even when the result seems unfair, with the explanation that the official had no other option. Moreover, an appeal to conventions cannot simply ignore the rules, since they are clearly an essential component to understanding sport.

An example reinforces the difficulties that each theory encounters. In a 1984 Major League Baseball game between the Oakland A's and the Minnesota Twins, the Minneapolis Metrodome became the story. Oakland slugger Dave Kingman hit a ball that never came down. Instead, his fourth inning popup went through an eight-inch drainage hole and became stuck in the roof. After discussion, the umpires awarded Kingman a ground-rule double for his feat.

The problem for the formalist is that no rule covered the situation; no rule directly addressed the matter of the ball becoming stuck in the roof.[22] Given no applicable rule, the formalist encounters two unsatisfactory options: the umpire could make no ruling because there is no rule to follow, or the umpire could use discretion to make some other ruling. In a case of discretion, formalism offers no explanation or guidance about the decision being made. While the case might seem a rare failure of the rules, upon reflection we find that analogous cases are relatively common.[23] In sporting events in which there are multiple referees or umpires, the officials often come together to discuss questionable plays. This suggests that a fair number of rulings either go beyond the written rules or require interpretation of the rules when situations are not exactly those prescribed by the rules. Thus, the applicability of formalism is limited in the real world.

The conventionalist faces a different set of difficulties in considering Kingman's "double." The conventionalist leaves our evaluation of the situation to social conventions. If Kingman's is the first to get lost in the roof, there are no conventions available for reference. At best, one could seek analogies to ground rules at other stadiums, but few would seem to involve awarding hits to routine fly balls. And while convention suggests an appeal to common practices and attitudes, the umpire has no clear means to discern these. Should umpires consult with each team? Or make a tentative ruling while waiting to see how teams respond? The problem goes deeper for innovation, which must be ruled out as untraditional, and therefore out of bounds. Ultimately, the conventionalist captures something about the spirit of the activity, but divorcing sport from the written rules appears impractical for any particular contest.

INTERPRETIVISM

John Russell offers a more attractive answer in the case of Kingman's fly ball. In sports like baseball the job of adjudication primarily falls to its officials. While some situations involve straightforward application of the rules, many cases require tact to achieve what appears to be the right outcome. In this case, Oakland manager Steve Boros described the ruling as "common sense."[24] However, it seems the decision was made through consideration of the spirit of the rules and the integrity of the game. Kingman cannot reasonably be called out for hitting the ball in play with no out recorded on the field. While interference rules do allow the umpires to make judgment calls, the stadium is not itself a cause of interference. Also, it would be unfair to make Kingman replay the at bat after hitting a ball into fair territory. In this case, the ground-rule double ruling fit best with how the game is played. Following Russell, we might conclude that the umpire's action, despite applying discretion beyond the rulebook, was an appropriate means to preserve the "good conduct and integrity of the game."[25]

The theory of sport that Russell introduced, in which an official or other individual must act based on an understanding of the rules and the spirit of the game, has become known as interpretivism. According to interpretivism, sports should be defined through both the written rules and a conception of what the sport is fundamentally about. By determining the essential aims of the activity, we are in better position to identify what the rules are intended to do. The interpretivist understands sport as organized around a goal and the means of attaining this goal. Distinct excellences are displayed through activities characteristic of that sport, such as the constitutive skills or capacities that comprise the means of goal attainment. These non-moral components of the sport undergird its normative outlook. Therefore, interpretivism entails that those involved in any particular sport should seek to cultivate, promote, and maintain its constitutive skills, related capacities, and distinct excellences.

Interpretivism has quickly changed the landscape of the philosophy of sport through its comprehensive nature and apparent success in practice. Against formalism and conventionalism, interpretivism presents a more compelling account of sporting principles that are essential to the sport itself.[26] It balances the concerns of other theories because, in the words of Cesar Torres, it "maintains that sport presupposes principles that are neither rules nor conventions, without which it is not fully coherent and intelligible."[27] It both characterizes the nature of sport and provides normative guidance to those who must interpret the rules. In recent years interpretivism has been used to address matters such as doping, FIFA's ban on playing soccer at high altitudes, intentional rules violations and strategic fouling, coaching style, and competition in youth sports.[28]

The success of interpretivism as a theory of sport is evident in two instructive applications. First, interpretivism offers a theory of officiating, describing how officials act from an external perspective but also guiding officials themselves. Mitchell Berman explores the interpretivist implications for sports officiating through a puzzle of strict rule adherence. Namely, some sports, like golf, include rule-adherence as a form of excellence, while other sports, like baseball, have a long history of accepting deception and trickery as legitimate forms of gamesmanship. At first glance, golf may seem best explained in formalist terms, given the well-known importance that the golf community places on strict adherence to promulgated rules. Nevertheless, Berman demonstrates that the few exceptions to literal rule adherence in golf serve to strengthen the interpretivist's overall case.[29]

One such rule exception involved dropping a ball at a safe distance from an alligator despite the overarching golf rule to play the ball as it lies. For Berman, the interpretation employed by a rules official to allow the drop away from an alligator makes sense when we consider our more general interpretation of golf. According to Berman, golf

> is designed to hone and test certain athletic excellences related to the ability to propel a small ball at great distance and with accuracy by the swing of a club. But it also embodies certain nonathletic excellences, in particular the willingness to subordinate one's tangible interests to the demands of authoritative—if arbitrary—rules.[30]

On this view, strict adherence to the rules is simply one excellence of golf, but this must be interpreted along with the central aim of golf as a test of certain athletic skills. Thus, even in golf, strict adherence to the rules does not take precedence over all other considerations. The formalist conception of sport cannot make sense of this rules exception since the action would seem to require a penalty—the ball was not played as it lay. On the other side, conventionalism does not adequately capture the importance that golf places on rule adherence. So golf officials appear to be formalist, but their interpretations of the rules are, in fact, non-formalist in nature.

Beyond the realm of officiating, Torres and Hager demonstrate the application of interpretivism in sport organization and championship systems. To determine the best interpretation of a sport, Torres and Hager utilize Alasdair MacIntyre's account of social practice as socially established, cooperative activity, through which goods internal to the activity are achieved. A sport's constitutive skills comprise its defining features because "in attempting to achieve excellence within a sport, individuals and teams must diligently hone and master those skills that make their sport a unique activity."[31] Constitutive skills are essential to the nature and function of sport, so they should be central to the evaluation and identification of athletic excellence and superiority. Yet most sports today use playoffs or tournaments to decide championships, which are often motivated by entertainment and economic values. Torres and Hager argue that playoffs and tournaments threaten to undermine "both the structural goal of sport and its internal goods of excellence" by disregarding the central features of the sport or by emphasizing skills peripheral to it.[32] In playoffs, the game changes to create more excitement, but through interpretivist eyes Torres and Hager see this as giving up what the sport is fundamentally about. Consequently, they maintain that the regular season, essentially a season-long tournament, is the most appropriate means for identifying a champion.

Interpretivism offers compelling answers to these problematic cases because it is both comprehensive and flexible. It gives significance to the written rules, but it also develops broad principles that provide further context to these rules. In Russell's initial article, he articulates the "internal principle," which seeks to foster and maintain the excellences embodied in achieving the lusory goal of the game.[33] He denotes other principles connected to competitive balance, fair play, and good conduct. Berman proposes a principle called the "athletic principle," which advocates, *ceteris paribus*, a competitive athletic contest.[34] Many of these interpretivist principles are general or abstract in that they apply broadly across sports, even though their application to any particular sport should be grounded in the specific excellences or skills tested therein. And some emphasize principles specific to a sport and its particular context, as with Berman's analysis of rulism in golf. All the while, interpretivism remains neutral toward other metaphysical issues in sport, allowing it to be consistent with a variety of philosophical approaches to sport.

LEGAL AND PHILOSOPHICAL FOUNDATIONS OF INTERPRETIVISM

Interpretivism has emerged as the most prominent philosophical theory of sport, seeming to accomplish two feats. First, it offers coherent and intelligible explanations in cases like those described above. Second, as a normative theory, it makes specific demands on those involved in sport, such as the umpires in the case of Kingman's fly ball. We can better understand interpretivism by exploring its parallels to the philosophy of law, especially its roots in Ronald Dworkin's legal theory.[35] Dworkin developed his theory of law as a response to both to legal positivism and legal formalism. Legal positivists hold that law is distinct from morality, with law existing as a social fact and human enactment. In the mid-twentieth century, legal positivism was modernized through the work of H. L. A. Hart, who held that the law is purely a system of rules. A legal system includes rules that people must follow (primary rules) along with rules that identify rules and specify their alteration and adjudication (secondary rules).

Hart's legal positivist theory does not entail legal formalism because he finds that not all rules can be applied in a straightforward manner. Some judicial decisions amount to hard cases where the outcome is not clearly dictated by statute or precedent. On Hart's view, hard cases arise due to indeterminacy or vagueness of a rule which prevent its straightforward application. In support, he offers the well-known example of a legal prohibition on vehicles in a park. Such a ban obviously applies to cars, but a skateboard or riding lawn mower is a more difficult instance to adjudicate. Cases of this sort emerge because legal rules have a core of settled meaning surrounded by a penumbra of uncertainty. That is, a legal rule applies clearly to some cases, but not so easily to those around the edges. With the park rule, the ban on cars is settled meaning, but the penumbra extends to other means of transportation that may or may not be included in ban. Hart believes a judge must use discretion in these cases.

Dworkin rejects the idea that judges rely on discretion, at least in the sense of discretion meaning unguided or unbounded decisions, and he denies the positivist view that the law is a system of rules. He advocates for a wider conception of law through a reassessment of hard cases. He presents *Riggs v. Palmer* as a representative case.[36] In *Riggs v. Palmer* a New York court was tasked with deciding whether an heir could inherit from his grandfather's will. While the man was named in the will, he had in fact murdered his grandfather. The court acknowledged that the rules regarding the will and inheritance were clear, and no rules addressed the circumstances of this case. The relevant statute simply directed inheritance to be given upon death according to its terms, so following the rules should lead the inheritance to be given to the heir. However, the court declined to give the inheritance, with appeal to a more fundamental maxim of common law. It held that "no one shall be permitted to profit by his own fraud, or to take advantage of his own wrong, or to found any claim upon his own iniquity, or to acquire property by his own crime."[37] In other words, the court set aside the rule on the basis of a more basic principle of fairness denying profit through means of fraud or wrong.

Dworkin sees hard cases as those in which the judge may need to look beyond the letter of the law to find a resolution. In *Riggs* and similar cases, this requires appeal to principles.[38] So Dworkin contends that the law is not a system of rules but an amalgamation of promulgated rules plus principles. While rules are spelled out, principles are typically unwritten and implied. Rules have an all-or-nothing application. Dworkin presents the rules of baseball as an example. A rule states that a batter is out if he has had three strikes. In contrast, principles are not all-or-nothing and do not necessitate particular decisions. Rather principles have weight and can apply to a case without determining it. Their relative weight also means that principles can be overridden or outweighed by other principles. Examples of proposed Dworkinian baseball principles include generosity toward other players and applying the rules evenly to all players.[39]

Since principles are not promulgated in the same manner as rules, the judge must decide when and where principles apply. Where some worry that this leads to an untenable degree of judicial discretion, Dworkin tries to avoid the problem by defining the role of the judge as fundamentally an interpretive endeavor. The judge must interpret the law in order to decide any hard case. By interpretation, Dworkin means that the judge articulates a coherent vision of the law, taking the rules and principles in light of their history and precedent. In developing such a conception of the law, the judge aims to interpret with integrity, which "instructs judges to identify legal rights and duties, so far as possible, on the assumption that they were all created by a single author—the community personified—expressing a coherent conception of justice and fairness."[40] The integrity of law provides the framework through which the judge identifies and applies relevant principles in hard cases.

Dworkin's notion of interpretive judging offers a clear alternative to formalist adjudication. He presents additional analogies to clarify the role of integrity and respond to worries of discretion. He imagines the ideal judge, Hercules, who exemplifies what the best judges aspire to be. Hercules approaches hard cases by first creating a theory, or interpretation, of the law.

He aims for an interpretation that best justifies the Constitution and the particular set of rules involved in the case. Hercules' interpretation also takes into account the society's past political decisions. This process of interpretation requires Hercules to develop a conception of the principles that underlie common law. He then applies these principles, rooted in his interpretation of the law, to the case at hand.[41] Elsewhere, Dworkin employs an analogy of adjudication to writing a chain novel.[42] Imagine a group of people writing a novel one chapter at a time. One person writes the first chapter, then sends it to another to write the next chapter, and so on. Each novelist has the dual tasks of interpreting and creating because each must read the preceding sections in order to determine what the novel is about, the motivations of its characters, and the like. Dworkin contends that judicial hard cases are similar. A judge must read through what other judges have written in order to reach an opinion about what they have collectively done. The new case before the judge is part of this enterprise that has these other structures, conventions, and practices as its history. Perhaps unlike the chain novel, the law may have foundational documents to serve as reference points. The judge's job is to advance the enterprise, not to strike out in some new direction. She must consider which theme is most important as a whole, then decide the case on these grounds. An interpretation of legal practice must both fit that practice and show its point or value, making choices about what is part of the interpretation.

Interpretivists in sport similarly define their activity as a combination of principles and rules. Just as Dworkin sought to refute formalist adjudication in law, Russell targeted the "vice of legal formalism" in sport adjudication in his article "Are Rules All an Umpire Has to Work With?"[43] While Dworkin employed legal cases in support of his view, Russell considers tricky cases from the history of baseball. Perhaps the most effective example Russell uses for support is among the most famous disputes in baseball history—the 1983 "Pine Tar Incident" in which George Brett of the Kansas City Royals hit a go-ahead home run in the ninth inning against the New York Yankees. Yankees manager Billy Martin challenged that Brett had used an illegal bat. Upon investigation, umpires determined that Brett's bat was covered in pine tar beyond the eighteen inches allowable in baseball rules. They decided that the bat was illegal, resulting in an illegally batted ball and nullification of the home run. Eventually, American League president Lee MacPhail reinstated the home run. While the bat was illegal, Brett gained no advantage from having pine tar that far up the bat. The rule was introduced as a cost-saving effort to avoid the need to replace baseballs covered in pine tar. With this history in mind, MacPhail ruled that the game should be decided on the field, not by a technicality. Therefore, he determined that allowing the home run was more consistent with the spirit of the game and the broader intent of the rules.

Building from such cases Russell argues that the best explanation of a sport includes principles beyond its promulgated rules, implying that baseball umpires require a similar approach to Dworkin's judges. Adjudication of sport by officials relies on an interpretation that aims to "generate a coherent and principled account of the point and purposes that underlie the game."[44] From this Dworkinian principle, Russell develops his aforementioned internal principle and further specifies its application.[45] According to this internal principle, integrity is found broadly in the excellences of the sport, and the practice of sport should maintain and foster these.[46] He considers this internal principle to be fundamental because, at root, a game requires the achievement of a goal through the development of certain excellences, including bodily skills, that are permitted by the rules. As with Dworkin, Russell's account of integrity includes an important backward-looking element. While the principles of a sport are not determined entirely by its practice, the best practices of a sport cannot be completely divorced from its past. The best account of any particular sport presumably will use history as precedent in order to tell the most complete and coherent story possible.

TYPES OF INTERPRETIVISM

Broadening Interpretivism

Russell's work laid the foundation for interpretivism, but, as is evident in the applications described earlier, it has evolved into diverse perspectives. Robert Simon is most responsible for making interpretivism into the dominant approach in philosophy of sport.[47] Simon sought an account of sport that explained its relationship to morality and value. Simon defends internalism, which is the view that "sport has a significant degree of autonomy from the wider society and supports, stands for, or expresses a set of values of its own which may run counter to the values dominant in the culture."[48] Simon rejects formalism as too narrow a version of internalism, instead advocating what he calls "broad internalism" that goes beyond the written rules.[49] He identifies varieties of broad internalism, including those rooted in social contracts and the interests of the game. Nonetheless, Simon considers the Dworkinian appeal to principles (which he terms "interpretive broad internalism") to be the most fundamental, since it shows how the best interpretation of a sport must presuppose certain principles or theories.

Simon's analysis of interpretivism as a form of broad internalism expanded the idea beyond baseball and umpires, transforming it into a comprehensive framework with distinct explanatory and normative components. Interpretivism is an explanatory theory because it offers an account of the nature and function of sport. Whether we understand this in terms of principles, excellences, or constitutive skills, developing a conception of any sport requires an investigation into its basic logic, purposes, and essential activities as they have developed over time. Ultimately, the sport should be given an interpretation or explanation that best makes sense of these and in terms of its central purpose and elements.[50] This interpretation then grounds normativity by providing a means of evaluating and adjudicating dilemmas that emerge within the sport, both in terms of its practice and management. In this capacity, it makes specific demands on those involved in sport.

Realism

In the past twenty years interpretivism has been further developed and sub-divided by various scholars, and it now admits of both moral realist and anti-realist formulations. Most of the leading proponents of interpretivism defend realist theories, although the nature of this realism is itself disputed. The common bond among realist interpretivists is that they are all committed to moral realism, in some form, which accepts the genuine existence of objective moral principles. Simon and Nicholas Dixon conceive of realism in terms of rational discourse theory. Dixon defines realism as "the belief that principles about the nature and purpose of sport . . . , supplemented where applicable with other factors such as general moral principles and the pertinent rules, dictate the best answer to moral and non-moral debates about sport."[51] This means that we seek principles to be used for the appraisal or adjudication of sport debates, and these principles should be general or abstract in nature. That is, the principles should be independent of the beliefs of those in the relevant athletic community.

For both Simon and Dixon, the principles of sport are discovered and justified through a process of rational dialogue. Their realism is a commitment to finding quality arguments for those principles that can be supported independently of any community's particular view. The underlying claim is that we have good reason to believe something is warranted or justified when a consensus is reached through rational agreement. Though we might worry the consensus is only among the participants, Simon insists,

> The more the consensus survives criticism, the broader and more diverse the viewpoints that have contributed to discussion, and the more defensible the values, principles, and forms of arguments have proved in other contexts . . . the more the discussants are entitled to have confidence in the intellectual merit of their views.[52]

Rational consensus must survive extended criticism from very different perspectives over a long period of time, and the rational dialogue is open to everyone, not just members of the community.[53] Simon and Dixon share the notion that rational dialogue about sport principles must begin in a particular social and historical context. However, they aim at universal principles that provide independent reasons or a reflective standard for means of evaluation and critique.[54]

Simon illustrates realist interpretivism with an example from basketball.[55] Two referees may have different conceptions of how much physical contact should be allowed in a basketball game, but they may agree that certain types of behavior are clearly prohibited on grounds that they would destroy the game. The realist presumes that a deeper disagreement between conceptions of the sport can be overcome through rational discussion. Perhaps a resolution is reached that all find agreeable. Or, at minimum, each side could abandon some value in order to reach a compromise. Simon and Dixon believe we should pursue a conception of sport through rational discourse, even though they accept that we may not, in fact, converge on one. They claim no privileged access to the truth. For Dixon, this realization should emphasize "the need for carefully constructed arguments" even when opposing positions also find convincing support.[56] After all, debates and interpretations of sport usually rely on the assumption that the relevant principles are supported by arguments with independent force.[57] Dialogue should lead toward increasingly defensible views of sport, even though convergence or universal validity are not guaranteed.

Russell finds the justificatory realism of discourse ethics too coherentist in nature. He defends an alternative conception of realist interpretivism that entails robust metaphysical and naturalist commitments. He advocates moral realism as a form of nonreductive ethical naturalism, in which moral facts supervene on other properties. That is, moral terms such as good, fair, or right refer to natural facts, including real properties, events, relations, or states of affairs.[58] Russell acknowledges that this kind of moral realism might initially seem an odd fit for sport, given that sports are human inventions, but he contends that invented activities still admit of moral facts. All sorts of human activities are invented, even as we consider their underlying principles to be discoverable and universal.

For sport, these principles "incorporate approximately true descriptions of facts about games."[59] Russell contends that his aforementioned internal principle of sport is precisely one such case. Russell finds another such principle in consent, which he calls the "external principle," that distinguishes participants from nonparticipants. In doing so, it regulates the conditions for game entry and exit. William Morgan elucidates how Russell's principles are built from Suits' conceptual account of sport.[60] The internal principle, discussed previously with the Pine Tar Incident, is rooted in the idea that each sport has a "clear underlying purpose" or conception.[61] The external principle derives from the voluntary nature of sport, regulating entrance into and exit from the game. Among other arguments, Russell defends his view with the claim that realist judgments underlie the moral discourse of sports. Arguments in sport typically appear as if they are referring to basic natural facts, such as arguing that a certain action was good or right.[62] He believes we should accept that justification would derive from these facts rather than satisfying certain justificatory conditions of a discursive community. He agrees with Simon and Dixon that discussion plays a role in moral inquiry, but on his account it amounts to a method of tracking the truth, which he compares to Rawls' idea of reflective equilibrium. A back-and-forth between theoretical commitments and considered judgments should lead to principles that approximate true descriptions of moral facts about sport.[63]

Aretism

The versions of interpretivism defended by Dixon, Simon, and Russell are not the only realist forms available. We saw earlier that Torres and Hager's work on tournaments utilizes MacIntyre's conception of a social practice to argue that constitutive skills are internal goods of the activity. Elsewhere, Torres picks up on this idea to argue that there are other intrinsic properties of sports related to their internal goods, such as an aesthetic dimension that cannot be separated from its moral component. He argues that since the best explanation of a sport includes an articulation of its intrinsic features, moral values and demands emerge from a conception that sport's integrity and are "intimately intertwined with aesthetics."[64] Quite plausibly, the aesthetic nature of sport takes its principles away from legal adjudication into a new moral-aesthetic framework of evaluation.

Many interpretivist works include some notion of virtue. The above use of MacIntyre highlights this connection, since MacIntyre's work has proven influential for many virtue ethicists. Moreover, Russell describes integrity, in sport and law, as a virtue.[65] To envision how a moral realist interpretivism might be put in terms of virtue ethics, we can consider the position that M. Andrew Holowchak and Heather Reid call Aretism.[66] While Holowchak and Reid do not identify their work as a version of interpretivism, their aims and methods are consistent with it. Their identification of virtues, values, and principles based on an interpretation of sport seems to fit within the interpretivist framework.[67] They develop their Aretic model of sport through an interpretation of the history of sport going back to the ancient world. The Greek origin of the term athlete indicates both contending for a prize but also enduring or suffering. Ancient sports emphasized the beauty, pleasure, and unity afforded by sport, whereas modern sport has become very competitive, individualistic, and commercialized.

Holowchak and Reid present their model of sport as a form of virtue ethics analogous to Aristotle's identification of the mean with vice in either direction. For instance, modern sport is too agonistic, which they term "panagonistic," with its win at all costs attitude. Yet sport cannot take place if competitors are indifferent to victory. Accordingly, the Aretic model identifies appropriate agonism in allowing that athletes pursue victory so long as they recognize the excellence is itself the primary achievement of sport. The Aretic model of sport makes normative demands on contemporary competitive sport. Holowchak and Reid identify these normative principles in conjunction with different levels at which the athlete is committed to excellence. Athletes can engage in competitive sport in a way consistent with global values like justice, societal values like respect, or a personal commitment to excellence and autonomy. Holowchak and Reid contend that these three aspects of excellence—global, social, personal—distinguish Aretism from other normative views.[68] Yet in making this claim they reveal the wide open landscape for other virtue-oriented forms of interpretivism, which may locate other interpretations or excellences in sport that ground a specific conception of virtue.

Anti-Realism

Anti-realist forms of interpretivism are relatively few in number, so the terrain has been little explored. Moral anti-realism is the view that moral principles cannot be validated from any external perspective. The requisite interpretations of sport are context-dependent and not tied to deeper values, reasons, or facts. In "Moral Antirealism, Internalism, and Sport," Morgan presents a form of anti-realist interpretivism with a different conception of rationality than that defended by Dixon and Simon. Morgan contends that all rational and normative judgments are historically qualified and socially dependent.[69] Conceptions of sport must depend on their historical and social context; no impersonal or objective reasons can be located to serve as the basis for rational inquiry. Since interpretivism aims at developing the best philosophical conceptions of sport, Morgan concludes that these must be "historically and socially freighted conceptions of sport," rather than realist interpretations that are more general or abstract in nature.[70]

Anti-realist interpretivism results in substantially different conceptions of sport that may be incommensurable across historical and social contexts. Morgan provides an example of two conceptions of sport he takes to be incommensurable in this way. In early twentieth century international sport, an amateur-gentleman conception of sport was in opposition to a conception of sport as primarily professional in nature. Each conception of sport emerged from a conventional understanding of athletic conduct, defined by its history and social context. Morgan allows that adherents to each conception of sport could understand the opposing view. However, understanding the other does not entail that the two views can rationally resolve their disagreement or find reason to agree on a shared conception of sport.[71] Nonetheless, that we must remain within our discursive framework need not result in a paralyzing relativism, since today few cultures and contexts are radically alien from each other. Although when we locate cultural agreement, Morgan suggests that we recognize it as providing the origin and boundary of moral investigation, within which arguments are appropriate means for pursuing justification.[72] Anti-realists retain the ability to give reasons and make persuasive arguments regarding excellence, albeit from within the practice of a particular sport. In fact, these reasons may aid deliberation because the goods of the community can inform and guide deliberation to make it more effective.[73]

In his 2004 article, Morgan described his view as in concert with the broad aims of interpretivism. He argued that interpretivism, or broad internalism, fared better than formalist or conventionalist views of sport.[74] In subsequent works, he has developed his position further and characterized his considered view as a form of conventionalism rather than interpretivism.[75] I will explore his conventionalist theory in Chapter 2. However, anti-realist interpretivism is not limited to Morgan's position. For instance, Francisco Javier López Frías locates the possibility of a hermeneutic anti-realist interpretivism. This kind of hermeneutics, with clearest expression in the work of Hans-Georg Gadamer, does not constitute an autonomous method or mechanical procedure. Instead, it aims to understand a text by reconstructing it from an interpreter's particular situation. The implication of this hermeneutic approach is that there is no best, or even relatively better, interpretation to be discovered. The goal is to understand the text "differently through time."[76] In the realm of sport, this hermeneutics points us to the subjective and intersubjective values and reasons that motivate individual responses and social practices. An interpretation of sport has no goal or criteria for guidance, since interpretation itself is a never-ending process.

ADDRESSING CHALLENGES TO INTERPRETIVISM

Fidelity to Rules

In this last section, I will explore the development of interpretivism through some proposed modifications made in response to criticism. Patrick Lenta and Simon Beck present one such critique concerning the nature of rules. They consider a dilemma in cricket in which the umpire must determine whether to call the batsman out. The umpire is sure that the batsman is out either by the "out Leg Before Wicket" rule or "out Caught" rule. However, the rules of cricket demand certainty and specification of the out, and the umpire cannot be sure which of the two is correct, since he is not certain whether the batsman hit the ball before he was struck in the leg. In this scenario, it seems the batsman should be out, though without certainty on the specific out, the rules appear to require the umpire to give the benefit of the doubt to the batsman.

Lenta and Beck demonstrate a Dworkinian response. In *Riggs v. Palmer* the court found a tacit exception to the law. In the cricket dilemma, the umpire might make an analogous move to "interpret the rules as tacitly incorporating the principle that if an umpire is certain that a batsman has transgressed one or other of the laws under which they would be out then they must be given out."[77] However, this principle would be inconsistent with the cricket rule that demands certainty regarding the specific out. A Dworkinian resolution thus requires an additional appeal or rule to reconcile the current rules with the relevant principle that transgressors should be given out.[78] Lenta and Beck believe that an additional rule should be included in the rulebook. But in the absence of a promulgated rule, the worry is that interpretivism requires the invention and insertion of a new rule.[79]

Ultimately, Lenta and Beck acknowledge that interpretivism can be employed by officials to resolve dilemmas, but they highlight costs of interpretivism that may be too steep to incur when compared to other theories of adjudication, such as those inspired by legal positivism. If interpretivism requires the invention of new rules, it might seem inconsistent with the judicial obligation of fidelity to the rules. In response, Russell contends that judges and umpires often must clarify the rules; a more faithful appeal to the written rules may not always fare better in terms of efficiency or predictability.[80] He agrees, nonetheless, that judicial and sport interpretation should be done with caution. This discussion leads Russell to clarify the nature of his realism and the source of our philosophical conceptions of sports between law and sport. Nonetheless, an interpretivist willing to accept that umpire intervention is needed, or that fidelity to rules isn't always possible, likely will not find this legal positivist challenge compelling.

Conventionalism

The conventionalist challenge to interpretivism has proven more difficult to dismiss. Conventionalists argue that the conventions, culture, or ethos of a sport contain the conditions of its evaluation. While conventionalism predates interpretivism as a theory of sport, it has gained new life in recent years as a response to perceived interpretivist flaws. Interpretivists attempt to develop a conception of sport sensitive to history and culture, but these apply to practices themselves situated in cultural contexts. Conventionalists conclude that interpretivist conceptions of sport operate at too abstract a level.[81] Instead, the social practices of sporting communities, and not principles, must be accounted for in a theory of sport.

Two recent essays aim to address the challenge by modifying interpretivism to include conventionalist elements.[82] Scott Kretchmar identifies six models of sport that attempt to capture different ways sport is encountered, played, and valued. These conceptions of sport include emphases on key elements like contest, aesthetics, knowledge, and meaning. The description of these six models are derived from personal and cultural experience, admitting of various permutations and combinations. However, Kretchmar argues that these models are not purely the result of history and culture. He connects each model to some scientifically grounded conception of human nature. The elements of human nature upon which these models of sport are built provide some constraint on our interpretations of sport, with the result that there is no indefinite number of models.[83] Accordingly, Kretchmar's interpretivism has a realist character.

Kretchmar's interpretivism, which he terms pluralistic internalism, accepts a much wider range of principles than other versions of interpretivism. Each model of sport resembles the principles other interpretivists identify in sport because they entail implications for individual behavior and sport structure. For example, what he calls the serendipitous model of sport treats sport primarily as a form of play. It advocates a relaxed attitude toward the rules with less pressure on winning, and it uses these as guiding principles in addressing issues that arise within sport. However, Kretchmar contends that other interpretivists typically draw their principles from what he calls the achievement model of sport, which emphasizes excellence and skill. In doing so, they wrongly privilege this ideal over other legitimate conceptions of sport.[84] His pluralist internalism moves toward conventionalism by embracing cultural influence and variation on sport. It is consistent with conventionalism "by identifying at least soft, non-metaphysical criteria for adjudicating different culturally influenced versions of sport."[85] Yet, against conventionalism, Kretchmar maintains that broad elements of human nature, represented in his models, provide the ultimate standards in sport, not the cultural consensus central to most forms of conventionalism.

Adam Berg goes further than Kretchmar by proposing a synthesis of interpretivism with conventionalism. Berg accepts that defining and defending particular conceptions of excellence comprise a central challenge to both conventionalism and interpretivism. Berg notes that the creators of a sport cannot appeal to any particular account of integrity or excellence, since the invention of a sport necessarily predates its tradition. Moreover, while a sport may be invented in order to support certain ideals, these are likely to transform through practice. He finds that "specific instantiations of athletic 'excellence' in sports are to a significant extent the consequence of a given sporting community's unwritten and perhaps even unspoken underlying agreements."[86] For support, Berg describes the transformation of basketball in Mormon and Navajo cultures. The Mormons primarily saw basketball as a means of moral and religious education, while the Navajo emphasized creativity, individualism, and entertainment. These are both legitimate interpretations of basketball, but the skills and excellences celebrated in each are not explained by the integrity of the sport or its essential features.

Berg contends that the normative force of specific instantiations of athletic excellence is best explained by the sporting community rather than some notion of integrity. Interpretivism actually depends on convention and culture to give specific content to the abstract concept of athletic excellence, with the result that any sport is likely to have multiple morally acceptable practices.[87] To assuage fears of relativism, Berg stresses that the interpretive appeal to excellence is not the only normative standard available in sports. Other, external principles remain to provide general obligations or parameters that constrain any sport ethos that strays too far.

We may wonder, at this point, how amenable Berg's modifications are to most interpretivists. In seeking to bolster interpretivism as the best explanation of sport, the significance he affords to conventionalism risks undermining the normative force of the theory. On many issues, it must now defer to conventions and culture. Furthermore, we must ask to whom Berg's conventionalism is most useful. Interpretivism is supposed to be applicable to officials, participants, and other sports organizers to help describe and understand the principles that underlie their sport. If this amounts to an investigation of the current conventions or ethos, then Berg's interpretivism may be less able to adjudicate hard cases with conflicting cultural norms. Ultimately, these alternative versions remind us of the twin challenges interpretivism aims to meet, of both explaining sport and providing normative guidance. To maintain a sound explanatory and predictive theory in light of conventionalist critiques, interpretivism may require modifications that actually diminish its normative effectiveness.

CONCLUSION

Interpretivism emerged first in the legal philosophy of Ronald Dworkin, but philosophers of sport have developed it in new and fruitful directions. Interpretivism in sport is the view that the nature of sport consists of both the written rules and implied principles. The identification of these principles requires an interpretation, taking note of features like the goals, skills, and excellences of sport. Interpretivism aims to satisfy both the descriptive and normative needs for a theory of sport. Its descriptive success is often evaluated in contrast to formalist and conventionalist positions. Analysis of Kipchoge's sub-2:00 run in Vienna shows how interpretivism compares favorably. Formalism, defining sport in terms of the rules or formal features of sport, can accept that the INEOS 1:59 Challenge differs from marathons sanctioned by World Athletics. By rule, it is evident that Kipchoge did not set an official world record in the event. Conventionalism supports a similar conclusion by looking to the tradition or ethos that surrounds marathons. Road races are expected to be run in ordinary settings without arranging ideal conditions. Some of the advantages organized for Kipchoge, including the pacemakers, shoes, and other support, violate traditional norms.

Formalism and conventionalism both support the conclusion that the INEOS 1:59 Challenge was not part of the sport of marathon. However, when compared to interpretivism, their explanations appear superficial. They offer no real insight about why certain runs count officially and others do not. And they do not provide means of evaluating whether current rules or conventions ought to be in place. While those theories emphasize only one feature of the sport, interpretivists show how the written and unwritten features of sport come together to more fully capture the nature of sport. Once principles of sport are identified, they can be used to offer normative guidance and to resolve debates within sport. Sport officials, governing bodies, philosophers, and even fans can interpret sport and draw conclusions regarding good, right, and appropriate actions in sport. The interpretivist likely reaches a similar conclusion about Kipchoge, but rooted in a conception of the sport. The spirit of the marathon is that an individual has to overcome the obstacles running 26.2 miles largely on one's own in natural conditions. Ideal conditions and advanced equipment undermine the basic test the race presents any runner.

This interpretivist answer appears compelling at first glance. Yet upon reflection the interpretivist position becomes more puzzling. As noted previously, there are competing definitions of excellence in the marathon, with some people inclined to count the 1:59:40. The purpose of the event seems similar to the purpose of any other road race, albeit with more focus on a specific goal time. And many races allow for the use of some strategies similar to those afforded to Kipchoge, including pacemakers, flat terrain, improved equipment, and scheduled times when the weather is expected to be accommodating. Determining precisely when a race crosses a line from official to unofficial appears, at times, arbitrary. Interpretivists need a conception of sport to ground these, but they face pressure from two directions. Successful interpretations must be broad enough to ground normative assessment while remaining specific enough to truly be an interpretation of the sport involved. In the next chapter I will pick up on these threads, although I will pursue them in underexplored directions. I will identify some situations in which interpretivism does not provide the best explanation of sport. Furthermore, I will argue that some cases pose greater trouble for interpretivist methodology, which I contend results in an inextricable dilemma. Accordingly, I will argue that interpretivism falls short in both its explanatory and normative aims.

NOTES

1. Dan Roan, "Nike Vaporfly Shoes are Not Banned but Kipchoge's Are," *BBC.com*, January 31, 2020, https://www.bbc.com/sport/athletics/51324991.

2. Paul Bisceglio offers a nice summary of the arrangements in "The Greatest, Fakest World Record," *The Atlantic*, October 13, 2019, https://www.theatlantic.com/health/archive/2019/10/kipchoges-sub-two-hour-marathon-how-legitimate-it/599974/.

3. Guinness World Records, "Eliud Kipchoge," *GuinnessWorldRecords.com*, accessed November 28, 2021, https://www.guinnessworldrecords.com/records/hall-of-fame/eliud-kipchoge-fastest-marathon-distance-male.

4. Bannister's run at Motspur Park on June 27, 1953 was a secretive affair with two other runners who served as pacemakers, neither of whom completed the race. Neal Bascomb provides a detailed account of the race and its aftermath in *The Perfect Mile* (Boston: Houghton Mifflin, 2004), 130–135, 139.

5. John Bale and P. David Howe, "Introduction: The Sporting Barrier: Historical and Cultural Interpretations of the Four-Minute Mile," in *The Four-Minute Mile*, ed. John Bale and P. David Howe (London: Routledge, 2008), 2. Bale offers discussion of the criticisms in "How Much of a Hero? The Fractured Image of Roger Bannister," in *The Four-Minute Mile*, ed. John Bale and P. David Howe (London: Routledge, 2008), 50–54.

6. Bernard Suits, "The Elements of Sport," in *The Philosophy of Sport: A Collection of Essays*, ed. Robert Osterhoudt (Springfield, IL: Charles C. Thomas, 1973) and *The Grasshopper: Games, Life and Utopia* (Peterborough, Ontario: Broadview Press, 2005).

7. Suits, in "The Elements of Sport," defends the view that all sports are effectively games, although not all games are sports. He offers four features of sports that differentiate them from games. Sports require skills, which must be physical skills, have a wide following, and are stable, which includes the development of institutions. I discuss the institutional structure of sport in the next section and again in Chapter 3.

8. When referring to legal formalism, I will always use the full name. Any subsequent references to "formalism" indicate the theory of sport.

9. Suri Ratnapala provides a clear and accessible overview of the relationship between legal formalism and legal positivism in *Jurisprudence*, 2nd ed. (Cambridge: Cambridge University Press, 2013), 104–106.

10. A view that either the nature of sport or law consists of nothing other than the rules does not necessarily entail a formalist approach to adjudication by other

judges or sport officials. However, a certain logic connects the two positions. If the activity is exhausted by a system of rules, one can understand how ideal adjudication might consist of simple, direct application of the rules. Thus, proponents of formalist adjudication in sport argue that these are comprised of a body of rules, and the job of officials is to apply the appropriate rule. For more on legal positivism and legal formalism in relation to formalism in sport, see Mitchell N. Berman, "On Interpretivism and Formalism in Sports Officiating: From General to Particular Jurisprudence," *Journal of the Philosophy of Sport* 38, no. 2 (2011): 179–180.

11. Unlike formalism, traditional conventionalism in sport is not closely related to any particular legal theory. While legal conventionalism is an approach to the nature of law, its focus has been with grounding obligations and authority. Until recently, conventionalists in sport made no direct use of legal conventionalism, as far as I am aware. In 2012, William Morgan published an article defending a position he calls deep conventionalism, which draws upon legal conventionalist work by Andrei Marmor. But Morgan's latest book differentiates his conventionalist theory from deep conventionalism. I will discuss Morgan's conventionalism both later in this chapter and throughout Chapter 2.

12. Fred D'Agostino, "The Ethos of Games," *Journal of the Philosophy of Sport* 8, no. 1 (1981): 14.

13. Examples include William J. Morgan, "The Logical Incompatibility Thesis and Rules: A Reconsideration of Formalism as an Account of Games," *Journal of the Philosophy of Sport* 14, no. 1 (1987): 13 and Robert L. Simon, "Internalism and Internal Values in Sport," *Journal of the Philosophy of Sport* 27, no. 1 (2000): 4–5.

14. For instance, Robert Simon, Cesar Torres, and Peter Hager argue that theories of sport have three functions: distinguishing sport from other activities, explaining the features of sport that make it of interest to people, and explaining the value of sport. The latter entails that a successful theory should provide resources for moral evaluation of sport and the ethical issues that arise within it. *Fair Play: The Ethics of Sport*, 4th ed. (Boulder, CO: Westview Press, 2015), 23–24. For another representative example, see Sinclair MacRae, "Toward a Shallow Interpretivist Model of Sport," *Journal of the Philosophy of Sport* 44, no. 3 (2017): 285.

15. Simon, Torres, and Hager, *Fair Play*, 29.

16. Klaus V. Meier, "Triad Trickery: Playing with Sports and Games," *Journal of the Philosophy of Sport* 15, no. 1 (1988): 15.

17. For instance, H. L. A. Hart allows that a legal system could exist without a legislature, courts, or officials, which he believes is the case in many "primitive communities." Hart, *The Concept of Law*, 3rd ed. (Oxford: Oxford University Press, 2012), 91. However, people in these communities must treat its standard behaviors like rules of obligation.

18. Others have made a similar argument against formalism, including Morgan, "Logical Incompatibility Thesis," 17–18; Simon, "Internalism," 3–4; and Simon, Torres, and Hager, *Fair Play*, 29–30.

19. Bogdan Ciomaga, "Conventionalism Revisited," *Sport, Ethics and Philosophy* 6, no. 4 (2012): 419.

20. At the end of this chapter I explore two recent attempts to incorporate conventions into other theories of sport. I return to Ciomaga's position in Chapter 2.

21. For further discussion see Craig K. Lehman, "Can Cheaters Play the Game?," *Journal of the Philosophy of Sport* 8, no. 1 (1981) and Morgan, "Logical Incompatibility Thesis."

22. The use of "rule" here includes controlling precedents that provide clear rules and principles. Of course, the notion of precedent in sport may not have the same weight given different institutions and the relatively short history of most sports when compared to constitutional law.

23. John Russell makes a similar argument against formalism, and he offers additional examples intended to show that interpretation is often required in rule application. Russell, "Are Rules All an Umpire Has to Work With?," *Journal of the Philosophy of Sport* 26, no. 1 (1999). I discuss Russell's view in detail throughout Chapters 1 and 2, beginning in the next section.

24. Carrie Muskat, "Dave Kingman Proved What Goes Up Does Not Necessarily . . . ," *United Press International*, May 5, 1984, http://www.upi.com/Archives/1984/05/05/Dave-Kingman-proved-what-goes-up-does-not-necessarily/4771452577600/.

25. Russell, "Umpire," 28.

26. Robert Simon and Nicholas Dixon elucidate a number of significant challenges that formalism and conventionalism face. See Simon, "Internalism" and Dixon, "Canadian Figure Skaters, French Judges, and Realism in Sport," *Journal of the Philosophy of Sport* 30, no. 2 (2003).

27. Cesar R. Torres, "Furthering Interpretivism's Integrity: Bringing Together Ethics and Aesthetics," *Journal of the Philosophy of Sport* 39, no. 2 (2012): 299.

28. On these applications, see, respectively, Carwyn Jones, "Doping in Cycling: Realism, Antirealism and Ethical Deliberation," *Journal of the Philosophy of Sport* 37, no. 1 (2010); Cesar R. Torres, "What Is Wrong with Playing High?," *Journal of the Philosophy of Sport* 36, no. 1 (2009); Warren P. Fraleigh, "Intentional Rules Violation—One More Time," *Journal of the Philosophy of Sport* 30, no. 2 (2003); Robert L. Simon, "The Ethical Coach: An Interpretive Account of the Ethics of Coaching," in *The Ethics of Coaching Sports*, ed. Robert L. Simon (Boulder, CO: Westview Press, 2013); and Cesar R. Torres and Peter F. Hager, "Competition, Ethics, and Coaching Youth," in *The Ethics of Coaching Sports*, ed. Robert L. Simon (Boulder, CO: Westview Press, 2013). Simon, Torres, and Hager offer a wide-ranging approach to sport through an interpretive lens in *Fair Play*, and they address many of the above issues.

29. Berman, "Interpretivism and Formalism," 185–190.

30. Ibid., 189.

31. Cesar R. Torres and Peter F. Hager, "The Desirability of the Season Long Tournament: A Response to Finn," *Journal of the Philosophy of Sport* 38, no. 1 (2011): 41–42.

32. Ibid., 47.

33. Russell, "Umpire," 35.

34. Berman, "Interpretivism and Formalism," 177.

35. Not all interpretivist philosophers engage with philosophy of law. But Russell's 1999 article "Are Rules All an Umpire Has to Work With?" and Simon's 2000 article

"Internalism and Internal Values of Sport," generally taken to be the foundational works of sport interpretivism, both engage with and draw inspiration from Dworkin's philosophy of law.

36. This is in "The Model of Rules," which was first published in 1967 and later included in Ronald Dworkin, *Taking Rights Seriously* (Cambridge, MA: Harvard University Press, 1977).

37. *Riggs v. Palmer*, 115 N.Y. 506, 22 N.E. 188, 511 (1889).

38. In "The Model of Rules" Dworkin utilizes *Henningsen v. Bloomfield Motors, Inc.* as another representative case to motivate his view.

39. William D. Blake, "Pine Tar and the Infield Fly Rule: An Umpire's Perspective on the Hart-Dworkin Jurisprudential Debate," in *The Cooperstown Symposium on Baseball and American Culture: 2013–2014*, ed. William J. Simons (Jefferson City, NC: McFarland, 2015), 250.

40. Ronald Dworkin, *Law's Empire* (Cambridge, MA: Harvard University Press, 1986), 225.

41. See Dworkin, *Taking Rights Seriously*, Chapter 4 "Hard Cases" and Dworkin, *Law's Empire*, Chapter 7 "Integrity in Law."

42. Ronald Dworkin, *A Matter of Principle* (Cambridge, MA: Harvard University Press, 1985), Chapter 6 "How Law Is Like Literature."

43. Russell, "Umpire," 31.

44. Ibid., 35.

45. Russell even suggests that Dworkin's notion of integrity may apply more easily in sport than it does in law, in "Broad Internalism and the Moral Foundations of Sport," in *Ethics in Sport*, 2nd ed., ed. William J. Morgan (Champaign, IL: Human Kinetics, 2007), 56.

46. Russell later amends the internal principle to refer to the practice of the game rather than just the interpretation of the rules. This amendment makes clearer that the internal principle has philosophical use and should be of general interest, not limited to umpires, officials, or other adjudicators of sport rules. Russell, "Moral Realism in Sport," *Journal of the Philosophy of Sport* 31, no. 2 (2004): 146.

47. Torres writes, "Sport philosophers engaged in interpretive efforts inspired by Dworkin's work on the philosophy of law, as well as Russell's and Simon's applications of such work to sport, have generally been regarded as working within the tenets of interpretivism." Torres, "Interpretivism's Integrity," 301.

48. Simon, "Internalism," 2.

49. While Simon suggests that the values of sport are distinct from those of the larger society, Russell argues in "Broad Internalism and the Moral Foundations of Sport" that the notion that sporting values are uniquely their own is a bold claim that likely goes too far. While internalism could imply this separation, Russell demonstrates that it also fits with the view that sporting values are consistent with those found outside sport. Sport may provide unique context and application, but the internal morality of sport expresses familiar values that are found in other institutions.

50. Torres, "Interpretivism's Integrity," 301.

51. Dixon, "Realism in Sport," 110.

52. Robert L. Simon, "From Ethnocentrism to Realism: Can Discourse Ethics Bridge the Gap?," *Journal of the Philosophy of Sport* 31, no. 2 (2004), 135.

53. Morgan explores in more detail Simon's and Dixon's reasons for opening rational dialogue to all comers, in opposition to his own view that such discussions are most successful when conducted amongst those within a particular practice community. *Sport and Moral Conflict* (Philadelphia: Temple University Press, 2020), 97–98.

54. Francisco Javier López Frías recognizes similarities in this kind of realist approach to principled hermeneutics. This hermeneutical approach holds that rules or criteria guide the interpretive process toward the goal of completely understanding the target. Thus, in a debate about sport, rational agreement is possible if all members presuppose the same discursive framework. López Frías, "Broad Internalism and Interpretation: A Plurality of Interpretivism Approaches," in *Defining Sport*, ed. Shawn E. Klein (Lanham, MD: Lexington Books, 2016), 31.

55. Simon, "Ethnocentrism," 136.

56. Dixon, "Realism in Sport," 113.

57. Ibid., 112.

58. Russell, "Moral Realism," 144.

59. Ibid., 146.

60. Morgan, *Moral Conflict*, 65–69.

61. J.S. Russell, "Limitations of the Sport-Law Comparison," *Journal of the Philosophy of Sport* 38, no. 2 (2011), 265. See also Russell, "Moral Realism," 146–147 and Russell, "Broad Internalism," 58–59.

62. Russell, "Moral Realism," 148–150.

63. Ibid., 155.

64. Torres, "Interpretivism's Integrity," 310.

65. Russell, "Broad Internalism," 56.

66. M. Andrew Holowchak and Heather L. Reid, *Aretism* (Lanham, MD: Lexington Books, 2011).

67. Dixon indicates the same for the Aretic principle that Holowchak defended in an earlier article in "Realism in Sport," 109. At the very least Aretism directs us to a nearby available interpretivist position.

68. Holowchak and Reid, *Aretism*, 178.

69. William J. Morgan, "Moral Antirealism, Internalism, and Sport," *Journal of the Philosophy of Sport* 31, no. 2 (2004): 170–172.

70. Ibid., 172.

71. William J. Morgan, "Broad Internalism, Deep Conventions, Moral Entrepreneurs, and Sport," *Journal of the Philosophy of Sport* 39, no. 1 (2012): 87–88 and Morgan, *Moral Conflict*, 106–109.

72. Morgan, "Moral Antirealism," 174–175.

73. Jones, "Doping in Cycling," 95–98.

74. Morgan, "Moral Antirealism," 180–181.

75. López Frías argues that Morgan's conventionalist position should be understood as a form of interpretivism, despite Morgan declining to recognize his later work in this way. López Frías, "Broad Internalism," 33–34.

76. Ibid., 33.

77. Patrick Lenta and Simon Beck, "A Sporting Dilemma and Its Jurisprudence," *Journal of the Philosophy of Sport* 33, no. 2 (2006): 135.

78. Ibid., 136.

79. Ibid., 136–137.

80. Russell, "Sport-Law," 266–267.

81. Morgan offers one such criticism of interpretivism. Morgan extends his account of rational inquiry in sport to show its emergence as a social practice is dependent upon historical contingencies. He rejects realist formulations of interpretivism on grounds that its principles are too abstract. See Morgan, "Broad Internalism," 66–70 and *Moral Conflict*, Chp. 3–4.

82. I offer critical analysis of these articles in Chapter 2.

83. Scott Kretchmar, "Pluralistic Internalism," *Journal of the Philosophy of Sport* 42, no. 1 (2015): 92.

84. Ibid., 93–94.

85. Ibid., 93.

86. Adam Berg, "The Ethos of Excellence," *Journal of the Philosophy of Sport* 42, no. 2 (2015): 242.

87. Ibid., 243.

Chapter 2

Hard Cases for Interpretivism

Interpretivism has become the dominant philosophical account of sport. It treats the rules as essential to sport, but it acknowledges that their application often requires interpretation within the context of the sport and the situation. Thus, it captures the intuitions many have concerning the significance of the rules of sport while also explaining cases in which deviation from the written rules seems appropriate. Interpretivists have done well to provide captivating cases showing how interpretivist strategies are employed by philosophers, and also where decisions from within sport by umpires, referees, and other officials reveal congruent reasoning. Above all, interpretivism makes a strong claim to be the most plausible theory of sport by linking its explanatory and normative elements. Its supporting examples, such as the George Brett pine tar incident, suggest that interpretivism helps us understand the nature of sport. Meanwhile, its account of interpretation provides a methodology for adjudicating dilemmas within a sporting community. As to its primary competitors, formalist theories rely too much on written rules to be realistic, and most conventionalist theories fail to give enough credence to the rules in describing how the game is played. Both approaches face difficulty in offering normative evaluation or guidance.

Despite the appeal and current influence of interpretivism, its dominance is not a foregone conclusion. Interpretivism ascended to prominence so rapidly due in part to the relatively clear limitations of competing theories. Most opposing accounts of sport have been unable to match both the explanatory and normative components of sport analysis.[1] Nonetheless, interpretivism demands further investigation into both components. Elsewhere, I have raised questions regarding the normative efficacy of interpretivism.[2] In this chapter, I will scrutinize its explanatory power. My primary interest for this chapter concerns the development of an interpretation of sport, which has been compared to a judge developing an interpretation of the law. Interpretations of sport face significant hurdles, above all a fundamental dilemma. An interpretation of sport has to address the specific features of the sport in question in conjunction with a broader normative stance. It must be sensitive to the practices of that sport while retaining a critical eye toward conventions. I will argue that walking this tightrope is effectively impossible; any interpretation is likely to satisfy one requirement while failing the other.

I cannot hope to investigate all instantiations of interpretivism, given the many versions of it along with the recent developments described in Chapter 1. I will analyze a position that I believe is amenable to most who characterize themselves as interpretivists and who build generally from the work of John Russell and Robert Simon. While much of the current literature has concerned the actions of umpires and other officials, a theory of sport must address all who adjudicate sporting dilemmas and issues—officials, official scorers, commissioners, players, and even fans. I will consider all such applications of it.

TWO HARD CASES

Two cases present important challenges for interpretivist analysis:

Foreign Substance on the Mound

On April 10, 2014, Michael Pineda pitched for the New York Yankees against the Boston Red Sox. During the game, television cameras spotted a brown mark on Pineda's pitching hand, which appeared to be pine tar. For that season, Major League Baseball Rule 8.02(b) stated that a pitcher shall not "have on his person, or in his possession, any foreign substance. For such infraction of this section the penalty shall be immediate ejection from the game. In addition, the pitcher shall be suspended automatically."[3] The Red Sox lodged no complaint, and Major League Baseball (MLB) took no action. Pineda faced the Red Sox at Fenway Park in Boston two weeks later. On a chilly night, Pineda gave up two runs in the first inning and felt that he could not get an adequate grip on the ball. In the second inning, the Red Sox noticed a brown spot in Pineda's neck that he went to before gripping the baseball. Red Sox manager John Farrell alerted home plate umpire Gerry Davis, who determined that the brown spot was pine tar. Davis ejected Pineda from the game, and MLB then suspended Pineda for 10 games.

Tiger's Drop

Tiger Woods was in contention on Friday at the 2013 Masters tournament. On the 15th hole, Woods hit a near-perfect third shot from the fairway, which looked on trajectory to settle near the hole for an easy birdie opportunity.

Luck was not in Woods' favor. The ball hit the flagstick and rolled into a water hazard. United States Golf Association (USGA) Rule 26–1a stated that in such cases a player who takes a drop must do so "as nearly as possible at the spot from which the original ball was last played."[4] The location of the previous shot was clearly identifiable by the divot it left. Woods played a drop about two yards behind the original shot, and after the round he explained that he did so because the area immediately around the divot was wet and muddy. He also indicated that by moving back two yards the distance better matched his preferred wedge play.

It became evident based on these post-round comments that Woods violated Rule 26–1a, so he should have been assessed a two stroke penalty. His scorecard did not reflect this penalty, meaning Woods signed an incorrect scorecard. Traditionally, the penalty for doing so has been disqualification from the tournament. However, a new interpretation of the rules gave the competition committee some flexibility. A revision to Rule 33, announced prior to the 2011 Masters, allowed the committee leeway to determine when a player should be disqualified. The rule reinterpretation was designed for cases in which the initial rule violation was not recognized until after the scorecard was signed. Following this revised rule, Woods was assessed a two stroke penalty but not disqualified from the tournament. Woods completed tournament and finished in fourth place, four shots behind Adam Scott and Angel Cabrera.

The Pineda incident may not even appear to be a hard case that requires interpretation. Pineda was caught obviously breaking a rule, and he was punished accordingly with ejection and suspension. The umpires and league officials did not need to appeal to any principles of sport to understand the rule, and the incident required no broader interpretation or philosophical conception of baseball. Simply put, the umpires and league officials saw Pineda's case as an isolated incident without controversy given his flagrant use of an illegal substance.

Players and coaches saw the incident in a different manner. Their reactions revealed a belief that Pineda's actions could only be understood in conjunction with his prior start against the Red Sox, in which television cameras caught Pineda with pine tar on his hand. The Red Sox elected not to make it an issue either during that game or afterward. Still, the problem went beyond Pineda being a repeat offender against them. The Red Sox bristled at the brazenness, or perhaps carelessness, with which Pineda used pine tar. Red Sox manager John Farrell explained, "I felt like it was necessary to say something. You know, I fully respect on a cold night you're trying to get a little bit of a grip. But when it's that obvious, something has got to be said."[5] For their part, the Yankees expressed regret over the situation. Yet again, their embarrassment concerned Pineda's audacious manner more than the action itself. General Manager Brian Cashman remarked, "We as a group are embarrassed because it takes place. Michael is embarrassed. I think we're embarrassed that somehow he took the field in a position with that like that."[6]

Players likewise offered nuanced reactions to Pineda's situation. Red Sox catcher A. J. Pierzynski explained that he has no problem with pitchers using substances on a cold night to better grip the ball, since he believes the pitcher losing grip would be more dangerous for the hitters. He acknowledged that "rules are rules," but his full answer included new strategies Pineda might try: "Put it on your hat, put it on your pants, your belt, put it on your glove—whatever you have to do. No one has an issue with him doing it. It's just more of a fact that it's so blatant."[7] We find similar analysis in the media. In a representative article from the *Boston Globe*, Christopher Gasper contended that the incident was mostly about "stupidity" and disregard for baseball's unwritten rules.[8] Articles written in the following days described baseball's long history of pitchers finding means to doctor baseballs, which have been viewed with a wink and a nod rather than genuine outcry and punishment.[9] Pineda's actions were characterized as those of a young kid who did not know how to better conceal his illegal, but accepted, actions.

One might wonder why it matters that other members of the baseball community viewed the situation differently from the umpires. The sporting community is essential to theories of sport for at least three reasons. First, theories of sport and adjudication are relevant to all participants and stakeholders. If we are examining a moral issue pertaining to sport, there is no reason to limit interpretivist methodology to umpires or officials, even though their decisions serve as motivating examples for interpretivism.[10] Second, debates in sport are not limited to the officials' interpretations of the rules. For instance, matters of sportsmanship almost always go beyond the purview of officials, as violations of each can be still be consistent with rules and a conception of the sport. Third, the activity of sport is not limited to the players and officials on the field. An explanation of sport that only considers officiating decisions is incomplete, since decisions made by others, including coaches, fans, media entities, etc., influence or affect the activity. Therefore, I believe the best interpretation should address the sport as a whole, including all members of the community.

In the Pineda case, the reactions of players, coaches, and media make it clear that we cannot fully understand what happened by looking only to the rules, or even to the umpires' decisions. Application of the rules without context or interpretation draws entirely the wrong conclusions about the nature of baseball. This is precisely the interpretivist claim. However, this case forces us to examine the interpretation employed by those in the baseball community. Principles of safety are espoused repeatedly; many advocate the use of pine tar in cold weather so pitchers do not hit batters with wild pitches. However, we find scant references to other principles applicable to Pineda, like those related to sportsmanship or fair play, that we might expect from an interpretation of baseball. Rather, members of the baseball community appeal to an ingrained sense of baseball tradition that allows the pitcher to use pine tar and other substances so long as he does so deftly or secretly. Those within the game are generally fine with attempts to break the rules so long as they conform to various baseball traditions and standards that characterize proper or appropriate efforts to deceive.

Those immersed in baseball evidently do not always address challenging cases through an interpretation of its integrity, excellences, or constitutive skills. While umpires may sometimes appeal to such interpretations, it is not clear that they always do so. Nor can we know the extent to which decisions are rooted in any philosophical conception of sport. Plus, umpires are not the only relevant constituency. We do not fully understand and explain the case until we take a wider perspective, which includes the traditions of the game. Likewise, we cannot predict future behavior and rule enforcement without appeal to conventions and a consideration of the entire baseball community.

Woods' Masters drop is more obviously a hard case lacking a straightforward or direct rule application. The relevant rule itself is part of the issue, with specifications like "as nearly as possible" that require interpretation or invite discretion. Additional complications make the resolution even more challenging than it first appears. Woods' drop, eventually deemed to be an illegal drop under Rule 26–1a, was initially found to be acceptable by officials on the course. To see how these rules were understood and later applied requires more details about this particular case and what the rules were meant to do.

The revised Rule 33 that gave the competition committee flexibility regarding disqualification was a product of technological innovation. Golf fans watching on television are known to call in rule violations. A precipitating event impacted Padraig Harrington at a tournament in Abu Dhabi in early 2011. As Harrington addressed the ball, a viewer noticed that the ball moved slightly; however, the players on the course did not observe the movement. After the round, officials were able to view the incident in high definition, and they determined that the ball rolled a distance of "three dimples."[11] The movement resulted in a penalty, which meant Harrington's scorecard was now deemed to have been signed incorrectly. Harrington was subsequently disqualified from the tournament. Thus, Rule 33–7 was revised to protect players from "exceptional circumstances" that were becoming far more common with high definition television and more outlets showing golf tournaments.[12] The rule still enforced the penalty but at least prevented players from being disqualified for signing scorecards later deemed incorrect based on post-round replay review.

Woods' drop at the Masters initially appeared to be headed for a similar resolution to that of Harrington. Champions tour golfer and experienced tournament director David Eger saw Woods' drop on television and believed it was too far from the original spot. He sought to ensure that the proper penalty was applied before Woods finished the round and signed his scorecard, in order to prevent disqualification. Eger called a PGA Tour official he knew to be working the Masters; eventually information reached the competition committee. Rules officials reviewed the drop before Woods finished his round and determined that it was close enough, therefore legal. Woods was not informed of any immediate controversy, since action was taken before Woods finished and signed his scorecard. The very kind of situation that Rule 33 was intended to cover was prevented.

The Woods case differed from the earlier Harrington case in two ways: the new information was the result of an (unknowing) admission rather than television, and the officials had already ruled the drop acceptable during the round before later ruling it illegal. Woods' illegal drop was brought to the competition committee again after the round due to Woods' post-round comments describing his reasons for dropping the ball two yards behind his divot. Officials determined, based on these comments, that his drop was not actually close enough. After all, Woods admitted that he could have dropped his ball closer to his original divot, but he moved back two yards to improve his position. This removed any doubt as to whether he dropped "as nearly as possible" to the original location. Thus, his action warranted a penalty, resulting in an inaccurate scorecard. Nevertheless, the competition committee believed Rule 33 gave it leeway to allow players to remain in the tournament, with penalty, when new information arises post-round.

A person unfamiliar with professional golf might find the entire controversy bizarre. The purpose of a golf tournament, it would seem, is to ascertain the person who best displays golfing skills, with the score being the best measure of these excellences. Therefore, a plausible interpretation of sport might find that golf's reliance on a signed scorecard is completely misplaced. Golf is unique among sports in maintaining that the official score must be kept by those playing it.[13] In the past, when scores were kept by individuals out of necessity, it made sense to emphasize fairness in doing so. In today's Masters the accuracy of a scorecard is not the only way to determine a player's score. Course scoreboards, television, and online sources all provide means of scorekeeping, making the act of signing an accurate scorecard outdated. From these developments, one might conclude that rule changes to prevent disqualification based on an inaccurate scorecard are appropriate ways to keep focus on the excellence of the game itself. Such an interpretation of golf would arguably resemble that applied to baseball by American League president Lee MacPhail in the George Brett pine tar incident. MacPhail allowed Brett's home run because he believed pine tar on the bat should not take precedence over the actions on the field. Perhaps golf should reinterpret itself in the modern world and completely remove the significance of signing a scorecard in professional tournaments so that excellence on the course is not overshadowed by technicalities.[14]

Most members of the golf community seem to reject the above interpretation of golf because they recognize adherence to rules as one of the particular values of the sport.[15] Golf, perhaps more than any other sport, values its conception of integrity. Calling one's own penalties is an essential component of this integrity. The most celebrated example is Bobby Jones, who called a penalty on himself that others did not see, then later deflected praise by explaining that he did not deserve congratulations for not robbing a bank. Golf has a long history of disqualifying or accepting higher scores from players who sign an incorrect scorecard, no matter their reasons for doing so. Famously, Roberto De Vicenzo signed an incorrect scorecard kept by his playing partner at the 1968 Masters. The card showed a 4, rather than his actual birdie 3, on the 17th hole, keeping him out of a playoff. Many in the golf community argued that Woods should have shown respect for the traditions of golf by removing himself from the tournament. For instance, Nick Faldo remarked, "He still has time. He is going to be watching this and he knows what has gone on. If he is smart and if he understands we have got to uphold the rules of this game, the gentlemanly conduct and the integrity of our game. He took advantage and he knows he took advantage and he knows you are not allowed to."[16] Others came to Tiger's defense, arguing that it was a fair ruling or noting that the ruling was consistent with the current written rules of golf.[17] Based on the evidence available, I suspect that most players are fine the rule application in a situation like Harrington's when the movement of the ball is not seen, whereas Woods' case was more controversial because it involved the misapplication of a rule that each player is expected to know.

The Woods incident at the Masters leaves us with a dilemma. An interpretation of sport in terms of general athletic excellence and fair play can explain the decision made to allow Woods to continue playing in the tournament on the grounds that application of a two stroke penalty is sufficient. But this interpretation is divorced from the history and traditions of golf. Many in the golf community interpret golf integrity to require the disqualification of those who sign a scorecard with a lower score than was earned. The case adds further complication in its differences from the baseball incidents described above, which appealed primarily to tradition. The resolution in Woods' case relied on neither tradition nor convention. In fact, tradition was repudiated in favor of Rule 33's new application. We are left to wonder how to philosophically explain or justify Woods continuation in the 2013 Masters. And how might interpretivists respond?

IMPLICATIONS FOR INTERPRETIVISM

The Dilemma of General and Particular Interpretations

In the previous section I illustrated disagreements between rules officials and the wider sporting community regarding the interpretation and application of rules. In this section, I will develop and explore the serious challenges these scenarios raise to the adequacy of interpretivism as a theory of sport. Others have presented extended arguments against interpretivism, most notably William Morgan. Among other concerns, Morgan has argued that interpretivist principles are too far removed from historical and social contexts, that there is no clear essence or purpose to sport, and that the theory is unable to explain rational persuasion or convergence. I agree with many of Morgan's criticisms, and I will show where my concerns overlap with his. Nevertheless, I offer here a unique argument that makes a case against interpretivism.

Interpretivism aims to serve as both an explanatory and normative theory of sport, yet it does not explain much about the Pineda incident. The actions taken by umpires and league officials made it seem an easy case with no interpretation required. The umpire applied the rule against foreign substances, and the league mandated a penalty it deemed appropriate. To decide the penalty, the league presumably looked to previous cases of pine tar usage by pitchers. These include an eight game suspension for Joel Peralta in 2012, ten days for Brendan Donnelly in 2005, and ten days for Julian Tavarez in 2004. Both Donnelly and Tavarez had their suspensions reduced to eight days after appeal. Pineda's suspension was slightly longer because he was a starting pitcher, not a relief pitcher. A ten game suspension is roughly equivalent to missing two starts. Pineda's suspension appears to be in line with these other cases, including an adjustment based on player position. Subsequent suspensions continued to be at the same level.[18] Understanding Pineda's ejection and suspension requires nothing beyond knowledge of the rule and MLB's treatment of prior cases.

While an easy case for umpires and officials, many players, coaches, and fans believed that the issue had nothing to do with rules. Pineda's mistake was in his failure to disguise his use of a foreign substance. The traditions of the sport provide the best explanation of the attitudes held by these various constituencies, needing no appeal to rules or principles. Interpretivism does not tell us much about these diverging conceptions of baseball, in which the umpires' understanding fails to match the interpretation of players or other participants. Importantly, there are no obvious reasons to prefer either conception as it pertains to the (open) use of pine tar by pitchers. The interpretivist view allows that we may encounter disagreements, but we should be able to identify a best, or at least better, interpretation to work from in determining the most relevant principles. In this disagreement, the umpires do not even see the matter as a hard case that requires interpretation. The implication for interpretivism is twofold. First, the interpretivist framework does not successfully explain the practices of the community, since these seem better captured by some notion of ethos or tradition rather than interpretation of the integrity of the game. At best, the explanation interpretivism provides of this case is incomplete because it tells us nothing about the umpires' perspective or how to reckon with this kind of dispute.

Second, it challenges the normative success of interpretivism. For example, which principles do we look to when analyzing proposed rule changes? Morgan makes a similar point, emphasizing the need for interpretivist principles to have broad agreement.[19] Interpretivism has shown itself to be a powerful theory of sport when the principles are shared. However, I believe this convergence is much rarer in practice than the interpretivist would like. And it's not just that we lack convergence, since this suggests disagreement that may be overcome. Many conflicts seem intractable. In Chapter 1, I presented Morgan's example of a conflict between conceptions of sport as essentially amateur or professional in nature. With a disagreement about the fundamental nature of the activity or contest, it is difficult to see how either could persuade others through realist, rational inquiry. My contention differs from Morgan's argument, at least in emphasis. Intractable disagreements between interpretations of sport are routine, and not just between broader philosophical positions. With Pineda, we encounter a common, internal dispute about how the rules should be understood and who applies them, with disagreement about whether a conception of sport is even needed. While we need not expect all within a sport to share the same interpretation, such fundamental disagreements suggest that the interpretivist account of sport does not provide the best explanation as was hoped for.

Interpretivism also fails to provide a clear explanation of the Woods case. One can argue that the competition committee followed interpretivist practice by utilizing the following interpretation: disqualification when penalties are discovered after the fact is inconsistent with the broader aims or excellences of sport. In seeking the correct score without disqualification, the competition committee ensured that the tournament would be decided on the course rather than after the round in the clubhouse where the scorecard is signed. This decision plausibly highlights the physical excellences of the game. Nonetheless, such an account faces a critical problem in that it relies on an interpretation of sport that is not specific to golf. As we have seen, many golfers believe that the actions of the type Woods performed must result in disqualification, allowing victory to be determined by something other than the physical skills of golf. Is the proper interpretation here one that applies a wider conception of physical excellence in sport, or must it defer to the unique demands of golf's traditions with its conception of integrity as one of the game's excellences?

Legal interpretations face the same basic challenge as those in sport. On Ronald Dworkin's account of law, the judge's interpretation must make sense of the law or legal system in which the ruling is being made, including that country's constitution and previous court rulings. Each judge is responsible for developing her own interpretation of the law, which explains how the court can make rulings that stake out new positions. Nevertheless, the aim is to develop an interpretation that is the most consistent with all aspects of law. In the same way, the best interpretation of golf must make sense of the rules and principles, including prior rulings and penalties. However, it is difficult to see this new rule as part of the interpretation of professional golf, given that it disregards traditions of golf and precedents regarding scorekeeping. Officials developed an interpretation of golf that is too detached from the sport to constitute the best interpretation of it. Morgan suggests that this kind of problem is endemic to sport because officials may "bypass the community's best interpretation" in working out their own answer to the case.[20] That may have happened here, but the competing interpretation has a problem, too. Critics of Woods appeal to integrity without any normative component beyond tradition, pushing convention above all other concerns. Perhaps the latter constitutes a better interpretation of golf, but it leaves no room for a wider interpretation of excellence or integrity. As I see it, the biggest problem is in how to navigate between these interpretations, both of which are supposed to be a part of the interpretivist's conception of sport.

In his essay on interpretivist officiating, Mitchell Berman implores philosophers to pay attention to both "the general jurisprudence of sport" and the "particular jurisprudence of individual sports."[21] I argue that the tension between these two levels is the source of a fundamental quandary for interpretivism. We see versions of this in both of the above cases. When developing an interpretation of a sport, many adopt a more general interpretation that supports principles of fairness in the pursuit of athletic excellence. These principles must remain at an abstract level, resulting in conflict with the traditions of that sport. The ability to criticize convention is one of the attractive features of interpretivism. Yet I contend that these general interpretations rarely comprise the best interpretation of the sport. On this I agree with Morgan—the resulting principles are often too far removed from the context to perform the normative tasks asked of them.[22] I diverge from Morgan because I accept that realist forms of interpretivism can allow for more specific conceptions of sport; interpretivists need not remain at the general level. Russell is right that interpretations of sport are supposed to understand integrity in light of social and historical context.[23] And I share Adam Berg's view that interpretivists have additional strategies available to connect their notion of integrity to historical developments and contextual factors.[24] However, my claim is that interpretations making greater use of precedent and tradition will need to leave out standards like constitutive skills, athletic excellence, and fair play. In this way, they come to look like conventions. Thus, the problem for interpretivism is not simply that its principles are too abstract to do the work. It's that when interpretations are needed to resolve hard cases, they must at the same time interpret sport in general and specific ways, employing a wide notion of athletic excellence and a particular conception of skills and traditions in the sport. This is not impossible in all cases, but I believe it creates an insurmountable challenge in many of them.

In law, the rejoinder to the dilemma may be located in its foundational principles. Dworkin indicates that law must presuppose some conception of justice and fairness.[25] This is not to say that justice and fairness cannot conflict, or that every community has the same notions of justice and fairness. Rather, any political community depends on a shared conception of justice and fairness.[26] The law presupposes justice and fairness, providing a wider context to the particulars of any legal tradition. Judges can develop an interpretation of law that weaves together the broader demands of law with the specifics of law because there is some basic agreement regarding the aims of law. In Chapter 1, I discussed two of Dworkin's strategies for constraining possible interpretations in the ideal judge Hercules and the creation of a chain novel. If successful, Dworkin's judges will interpret law to successfully apply general principles of law to the context of a particular case.

I believe the dilemma between principles too general and too specific is more intransigent in sport than in law. Sport officials cannot appeal to foundational principles as easily as judges in a legal system. Competitive sports may share some basic aims, and perhaps even similar excellences, but they generally lack the shared adjudicatory frameworks and core documents we find in law.[27] There is nothing like a Constitution or case history shared between sporting entities like MLB and the NBA. The difference is largely a matter of how the relevant community is defined. In law, the community consists of an entire legal system, while in sport it is the members or interested parties of a subset of some sport (e.g., professional baseball or college swimming). There are countless examples of sport teams or leagues shifting affiliation or realigning, or changing their most basic rules with relative ease. Consequently, interpretations of law may presuppose justice or fairness, even as basic notions like fair play are debated within the context of sport. Interpretations that remain closely tied to the norms of the community will tend toward the particular and be too narrow. Attempts to expand beyond the community to general principles and broad excellences provide normative guidance, but I argue that these are rarely the best interpretations of the sport in question.

The difficulty integrating universal and contextual excellences also threatens to undermine normative evaluation. Another example highlights the depth of the problem. Bill Belichick of the New England Patriots in the National Football League (NFL) has employed a number of novel formations to take advantage of rules regarding which players are eligible receivers, most famously in a 2015 playoff game against the Baltimore Ravens. Some players and media praised Belichick's precise knowledge of the rules, with Patriots' quarterback Tom Brady remarking that "maybe those guys got to study the rule book and figure it out."[28] The Ravens complained that these formations undermined the spirit of the rules, and some in football and the media agreed.[29] Following an interpretivist approach, it is tempting to argue that the excellences of football, in this case the physical skills required on both offense and defense, were overwhelmed by a surprising offensive formation, obscuring the excellences of the sport. This would constitute an argument against the Patriots' formations. However, other interpretations might emphasize how Belichick's maneuvers test the defense in various ways, such as their ability to read the offensive formation, or to keep them from ignoring certain players or positions on the field. These considerations all suggest that we should applaud Belichick's innovations.

The interpretivist believes that some excellences can be recognized as more central to sport than others, resolving the tension. I think the kinds of examples discussed here show how the problem goes beyond a debate between competing conceptions of sport. The problem is that a contextual understanding of the traditions and norms of sport reveals additional excellences that are worth pursuing, pushing against the broader notion of integrity. Beyond this dilemma, we might wonder whether interpretivism really explains anything here at all. As a matter of the rules, the Patriots' actions were perfectly acceptable. Many within and surrounding football questioned whether the Patriots were being inappropriately deceptive, and Belichick's reputation may have contributed to these worries. Still, these questions were raised in the context of whether the Patriots followed the rules, not whether their actions violated the integrity of the game. It is not clear that interpretivism explicates the situation or provides any insight into it.

Russell's Internal Principle

Interpretivists aim to develop abstract principles rooted in an interpretation that can be applied across sport. At the same time, these interpretations are supposed to be grounded in excellences tied to the particular history and context of a specific sport. I argue that an adequate interpretation cannot generally do both. A conception of sport that emphasizes athletic excellence more broadly is likely to run afoul of the interpretation provided within the community, so it is not the best explanation of (the) sport. Yet relying on local interpretations limits the wider explanatory and normative work that interpretivism seeks. It seems the best interpretation of the sport is unlikely to be found by moving in either direction. Given that there are numerous types of interpretivism, I want to explore how this challenge manifests in some different interpretivist accounts, beginning with Russell's internal principle.[30]

Russell's amended internal principle reads "*The practice of any game should be undertaken* in such a manner that the excellences embodied in achieving the lusory goal of the game are not undermined but maintained and fostered."[31] This rendering widens application from rules officials, for whom he first characterized an earlier version of the principle, to rule interpretation that broadly regulates the conduct of participants. The resulting interpretation of the sport has clear moral content, providing duties to preserve and uphold the context in which excellences are fostered. Not all sports have the same lusory goals and excellences, so the same interpretation cannot be developed in each case. Therefore, the internal principle requires specific excellences to be given a particular interpretation, even though the internal principle is presented as true of sport overall. As we saw with the 2013 Masters, interpretations of golf that are sensitive to the excellences recognized within golf conflict with the internal principle's maxim to foster what Russell calls "game-specific physical excellences."[32] If sport does admit of a clear purpose, then this should provide the resolution. However, I am skeptical about locating any. Even if there is a clear purpose of golf, it may not be consistent with the idea of a clear purpose of sport in general, shown through the disagreement about the status of a scorecard.

Morgan contends Russell's internal principle has trouble taking into account strategy. I concur, and I want to focus on gamesmanship, especially when the test is primarily psychological in nature. Leslie Howe defines gamesmanship as "the attempt to gain competitive advantage either by an artful manipulation of the rules that does not actually violate them or by the psychological manipulation or unsettling of the opponent."[33] Many forms of gamesmanship favor knowledge of the rules over the physical excellences of the activity that are derived from its lusory goal. Russell shows how interpretivism deals with some instances of gamesmanship when discussing Billy Martin's complaint about George Brett's illegal bat. Other scenarios prove more troubling.[34] Consider the practice of bluffing in poker. Many take bluffing to be an essential component of the game, but it is not evident that bluffing derives from any excellences inherent to the game. If we interpret poker as an attempt to gain the best poker hand, then bluffing actually hinders the activity by convincing those with better hands to fold.

The appropriateness of bluffing is not easily provided by an interpretation of the sport, since we have a fundamental disagreement between a general conception of competitive excellence and traditional strategies that have become accepted over time. Any interpretation of poker must make sense of the practice, but doing so requires a contextual analysis of excellence in poker at the expense of normative assessment. The interpretivist may be able to offer principles as guidelines to assess some forms of gamesmanship, but it does not seem able to address the more basic question of why some forms of gamesmanship make us uncomfortable even as others are seen as essential to the sport itself.[35]

Torres and Hager

For another illustration I turn to Cesar Torres and Peter Hager, who build from Alasdair MacIntyre's account of internal and external goods. The constitutive skills of a sport function as its internal goods, and these constitutive skills derive from the sport's constitutive rules and corresponding logic. Sporting communities should act for the best interests of these internal goods.[36] Initially, Torres and Hager's approach looks better suited to overcome the problem of interpretations being too general or too specific. Many sports have similar constitutive rules or aims, allowing for common analyses of them. For instance, one might argue that sports like soccer and hockey are defined in terms of speed, precision, and strategy all organized around a goal. Baseball and softball share similar goals and skills of pitching, batting, and fielding. Nevertheless, no two sports are identical, allowing the evaluation of each sport to consider its unique internal goods.

Torres and Hager's view does not fully avoid the problem. The telos of a sport is historically determined, at least to some degree, and I am not convinced that this can be accounted for. While it might seem that the aims and skills of a sport can be defined in the abstract, sports develop in different contexts, leading to competing conceptions of the relevant skills and goals. For instance, we find noteworthy differences in strategy and culture between Japanese and American versions of baseball. Japanese baseball tends to focus on what American fans call "small ball," including bunts, stolen bases, and sacrifice flies. American baseball, in contrast, holds strength in the highest regard, including home runs and power pitching. These differences, plus variances in the baseballs themselves, have resulted in very different games not captured by analysis of constitutive skills.[37] Although Japanese and American baseball teams are able to compete on the field at the Olympics or World Baseball Classic, the leagues themselves emphasize diverse skills and principles. These forms of baseball require distinct interpretations that reflect cultural differences.

Torres and Hager's approach also precludes the plurality of teloi in sport when defining excellence. American sports fans value both athletic excellence embodied over the course of a season and that of a high-level peak performance, the latter of which is often revealed in a playoff or tournament. The organization of a sport's championship itself determines some of the skills and excellences exemplified in that activity, leaving the interpretivist with no clear means to adjudicate between interpretations.[38] A similar conflict emerges surrounding the Woods case. Officials recognize the game is being changed by technology, specifically the ability of individuals to call in rule violations that would have otherwise gone unnoticed. A sport like golf might embrace the increased number of violations as a way to make the sport more accurate. Another sport might stick to tradition, allowing only violations that are recognized on the course in real time.[39] If the sport allows violations to be called in, it might modify the rules to prevent an increased number of disqualifications, which is the path professional golf associations have attempted to take, or it might continue to demand disqualification for a mistaken scorecard.

In the end, evaluating sport in terms of constitutive skills and internal goods remains too abstract to ground the best explanation of sport because the teloi of a sport are neither singular nor universal. Incorporating these into an interpretation requires a strategy reminiscent of conventionalism. I find that Torres and Hager successfully offer guidance and constraint to developing an interpretation of sport through internal goods, but we are not always able to decide between competing interpretations, which undermines the claim to offer the best explanation of sport.

PARTICULARIST INTERPRETATIONS AND CONVENTIONS

Kretchmar and Berg

I have argued that interpretivists occupy an untenable position in developing conceptions of sport that are close enough to a sport to be accepted but retain a critical distance. At least two recent views that I discussed in Chapter 1, Kretchmar and Berg, can be read as modifications of the interpretive approach that take on one horn of the dilemma I have presented.

Scott Kretchmar's pluralism moves in the direction of offering general interpretations of sport rather than those more closely tied to a sport's tradition. Kretchmar presents six models of sport that reflect various ways in which sport is played and valued. Rather than connecting these to history, culture, or tradition, Kretchmar grounds these in distinct conceptions of human nature. Kretchmar calls his account interpretivist largely because it resists conventionalism with a theoretical conception of sport. Its continuity with Dworkin seems to begin and end with the idea that the purposes of sport can be identified through "careful reflection and reason-based discussion."[40] On reflection, Kretchmar's position is internalist but not obviously a form of interpretivism. In any case, he encounters some familiar challenges when he appeals to conceptions of sport derived from human nature. He notes that sports may be understood through different value frameworks, yet this flexibility remains abstract from the particular sport in question. It is not clear that adopting any specific model of sport constitutes an interpretation of a sport, leaving an open question concerning how these models resolve hard cases.

Berg's version of interpretivism is particularist in nature. Recall that for Berg the particular sporting community, not a broader notion of integrity, provides the best explanation of specific instantiations of excellence. He characterizes excellence as a historical question as much as a philosophical one. For instance, he shows how basketball developed as a product of its cultural and historical context, responding to changes in work and politics at the turn of the twentieth century.[41] So concepts like excellence or integrity should be understood in terms of convention rather than a sport's telos, central purpose, or constitutive skills. He concludes, "Under the cover of the abstract notion of 'excellence' a good measure of culturally shaped ethos has been embedded within interpretivist schemes. It is not that interpretivism in sports is wrong . . . just that this principle functions through a sizeable dependency on conventionalism."[42]

Berg advocates a method of interpretation that depends on the particular culture and conventions of the local sporting community. I am skeptical that other interpretivists will accept Berg's account of excellence. However, the more general puzzle might be whether his notion of excellence requires any interpretation at all. When dealing with debates or making rulings in sport, Berg's view amounts to an investigation of the relevant conventions. This eliminates the traditional kinds of hard cases we have been dealing with by resolving them via the community's practices and concepts. Situations that become hard cases, through this framework, are those in which either there are no current conventions or those about which the culture disagrees. However, there appears to be no clear way to deal with such cases using Berg's tools. At the very least, there is little room for the kind of interpretation advocated by the likes of Russell or Simon with reference to excellences of sport more generally, and no normative assessment from principles beyond those of the sport in question.

Berg allows for additional normative principles beyond the ethos of a sport, but he limits these to external principles and values.[43] Consequently, Berg's interpretivism also faces an explanatory challenge. If cases are resolved through the community's practices, an interpretation of sport is an unnecessary complication to determining which conventions take precedence. If so, his interpretivism adds nothing that other forms of conventionalism cannot also accept. Therefore, it offers no reason to believe interpretivism provides the best explanation of an event.

While Kretchmar and Berg interpret sports at different levels, both face the same basic problem. Their appeal to pluralism or conventions might improve their ability to explain sport in some respect, but both come with significant cost, risking the overall explanatory power and normative authority of interpretivism. Furthermore, both manage only to provide some minimal constraint to avoid slipping completely into relativism. For Kretchmar, adjudication can adopt various value frameworks, all constrained by having some broad connection to human nature. But he does not believe there is good reason to prefer one model of sport to any others. Hard cases may be perceived differently by competing models. For Berg, constraints on sport are found through external principles, such as consent or cosmopolitanism. External principles and values have a wider application that is not specific to sport application. That is, these principles are not limited to the realm of sport but are applied also to other human activities. This does not meet the needs of a theory of sport for internalists or interpretivists.

Conventionalism Revisited

At this point conventionalism deserves a new hearing. I dismissed early forms of conventionalism because they offer little normative evaluation. Yet, attempts to improve interpretivism have reintroduced concepts like conventions and ethos. And conventionalism might provide a better explanation of some situations, such as the Pineda case. I introduced this example to show a tension between more general and more particular interpretations of sport. I found it puzzling that the umpire's ruling could be so straightforward and different from the interpretation offered by other stakeholders, like players and coaches. A conventionalist offers a reasonable explanation of it. Players and coaches reflect a distinct tradition of how the game is played, an ethos of the sport that looks the other way when pitchers use certain substances to improve grip in colder weather. Thus, I want to distinguish my approach from some more recent defenses of conventionalist theories before moving on to develop my own theory.

Bogdan Ciomaga defends a version of sport conventionalism inspired by that found in geometry rather than the law. The agreement of a community does not override all other considerations, including empirical data. Rather, wide acceptance is "only a source of prima facie normativity" that can be overridden by other norms or considerations.[44] In the context of sport Ciomaga proposes that some such moral norms would include life, freedom, and justice. For instance, a storm that risks the lives of the players overrides any conventions regarding playing the sport in all sorts of weather.

I anticipate that Ciomaga's revised conventionalism appeases neither interpretivists nor most conventionalists. Even if he has shown that conventionalists can, in fact, appeal to non-conventional norms to resolve normative dilemmas, these external values need to be justified. There is no reason to think that an interpretation of sport would be the appropriate means to do so. Ciomaga himself appeals to the "relative normative prima facie strengths of these norms" to determine when community agreement will be outweighed, which requires an account of universal moral norms and nothing regarding the excellences of sport.[45] I see no way to make interpretivism the source of weighty prima facie norms as this conventionalism requires, since the interpretation of sport would itself need to take the context into account. On the other side, we have seen that many philosophers accept that conventions bear significance in our understanding of sport. Reducing conventionalism to only this aspect of sport removes its unique feature, resulting in a conventionalism that does not appear to provide any unique insight into the nature of sport.

Morgan offers a more robust conventionalist theory. In Chapter 1 we encountered Morgan's anti-realist interpretivism that defended historically dependent and socially qualified interpretations of sport. As Morgan worked through the implications of these ideas, he found interpretivist framework was no longer the best characterization for his view, since its normative principles are too abstract. He developed an alternative position initially termed deep conventionalism, although his most recent work moves away from deep conventions and regards itself as a distinct kind of conventionalist theory.

Morgan argues that previous conventionalist theories focused on the wrong kinds of conventions. They mainly considered conventions that amount to practical agreements to do things a certain way. He identifies these as coordinating conventions, which aim to harmonize behavior with others to avoid large-scale coordination problems.[46] These conventions work through appeal to our desires and preferences. As we have seen, they offer little help in considering whether the conventions themselves ought to be changed. In contrast, Morgan defends different kinds of conventions that structure our ways of thinking, reasoning, and communicating. These conventions "are embedded in and inform the actual ethical life of sport and the other collective practices of society in which they figure," meaning they reflect the community itself and not the individual members.[47] Conventions are social norms that relate to the beliefs and values of the members of a social group. When it comes to sport, conventions are rooted in a shared background understanding of the practice, its purpose, and the way things are done.

These conventions explain sport by showing how disagreements arise, such as the aforementioned example regarding amateur and professional conceptions of sport. He sees these as incongruent conceptions of the purpose of sport or the nature of athletic endeavor. The two views may understand each other, but there is no rational way to persuade one framework to adopt the other. Each has a fully formed conception of the sport and neither can be considered a better interpretation than the other. Morgan also believes his conventionalism can provide an adequate normative standpoint, unlike traditional conventionalist theories. Conventions provide moral norms independent of desires because a sporting community holds people to standards they would prefer not to follow. Participants commit to a particular community and conception of purpose, but then must adhere to the community norms. A player in the community who strays from the way things are done will be criticized accordingly. Since conventions establish the worth and value of sport, they serve similar functions to interpretivist principles. However, adjudication of sport dilemmas is possible only when the conflict occurs within the community or form of life. Although the purpose identified in deep conventions may be rationally investigated, at root conventions remain forms of social agreement. Rational inquiry into deep conventions is historically contingent; different schematics of conventions are incommensurable, precluding rational inquiry and discussion between them. And there is no rational way to decide whether shifts from one conception of sport to another entail moral progress.[48]

I share with Morgan a concern that interpretivism's principles may to be too abstract or general to accomplish its goals. Many of our arguments against interpretivism have similar targets. In subsequent chapters I will defend a view that, like Morgan, appeals to some pragmatist elements. Nevertheless, I do not agree with Morgan that conventionalism provides the best alternative theory. I want to differentiate my theory of sport from Morgan's conventionalism and motivate the need to look elsewhere. For one, I am skeptical that the conventionalist explanation of the above cases is as convincing as it first appears. Let's return to the issue of pine tar use by pitchers. In the Pineda case, there is a disconnect between the application of rules by the umpire and the players and coaches, although only the latter seems to reflect a distinct community or conception of purpose. The umpires made a ruling but don't seem invested in any community of sport, nor does their position seem to rely on any purposeful view of the activity. Morgan acknowledges that sports can be fragmented when its devotees disagree about the purpose and value of sport.[49] However, this case goes beyond fragmentation when some don't rely on a conception of purpose or value in the first place.

This becomes even clearer when we look to changes made during the 2021 MLB season. Additional rules were put into place to limit substance use by pitchers, including checking pitchers throughout the game and increasing penalties. These changes are in tension with the view that many espoused defending pitcher use of certain sticky substances, at least in cold weather. I do not believe the 2021 rule changes reflect a disagreement about the purpose of baseball or the nature of athletic endeavor. While not explicitly stated, one can reasonably argue that the changes were intended to address concerns about gameplay, such as poor offensive production perceived to damage the entertainment value of the game. If so, then conventionalism does not provide the best explanation for this kind of significant rule change or application. We need a different approach to better capture this kind of reasoning.

My deeper disagreement with conventionalism stems from its appeal to purpose in sport. Morgan and I both critique the interpretivist ideal of a clear purpose, aim, or telos in sport which all should assent to. But Morgan accepts that a conception of purpose is essential to understanding sport and developing moral norms. He moves away from interpretivism by arguing that a sport's purpose makes sense only through a community's conventions. He explains, "Committing to the overriding purpose, ethical norms, and internal goods of a sport practice is a self-transformative process, a process by which, to parrot Hegel, an 'I' becomes a 'we,' a tightly knit, normatively like-minded practice community."[50] Different practice communities may identify different purposes of sports, even when the rules and institutions are in place.[51] I disagree that a sense of purpose or endeavor is the driving force behind many decisions in sport, and I will expand on this in the next chapter. Some disputes and rule changes to sport surely involve competing frameworks or conceptions of purpose. But I contend that many clashes are better understood in different terms. We see this most clearly when we look to the officials who adjudicate these hard cases. I argue that their reasons are most often practical, selfish, economic, moral, or otherwise, but not dependent on the ideas or vocabulary of any particular conception of sport or its traditions.

My suggestion that the best explanation of sport does not include any conception of purpose is a radical break from both interpretivism and Morgan's conventionalism. The interpretivist believes we must interpret sport in a purposeful manner in order to make sense of the activity. Similarly, Morgan treats sport as a "moral laboratory" precisely because communities disagree about purpose and athletic excellence.[52] Yet this normative approach to sport, through interpretations of purpose, is precisely where I believe we go astray in attempting to explain sport. These theories use the purpose of sport to build normativity into an explanation of sport. Doing so obscures many decisions that are not made from such philosophical viewpoints.

Finally, Morgan's move back toward conventionalism abandons an important insight; interpretivists were right to look to the law as a model for sport. Theories of law do not apply directly to sport, but philosophical attempts to understand law can illuminate parallel features of sport. While I have argued that interpretivists chose the wrong legal theory in applying Dworkin to sports, the basic idea was fruitful and is worth revisiting. Furthermore, interpretivists were right, generally speaking, to consider the manner of adjudication employed in sports, such as that performed by umpires and officials. Instead of considering parallels to law, Morgan's conventionalism introduces a number of controversial metaphysical and epistemological claims. These include his use of Hegel's *Sittlichkeit* to characterize how norms are embedded in social practices.[53] And he relies on a Rortian pragmatism in his account of practical reasoning about sport.[54] In contrast, I propose that drawing from philosophy of law can avoid some of these complicating background assumptions.

CONCLUSION

Russell defended interpretivism initially by showing where it best explained the decisions made by umpires, officials, or other adjudicators. It developed into a theory aiming both to explain sport and guide decision-making for officials and others in the sporting community. I have raised questions concerning its success in both arenas. My central goal in this chapter has been to show that interpretivism does not provide a sufficient explanation of sport. The cases I presented in this chapter highlight some important problems. In the pitching scenario, interpretivism can easily explain the umpires' straightforward application of the rule, but the debate in the community did not include rules, principles, or any interpretation of sport beyond an appeal to tradition. In the Woods incident at the Masters, rules officials made decisions for their sport based on principles implied by the nature of sport, including those of fair play and deciding championships by results on the course. However, while this decision was based on an interpretation of sport, it is not clear that this actually constitutes the best interpretation of golf. The sport of golf takes great pride in its self-enforcement of rules, and the new rules interpretation, as applied to Woods, is inconsistent with values and precedent that many find central to it.

These considerations reveal a dilemma for interpretivism. To offer the best explanation of sport, it must adhere closely to norms and traditions of the activity, undercutting the ability to offer normative guidance. Accordingly, interpretations may work with broader conceptions of excellence in order to ground normative judgments, but these are unlikely to constitute the best interpretation and explanation of the sport in question.

Based on these and similar cases, we need a wider perspective of sport that accounts for all stakeholders. It is evident that when hard cases arise, players, coaches, officials, the media, and fans do not always appeal to an interpretation of sport and its integrity. Moreover, the disagreements we find in such cases emphasize the fact that the interpretive approach is nowhere near making sense of these opposing constituencies. The Woods case reveals an intriguing path forward. After the decision was made to allow Woods to remain in the tournament, fellow golfer and previous Major Champion Graeme McDowell tweeted the following: "Take the fact that it was Tiger out of the equation and it is a fair ruling. Since it is him the debate begins about TV ratings etc etc."[55] McDowell's tweet reminds us that decisions about sport are not made in a vacuum, nor are they made entirely within the sporting world. Sports are significant political and cultural institutions, and we cannot ignore these other elements and their potential influences. In the next chapter, I will provide an account of sport that takes what sport is today as its central focus.

NOTES

1. An exception to this is the form of conventionalism developed by William Morgan. I will discuss his recent work later in this chapter.

2. In a previous article, I examine the application of interpretivism to a rejection of playoffs and tournaments in favor of the regular season. I argue that interpretivists like Cesar Torres and Peter Hager (see Chapter 1 for a description of their view) cannot defend only a single conception of excellence in sport. Essentially, numerous interpretations of the sport emerge from its skills and excellences, some of which find expression most fully in playoffs and tournaments. See Aaron Harper, "'You're the Best Around': An Argument for Playoffs and Tournaments," *Journal of the Philosophy of Sport* 43, no. 2 (2016).

3. Office of the Commissioner of Baseball, *Official Baseball Rulebook*, Major League Baseball 2014 Edition, http://mlb.mlb.com/mlb/downloads/y2014/official_baseball_rules.pdf.

4. United States Golf Association, *Decisions on the Rules of Golf 2012–2013* (The United States Golf Association and The R&A, 2011).

5. Bryan Hoch, "Pineda Gets 10-game Suspension for Pine Tar on Neck," *MLB.com*, April 24, 2014, https://www.mlb.com/news/yankees-michael-pineda-gets-10-game-suspension-for-using-pine-tar/c-73202466.

6. Christopher L. Gasper, "What a Foolish Mistake by Michael Pineda," *The Boston Globe*, April 24, 2014, http://www.bostonglobe.com/sports/2014/04/23/yankees-pitcher-michael-pineda-ejected-what-sticky-situation/bi1m0aruFUrLekQTeaFy7L/story.html.

7. Scott Lauber, "Nieves: Red Sox Pitchers 'Don't Have to Worry' About Being Accused of Using Illegal Substances," *Boston Herald*, April 24, 2014, https://www.bostonherald.com/2014/04/24/nieves-red-sox-pitchers-dont-have-to-worry-about-being-accused-of-using-illegal-substances/.

8. Gasper, "Foolish Mistake."

9. Examples include Ted Berg, "Pine Tar Still isn't a Big Deal, but Michael Pineda Deserves his Suspension," *USA Today*, April 24, 2014, https://ftw.usatoday.com/2014/04/michael-pineda-pine-tar-suspension-new-york-yankees-mlb; Cindy Boren, "Michael Pineda Ejected for Pine Tar, Leaving Yankees with a Sticky Situation," *Washington Post*, April 24, 2014, https://www.washingtonpost.com/news/early-lead/wp/2014/04/24/michael-pineda-ejected-for-pine-tar-leaving-yankees-with-a-mess/; and David Lengel, "Tar for the Course," *The Guardian*, April 24, 2014, https://www.theguardian.com/sport/blog/2014/apr/24/pine-tar-for-the-course-yankees-pitcher-michael-pineda-busted-for-using-foreign-substance.

10. Interpretivism has been applied to other sub-communities of sport, including coaches. Two examples are Robert L. Simon, "The Ethical Coach: An Interpretive Account of the Ethics of Coaching," in *The Ethics of Coaching Sports*, ed. Robert L. Simon (Boulder, CO: Westview Press, 2013) and William J. Morgan, "Interpretivism, Conventionalism, and the Ethical Coach," in *The Ethics of Coaching Sports*, ed. Robert L. Simon (Boulder, CO: Westview Press, 2013).

11. Bernie McGuire, "Padraig Harrington Disqualified Over Marker Incident," *Reuters*, January 21, 2011, https://www.reuters.com/article/us-golf-european-harrington/padraig-harrington-disqualified-over-marker-incident-idUSTRE70K1LS20110121.

12. USGA, *Rules of Golf 2012–2013*.

13. Actually, this is not entirely the case, as is evidenced in the two different ways a scorecard can be inaccurate. A scorecard that gives a worse score than the player actually made on the course becomes the score of record. A scorecard that gives a better score than the player actually made on the course results in disqualification. In the latter scenario, an independent scorekeeping mechanism is implicitly used as a standard.

14. The professional golf associations of the PGA and R&A made rule changes for 2019 to move in this direction. The new 1.3b(2) states that players should be held to a standard of reasonable judgment and not held to the standard of precision created by technology in estimation or measurement. United States Golf Association, *The Rules of Golf for 2019* (R&A Rules Limited and the United States Golf Association, 2018), https://www.usga.org/content/dam/usga/images/rules/rules-modernization/golf-new-rules/Rules%20of%20Golf%20for%202019%20(Final).pdf.

15. Mitchell N. Berman, "On Interpretivism and Formalism in Sports Officiating: From General to Particular Jurisprudence," *Journal of the Philosophy of Sport* 38, no. 2 (2011): 189.

16. "Masters 2013: Tiger Woods Given Two-shot Masters Penalty," *BBC.com*, April 13, 2013, http://www.bbc.com/sport/golf/22134938.

17. Examples include Graeme McDowell's statement quoted in "Masters 2013" and Thomas Boswell, "Tiger Woods Deserved Penalty, Not Disqualification, at 2013 Masters," *Washington Post*, April 13, 2013, https://www.washingtonpost.com/sports/othersports/tiger-woods-deserved-penalty-not-disqualificiation-at-2013-masters/2013/04/13/539c180c-a486-11e2-be47-b44febada3a8_story.html.

18. In 2015 Will Smith and Brian Matusz, both relief pitchers, received eight game suspensions for use of a foreign substance.

19. William J. Morgan, *Sport and Moral Conflict* (Philadelphia: Temple University Press, 220), 73–76, 101–102.

20. Morgan, *Moral Conflict*, 89.

21. Berman, "Interpretivism and Formalism," 179.

22. William J. Morgan, "Broad Internalism, Deep Conventions, Moral Entrepreneurs, and Sport," *Journal of the Philosophy of Sport* 39, no. 1 (2012): 67–68 and Morgan, *Moral Conflict*, 85, 105. Morgan argues that principles must ground their normative judgments in the basic nature of sport rather than those considerations approved by the community. This makes the normative force of principles independent of the historical and social context.

23. J.S. Russell, "A Critique of Conventionalist Broad Internalism," *Sport, Ethics and Philosophy* 12, no. 4 (2018): 455–456.

24. Adam Berg, "The Ethos of Excellence," *Journal of the Philosophy of Sport* 42, no. 2 (2015): 235–236.

25. Ronald Dworkin, *Law's Empire* (Cambridge, MA: Harvard University Press, 1986), 176–178.

26. Additionally, as Berg writes, its institutions are "set up to cope with actions that might challenge or weaken the normative legitimacy of a given legal system." Berg, "Ethos," 239.

27. There are some sport institutions that more closely resemble legal and political institutions, such as the Court of Arbitration for Sport. These are the exception, not the rule, and those that exist are often relatively recent creations with limited case histories and emerging authority.

28. Aaron Wilson, "Ravens Coach John Harbaugh Tried to Stop Patriots Line's 'Deception' with Penalty," *The Baltimore Sun*, January 11, 2015, https://www.baltimoresun.com/sports/orioles/bal-baltimore-ravens-coach-john-harbaugh-tries-to-stop-new-england-patriots-deception-with-penalty-20150110-story.html.

29. For instance, Bill Barnwell wrote, "The Patriots weren't technically doing anything illegal, because the rulebook doesn't account for a change in receiver eligibility, even if the spirit of the law would seem to suggest that the Ravens should have had more of a chance to identify the Patriots' formation. I suspect that the league will quietly tell the Patriots to cut that out and make an according change to the rulebook this offseason." Barnwell, "Divisional Wrap-Up: A Crop of Classics," *Grantland*, January 12, 2015, https://grantland.com/the-triangle/nfl-divisional-cowboys-packers-panthers-seahawks-colts-broncos-patriots-ravens/.

30. For previous discussion of Russell's internal principle, see Chapter 1 section "Legal and Philosophical Foundations of Interpretivism."

31. J.S. Russell, "Moral Realism in Sport," *Journal of the Philosophy of Sport* 31, no. 2 (2004): 146.

32. Ibid., 146.

33. Leslie Howe, "Gamesmanship," *Journal of the Philosophy of Sport* 31, no. 2 (2004): 213.

34. Morgan finds Russell's analysis of Martin's strategy to be less persuasive than I do in *Moral Conflict*, 75. Morgan points out that Martin suspected Brett's bat to have too much pine tar at a point earlier in the season, but he did not notify the umpire until

an opportune time. Managerial tactics of this sort might be accepted as a legitimate strategy.

35. Howe offers a different distinction between acceptable (weak) and unacceptable (strong) gamesmanship. She argues that gamesmanship is appropriate, even necessary, when it improves participants from both sides in a competition. Howe, "Gamesmanship," 220–222. At first glance, Howe's approach might seem interpretivist due to her appeal to excellence, but her notion of improvement does not require any interpretation of the activity. Rather one considers whether the act of gamesmanship improves or diminishes the player's development or causes the deterioration of skills.

36. Cesar R. Torres and Peter F. Hager, "The Desirability of the Season Long Tournament: A Response to Finn," *Journal of the Philosophy of Sport* 38, no. 1 (2011): 45.

37. Berg's example of basketball, discussed in Chapter 1, offers another instance of this phenomenon. Basketball was initially developed to promote certain upper-class, broadly religious ideals related to discipline and bodily health. However, when the game was introduced to the Navajo, creativity and individuality became central to their conception of the game. These changes to basketball excellence are unrelated to the essential features of the sport. Berg, "Ethos," 239–242.

38. Harper, "Playoffs and Tournaments," 303–304.

39. A similar debate is currently taking place in baseball concerning both replay and the possibility of balls and strikes called electronically instead of being determined by the home plate umpire.

40. Scott Kretchmar, "Pluralistic Internalism," *Journal of the Philosophy of Sport* 42, no. 1 (2015): 83.

41. Berg, "Ethos," 240.

42. Ibid., 243.

43. Ibid., 244.

44. Bogdan Ciomaga, "Conventionalism Revisited," *Sport, Ethics and Philosophy* 6, no. 4 (2012): 415.

45. Ibid., 416.

46. Morgan, "Broad Internalism," 71–72 and *Moral Conflict*, 129–131.

47. Morgan, *Moral Conflict*, 156.

48. Ibid., 194.

49. William J. Morgan, "The Normativity of Sport: A Historicist Take on Broad Internalism," *Journal of the Philosophy of Sport* 43, no. 1 (2016): 30.

50. Morgan, *Moral Conflict*, 162.

51. Ibid., 145.

52. Ibid., 1–2.

53. Ibid., 156–157.

54. Eric Moore also raises questions about Morgan's reliance on Rorty's views of truth and rationality, which Morgan responded to in a subsequent article. For this debate see Eric Moore, "Against Deep Conventionalism," *Journal of the Philosophy of Sport* 45, no. 3 (2018): 236–238 and William Morgan, "Conventionalism Defended: A Reply to Moore," *Journal of the Philosophy of Sport* 46, no. 1 (2019): 101–104.

55. "Masters 2013."

Chapter 3

Legal Realism and Sport Realism

Theories of sport seek both to explain what happens in sport and to offer normative guidance for those invested in sport or who resolve its disputes. I have argued that these goals have not been attained by current theories. In this chapter I offer my own theory of sport, which I call sport realism, to better explain sport and to provide for effective adjudication.[1] This chapter is divided into three major sections. In the first section I investigate work in legal theory that provides important background for my own position. Next, I build from some insights of legal theory, specifically legal realism, to construct a successful, useful, and improved theory of sport. I argue that my position is better suited than other theories to address sports of all kinds, across professional organizations, amateur sports, and even informal pick-up games. Finally, I offer case studies to show the explanatory power of sport realism.

I propose to make progress by moving away from the language of principles or purposes. In doing so, I seek inspiration from the tradition of American legal realism.[2] Earlier I contended that philosophers of sport are right to see legal theory as a model, despite the evident differences between the two fields, due to the overlapping and parallel features of these two kinds of human activity. This does not mean that all aspects legal realism should be accepted as accurate or applicable to sport. Rather, I believe that it makes claims about law that reveal comparable insights regarding sport, which I organize into an account of the nature of sport and its distinct kinds of adjudication.

Three legal realist insights are central to my theory of sport. First, legal realism defines law in terms of how it functions rather than its constitutive rules or principles. For legal realists this involves understanding law through the actions of the courts and various legal officials. Similarly, sport realism defines sport through the actions of its officials who adjudicate or otherwise resolve disputes in sport. Second, to best explain the actions taken by courts, legal realists do away with any distinction between legal and non-legal reasons, acknowledging that judges may be motivated by any number of factors.

Comparably, sport realism has wide explanatory power in recognizing that sport officials have motivating reasons that may go beyond the rules and principles of sport. It explains the role of organizations and officials in sports, along with how and why they act. Finally, legal realists approach law as a profession, with its members most interested in predicting future decisions or rulings. Sport realism aims to predict future outcomes and resolutions, since people involved in sport are most interested in what will happen in upcoming disputes.

A REALIST APPROACH TO LAW

Preliminaries

Legal realism might seem an odd choice given that its height of popularity in American jurisprudence was attained in the first half of the twentieth century before fading from prominence. Today, legal realism is regarded as an "adolescent phase" of American law.[3] Its value is acknowledged by the common refrain that "we are all realists now," but its contemporary significance has been largely reduced to being a forerunner to subsequent movements like critical legal studies (CLS) and critical race theory (CRT). Such an attitude toward legal realism is understandable but misguided. Its core tenets were not simply ideas to move beyond, and its main features have not been incorporated into legal study. Legal realism has become more visible in recent years as scholars have rehabilitated and reconstructed key realist insights. Before constructing my theory of sport, I will explore the aims of legal realism and its merits as a theory of law.

Legal realism is not a school of thought with a clear manifesto or program.[4] On its simplest definition, it is the view that judges respond primarily to the facts in concrete cases or decide based on the facts of the case, rather than doing so on the rules (or principles) of law. A frequent rendering is that judges respond primarily to "the stimulus of the facts," which emphasizes the role of particular judges in deciding cases.[5] Legal realists claim to study the law as it really exists as opposed to some ideal of law that proves inconsistent with the facts on the ground. They take judicial decisions to represent how the law really works. With this focus, some consider the development of a theory of adjudication to be the central realist project.[6] Realists argue that judges often respond to non-legal reasons and inputs in making their decisions, so these must be included in any account of the law or legal reasoning.

In accepting that judges decide based on many reasons and influences, legal realism undermines the idea that legal reasoning is deductive in nature, a view typically associated with legal formalism.[7] Moreover, the legal realist approach reduces the explanatory power of legal features like statutes and precedents by holding that these are often not deciding factors in law. So legal realists do not accept that the law can be fully defined through its formal features. As we saw in Chapter 1, legal positivists typically define law in terms of its rules. Ronald Dworkin rejected the positivist definition, finding that law included both rules and principles. Legal realism is comparable to Dworkin in contending that the rules do not exhaust the law, although realists deny that principles are the missing piece. For realists, the law is found in the activity and profession of law, including the actual processes by which legal disputes are resolved.

In its most basic form, the realist finds law in what judges (or courts) actually do, not merely what is written down. This maxim has been understood to embrace or justify wide judicial discretion. Realists do identify areas of uncertainty in law, but realism is not equivalent with judicial discretion. Realists expect that law is generally predictable; they anticipate how legal reasoning and decision-making will occur. Wide judicial discretion would undermine this basic aim of predicting legal outcomes. Thus, it is *prima facie* implausible to associate realism with discretion.[8] Rather, legal realists pursue identification of patterns of adjudication in order to better understand the mechanisms by which courts act. Judges respond to the facts of cases in unique and personal manners, but this does not entail that judges decide based on nothing other than personal or political biases. Judges act in identifiable and accessible ways, even if these are not always explained through appeal to rules and legal reasons.

Realists connect this predictability of law to its expediency; law cannot be practiced effectively if its decisions are mysterious or unexpected. This approach has been termed functionalist, meaning it "reflected an attempt to understand law in terms of its factual context and economic and social consequences."[9] Functionalism makes central the usefulness of law for those who work with it. A theory of law succeeds only if it simultaneously explains legal decisions and envisages those that are forthcoming. As a result, legal realists do not focus on developing a conception of law or see it as an abstract object to study.[10] As Brian Leiter notes, interest in the concept of law did not become popular until Hart's work. To construe realism as a conceptual account of law would seem to have it answering a question that had yet to emerge.[11] And we risk losing sight of legal realism if we imagine its proponents providing a direct response, without reconstruction, to the later concerns of those like Hart and Dworkin.[12] Instead, we should recognize legal realism as pursuing a more useful way of approaching the law by describing how it operates, not as an attempt to define the law.

Oliver Wendell Holmes, Jr.

My interest is not limited to scholars under the label of legal realism. I also find influence in their precursor Oliver Wendell Holmes, Jr., who legal realists came to see as a forerunner of their own view on questions of law and adjudication. Here, I will focus on the position Holmes advocated in his groundbreaking essay "The Path of the Law."[13] Holmes criticized other jurists for misrepresenting the role of principles in judicial decisions. Decisions are often made for political and economic reasons, with appeals to principles serving only to cloak them in legal language. Principles can disguise the deeper motives that judges employ in their reasoning.[14] Holmes did not mean that rules and principles are not part of the law, but that they offer at best an incomplete account of law. Holmes sought to understand law as it actually functioned in the world, leading him to adopt what we today recognize as an evolutionary account. The law emerges through human actions, sometimes even without direction from lawmakers. Thus, it is essential to understand the social context in which laws and decisions are made.

Holmes did not criticize other jurists for acting on political and economic motives. Rather, he took issue with how they hid or ignored the fact that their motives did not match their judicial opinions. He encouraged them to take ownership of their methods. Holmes believed that cases are decided on their facts, one case at a time. His contextualist view of law removes the boundaries that legal positivists associate with it; the appropriate reasons are determined by the needs of the case, not constrained by a prior definition of the law.[15] And he broke with legal formalists on the nature of legal reasoning. Where formalists attempt to delineate a distinct manner of adjudication, Holmes insisted that legal outcomes can be reached in many ways.

Holmes provided perhaps his most well-known analysis of these features of jurisprudence in his dissent from *Lochner v. New York*, which included his oft-quoted statement "general principles do not decide concrete cases."[16] In *Lochner* a majority of the Supreme Court rejected as unconstitutional a law limiting employees from working more than 10 hours a day or 60 hours a week. The majority's decision was grounded in an interpretation of the Fourteenth Amendment, based on an expansive concept of freedom and the court's role in protecting that freedom. Justice John Marshall Harlan's dissent held that the majority was mistaken, but he accepted the majority's conception of freedom. He dissented because the state may have had other good reasons for the law. Harlan appealed to additional non-legal sources in making this case, including a scientific treatise called "Diseases of the Workers." Holmes argued that both the majority and Harlan's dissent were engaged primarily in policy analysis rather than traditional adjudication, and that they made no distinction between legal and non-legal reasons in doing so. He criticized the other justices for obscuring their policymaking. In doing so, the Court acted undemocratically and under false pretenses, so Holmes found that the Court should defer to the legislature that had engaged more thoroughly in a policy debate on the issue. The justices were not wrong to use economic theory, but they should defer to the legislature when possible. Thus, Holmes accepted that a policymaking approach is best suited in this case, but his dissent was ambivalent about where precisely this analysis must occur.

Holmes expressed skepticism about the possibility of identifying anything like the nature of law, at least as others understood it. Holmes characterized law as, essentially, how the courts act. The decision made in any case depends largely on the surrounding social conditions, including whether they are ready or untimely for various outcomes. This makes appellate courts the true arbiters of law. At that level, judges act akin to legislators, making decisions based on their expediency for the community. In practice, judges weigh competing policy alternatives. More abstract rules and rationales generally emerge after the contours of the issue have been developed through specific cases, or when gray areas need to be removed. This element of Holmes' view reflects influence from the American pragmatist tradition, as the law works through custom and practice to develop clarity and abstraction over time.[17]

Holmes innovated by examining law as profession. He did not find value in treating law as an abstract body of rules or concepts. Instead, one studies law for practical reasons. He put this in terms of lawyers who study the law not to know how the laws read but in order to best advise clients. These individuals "want to know under what circumstances and how far they will run the risk of coming against what is so much stronger than themselves," namely the legal consequences that may occur.[18] This perspective views the courts in an instrumental manner. Understanding the law entails successful prediction of how courts will act in deciding cases. It is tempting to say that the nature of law amounts to recognizing which actions will, in fact, prompt sanction by a court. Such a definition might be too narrow because we may not construe every judicial decision as a matter of sanction, but the sentiment is right. The nature of law is not found in what the law says but in knowing how it will manifest in particular cases, given the facts of the case and the social conditions in which it arises.

Holmes simplified his position through his memorable "bad man" example:

> If you want to know the law and nothing else, you must look at it as a bad man, who cares only for the material consequences which such knowledge enables him to predict, not as a good one, who finds his reasons for conduct, whether inside the law or outside of it, in the vaguer sanctions of conscience.[19]

Despite all the talk of rules, only the consequences truly matter to the bad man, since the law amounts to what will be done. By studying the law from this perspective, we gain a new understanding of what parts of law really matter. For Holmes, the bad man perspective also provided the clearest distinction between law and morality. Morality does not, and should not, provide insight into the nature of law as it is actually practiced in the courts.

We should keep in mind that while Holmes' bad man example accentuates features of his perspective, the example is limited and does not reflect the broader realist view. First, it is too narrow to reflect the law as a whole. Namely, the law exists outside the court, as the processes of making law and its interpretation by other officials seem relevant. Second, the example overstates his position, making it appear more cynical in nature. Holmes himself was aware of this portrayal.[20] Jack Balkin and Sanford Levinson argue that the bad man is not a unique figure in Holmes' thought; on his account both the bad man and the good man respond to the threat of sanction and require a practical conception of the law.[21] Holmes' insistence in looking at the bad man has resulted in a more negative, skeptical view of the law than he is actually committed to. The larger point he wants to get across through the example is that studying law entails an unsentimental and accurate conception of human action and motivation. His vision influenced the later legal realist tradition, and I will argue that its core elements and examples also should inform our view of sport.

Development of Legal Realism

Legal realism emerged as an identifiable approach to law in the early twentieth century, especially the 1920s and 1930s. We can best understand the most important (for current purposes) themes and ideas of legal realism by examining what it sought to accomplish. Scholars today frame legal realism as a response to the classical legal theory that dominated the nineteenth century, and specifically to its prominent defender Christopher Columbus Langdell. Classicists approached law in the same manner as a rational science like geometry, in which fundamental axioms—often derived from empirical observation—could reveal specific rules or corollaries when approached through deduction and similar reasoning processes.[22] The presumption of a well-ordered and complete system made classicism into a formalist exercise. Langdell himself drew upon disciplines like zoology and botany to show how law was a rational science of classification. Since he found "that all law should be reduced to a set of well-categorized rules and principles," he sought to revolutionize the study and teaching of law.[23] He eschewed apprenticeship in favor of the case method. By collecting cases on various topics and identifying the significant and inconsequential ones, scholars could deduce the general legal principle to be drawn from each case. Langdell's science of law served to legitimate the study of law at universities, and it removed law from the political realm.[24]

Legal realists did not oppose the broadly scientific nature of law, but they found it to be a different kind of science. Laura Kalman observes that this shift mirrored that of economics, in which many economists repudiated the abstractions of classical economic theory in order to focus on social processes, including societal institutions.[25] Legal realists considered social processes essential to law, and they were inspired more generally by the empirical methods of social sciences. To use contemporary terminology, the shift in the scientific foundation of law resulted in its naturalization. Realists sought to study and explain law in the same manner as these other sciences, burgeoned by insights of the sciences of human behavior.[26] On Leiter's interpretation, realists maintained that the law is rationally indeterminate because the class of legitimate legal reasons does not justify a unique outcome in each case.[27] Thus, realists denied that a formalist method of deduction or reasoning could help us understand or explain the law in practice.

Legal realists held that law exists imperfectly in a social world; lawyers cannot deduce the law but still must make sense of it. Accordingly, realists adopted "predictivism." Following the example set by Holmes, they aimed to develop "accurate scientific knowledge about judicial behavior patterns" so they could predict the law and advise their clients.[28] As a result, a sense of usefulness or pragmatism is inherent to their approach. Their emphasis on social processes and prediction led them to diminish the importance of legal rules and concepts, which are not entirely predictive. The rules should be compared to what officials actually do in order to see which have practical import.

The nature of this rule skepticism often has been misunderstood or overemphasized. Legal realists investigated the uncertainties of the rules that make up the law, and they concluded that the rules do not fully capture the way courts actually decide cases.[29] Suri Ratnapala presents three reasons why a rule may not be followed by courts: the court may not wish to follow it, it may think that earlier opinions got the law wrong, or it may find that the relevant social conditions have changed.[30] Yet realists did not reject entirely rules and concepts, since they can be useful in predicting judicial decisions.[31] For example, Karl Llewellyn argued that defining law in terms of what courts or other officials do reframes the importance of rules, writing "judges think that they must follow rules, and people highly approve of that thinking."[32] Accordingly, rules and their manipulation remain central features of law, even as realists found that other factors were equally relevant or useful. That is, rules and concepts are not the sole determinants of law, and non-legal reasons can explain and justify judicial decisions within the practice of law.

Some scholars argue that rules and concepts are not entirely predictive due to judicial idiosyncrasy. If judges decide based on their feelings or psychological dispositions, rules and concepts will not fully explain judicial behavior. However, we should resist interpreting legal realists as focused entirely on idiosyncrasies, since the claim that judges rule primarily by unique individual factors would preclude precisely the kind of predictions that realists aimed to make. Most realists explored the political, economic, and moral biases and policy considerations that might influence, subconsciously, judicial behavior.[33] To this end, Leiter contends that we best understand the realist project as a search for patterns that judicial decisions fall into. We can identify these patterns if we recognize different "situation types," since judges are responding to the underlying facts of legal disputes.[34] Thus, legal realists sought to understand the features of cases that result in certain judicial actions.

Moreover, predicting behavior need not be limited to identification of subconscious influences. Realists made no distinction between legal and non-legal reasons because they found judges who acted based on reasons outside the law. For example, judges may overtly act in ways motivated by morality or politics, which are not limited to subconscious influence. Typically, judges are wary of their discretionary power, but American judges tend to think of themselves as lawmakers.[35] Consequently, there are many tools at their disposal to reach the right or best outcome in a case.

The primary goal of legal realism was to develop an accurate understanding of the law beyond the pretense of formalism or legal reasoning. Yet, many realists maintained that law was not an end itself, instead viewing the law as an instrument to promote social welfare. The empirical knowledge of social and economic conditions that legal realists pursued could then be used to direct legal and social reform.[36] Additionally, by discovering that judges engage in lawmaking, some realists advocated that courts revise law to better keep up with a changing society.[37] Likewise, courts could make legal rules sharper and narrower so they might be more useful in practice. Other realists went further, connecting the need for legal reform to the demands of justice. After all, the law was meant to promote justice in the first place, so if society's notion of justice changes, the law should change accordingly.[38] However, we might wonder if there is a tension in the predictive and justice-oriented aspects of realism. The pursuit of justice might allow for more political and moral biases, making it harder to predict judicial behavior. This tension is reduced if legal realists emphasize the pursuit of justice found in revising law to keep up with the wider society.

People may want to continue debating the merits of legal realism, which I have only here sketched as a theory of law. But we need not resolve all such concerns in order to locate the implications for sport. I find legal realism a plausible theory of law, but it does not need to be shown the best theory of law for it to serve as a viable touchstone for what I will maintain is a more successful theory of sport, with emphasis on predicting how decisions in sport will be made.

A REALIST APPROACH TO SPORT

Basic Commitments of Sport Realism

To move from realism in law to realism in sport, we can begin with a description offered by Llewellyn, first referenced in the Introduction, regarding some similarities between umpires and legal officials:

> Like an umpire in that he does not always see the breach of the rules. Like an umpire in that at times he is severely partial to one side, or stubborn, or ignorant, or ill tempered . . . Like an umpire finally in that his decision is made only after the event, and that play is held up while he is making it, and that he is cursed roundly by the losing party and gets little enough thanks from the winner.[39]

Llewellyn does not imply that either activity is undermined by suggesting that an umpire or jurist may be partial, stubborn, or ignorant. In fact, recognition of these human influences improves our understanding of the activity. Both umpires and judges are entrusted to ensure their "game" continues, broadly in accord with the practices laid out by respective authorities. The decisions made by umpires and judges occur in concrete situations, with numerous inputs into their decision-making processes. According to Llewellyn and other legal realists, understanding why a legal ruling is made may require consideration of the context and individuals involved in the ruling, along with the relevant rules. I contend that a comparable approach is needed to explain decisions made in sport.

The central idea of my realist theory is that sport should be defined in the manner that it occurs, or as the activities of sport actually take place. To do so, I look to decisions made by sport officials of all sorts and how participants use past adjudications. These decisions orient and motivate the participants of sport. When participants recognize how certain actions are judged, they modify their behavior accordingly. Whether these decisions are based on rules, principles, or other factors is irrelevant. Those involved in sport aim to identify how future disputes will be addressed, and they characterize sport in these terms.

Sport realism places emphasis on the people and communities that comprise sport, along with the decisions that are made within and surrounding them by individuals and institutions. This is not to say that formal analysis of sport is impossible, or that the rules have no role in a theory of sport. Legal realists accepted that the written rules, and the pressure to follow them, have predictive significance. We can say the same for sport. In situations where the rules are largely predictive, we find what Hanoch Dagan calls a "rule-oriented realism."[40] In simple cases, the rules typically provide the best explanation for why some decision is made or some action occurs. Although even here the rules are not really the main source of the explanation. The stability of the rules depends on a convergence of the background understanding of the practitioners. The rules explain why a certain action is performed or decision made when there is a shared expectation to keep and follow the rules as written, regardless of the participants' reasons for doing so. In complex cases, the rules may or may not provide the most significant influence on the decision—on this I agree with interpretivism. Yet the same limitations apply to principles and abstract concepts; these surely influence and motivate some individuals, and they undergird dominant ideologies within sport, even if they are not the exclusive reasons for decisions.

Legal realists hold that judicial decisions are motivated by legal and non-legal reasons, which include factors like social pressure or political belief, and these are included in an analysis of the ever-evolving practice of law. Sports do not have comparable terminology, but the same idea applies for sport realism. Other theories try to delineate the category of reasons internal to sport by identifying those rules and principles that are appropriate for consideration. However, a realist approach to sport recognizes that such a distinction is untenable in practice. Sport adjudicators make decisions based on all sorts of reasons, and an adequate explanation of sport must account for all of these. Acknowledging how sport adjudication actually happens, and revealing that sport is not always organized around its rules, principles, or sense of purpose, will not undermine sport in any way. It is already commonplace for people to note imperfections in sport adjudication, including complaints of bias, obvious mistaken calls, and technological limitations. Moreover, sport officials do not have the perceived authority of judges, and sporting systems do not require such a high standard of legitimacy. Yet sports continue, with immense popularity. So realism does not threaten to deconstruct sport when it accepts that the sport equivalent of legal and non-legal reasons both motivate action with the practice of sport.

An examination of U.S. intercollegiate athletics provides an initial example of how realism shifts our conception of sport. The National Collegiate Athletic Association (NCAA) purports to promote the interests of student athletes through the development of rules and guidelines that govern collegiate sports. There is no doubt that NCAA institutions provide athletic opportunities that would otherwise not exist. To understand various NCAA decisions, it may be tempting to interpret them in light of its seeming core principles of fairness, amateurism, and the benefit of student athletes. Many cases reveal the limited explanatory power of such principles. Consider the continual expansion of NCAA playoffs, such as the recent creation of a Division I football championship. These playoffs, along with countless bowl games, provide opportunities for more teams to play additional games at neutral sites. But the desire for additional games is at odds with the "student" aspect of student athletes. In the 2017–2018 season eighty Division I football teams—well more than half of all teams—participated in a bowl game. These bowls involve weeks of extra practice, with the playoff games now stretching into the spring semester for many universities. Surely these do not benefit the student-athlete qua student.

The more plausible explanation is a monetary one. Even though many bowl games have meager attendance and low television ratings, partnerships between the NCAA, conferences, and media outlets require ample football content, including an additional week for an official championship. I am not claiming that sport realism is the only theory to recognize how the NCAA truly acts, but I do believe it gets to that conclusion most straightforwardly. For one, by rejecting the sport equivalent of a legal/non-legal distinction of reasons, sport realism pays attention to all of the inputs and motivations. It seems evident that many of the guiding reasons go outside sport to include additional social and economic reasons. These other motivations appear to dwarf interest in maximizing athletic excellence, skills, or other such principles, which are surely considerations but not decisive. Thus, an account of decisions made within the realm of NCAA athletics will have to take into account the history of the NCAA athletics being run primarily as a business, not as a romanticized realm of amateur athletic virtues. A complete explanation of these sports cannot be satisfied if our theory of sport approaches them through the lenses of the rules or excellence alone.

Legal realists were inspired by the empiricism of social science, in contrast to the rational, deductive approach of the nineteenth century. Sport realism is a philosophical theory, not a social scientific account of sport, since its focus remains primarily on philosophical questions and methods. Realism, nonetheless, implies a naturalization of sport in the sense that a theory of sport should be consistent with our best accounts of human behavior and motivation. The overall bent of sport realism is empirical in its pursuit of the best explanation of decisions as supported by available evidence. Sport realism is anti-foundationalist in that the facts of specific cases generally will not lead to a single "best" decision or outcome that can be rationally deduced. Instead, realists use philosophical and scientific investigation to ascertain the motivating reasons that underlie sport.

Sport realism is functionalist in nature. For some legal realists, functionalism provided a theory of meaning, that concepts should be defined in terms of actual experience.[41] More broadly, a functionalist approach aims to understand sport in its context, with an eye toward its social consequences.[42] Abstract concepts and rules should be redefined in terms of recognizable patterns and arrangements, which we can ascertain from studying individual cases. In other words, cases take precedent, and only from these can we recognize patterns of decision-making within sport. A functionalist sport realism turns the question of the nature of sport into one of what decision-makers will actually do, including how legal rules and principles actually influence actions, along with what other sorts of reasons are involved. Functionalism in sport shifts its examination to figuring out what will happen, how activities will occur, or which decisions will be made, since these conclusions are most significant to those involved in the situation. Simply put, sport realism defines sport in terms of the decisions, and predictions thereof, that are made (or tend to be made).

To sum up, sport realism defines sport in terms of its operation. It rejects the idea that sport can be defined by its formal features such as rules, or even the introduction of principles. Realism views sport in its context, but without appeal to conventions or the purposes people attribute to sport. Instead, the primary goal of realism is to explain sport for those involved in it. A successful explanation is one that allows for prediction of how decisions will be made by sports officials. Sport realists accept that decisions will derive from all sorts of reasons, not those limited to a specific category or class of reasons. So sports decisions should be recognized as more similar to policymaking actions than to neutral or passive adjudication.

Predictivism

Predictivism, as noted earlier, was the name for the legal realist view about developing knowledge of patterns in judicial decisions in order to better predict and practice law. Predictivism proved one of legal realism's most controversial ideas, often because it was taken to comprise the entire theory rather than simply one interest of legal scholars. Sport realism treats sport in comparable terms, with participants predicting the decisions made by all sorts of sport officials. The predictive aim compares to Holmes' claim that law should be treated as a profession because lawyers try to predict outcomes as a means to help their clients. Similarly, decisions in sport matter because individuals are invested in them, often professionally. The profession of sport includes players, managers, owners, media outlets, and fans, all of whom benefit from understanding and predicting decisions made throughout sport.

Holmes' key insight into legal theory, which spurred the subsequent realist movement, entailed the identification of law with the (appellate) court system rather than the rules themselves. Since sports lack a legal judicial system, one might wonder how a theory of sport can draw meaningfully from the legal realist account of law. Llewellyn's legal theory offers an idea of how to do so. He argues that the proper scope of the law is disputes, with the business of law being to do something about disputes that do, or may, arise. Consequently, we should recognize that some legal disputes are not resolved by court action, but rather by individuals he calls officials. In his words, those who deal with disputes "whether they be judges or sheriffs or clerks or jailers or lawyers, are officials of the law. *What these officials do about disputes is, to my mind, the law itself.*"[43] I propose that we incorporate this into sport realism by broadening our sense of who or what functions in a manner comparable to a court or law official in the context of sport. According to sport realism, a sport is not defined by rules, conventions, or principles but as a system in which the rules and their corresponding punishments and penalties will be applied in predictable ways to resolve disputes.

We can identify numerous officials in sport that resolve disputes and issue punishments, along with individuals and institutions that serve these same ends. Referees and umpires are the most obvious embodiment of these functions, since they perform them on the field, court, or ice. For instance, a soccer referee who gives a red card acts like a judge in both ways, deciding or interpreting the rule in the context of some action, and issuing a corresponding penalty. However, in some cases the referee does not have the last word. Holmes targeted the appellate court because it has the power to overrule lower court decisions while its own decisions are final in most cases. Most organized sports have some procedure by which actions during a game can be reviewed, and subsequent punishment given or modified. The primary cases from Chapter 2 exemplify such further adjudication by league officials or a rules committee. Yet we cannot choose to look for sport at only this level because this additional review does not occur in all situations. Most often the referee's ruling is the final one. The courts comprise one judicial system with a clear order of operations; in sport we should treat these levels as relatively distinct forms of adjudication, both of which are essential to defining and understanding sport.

Sport includes additional levels or locations at which disputes and punishment are resolved beyond referees, umpires, and official league reviews. One such location is the locker room. Coaches and managers regularly determine what will be done in certain circumstances. They perform roles of a judge in that their decisions are often final and lack external review. At other times, team officials serve this function. For instance, the team (i.e., general manager, president, owner, etc.) may suspend players if it deems they have violated certain rules or protocols. Sport disputes occur in many forms, with officials and institutions making rulings that are rarely subject to additional review. Each category entails its own fiefdom as it were, with only occasional overlap.

Still other matters are resolved "on the field" in the form of response by other players. Major League Baseball, for example, is known for having players attempt to make up for perceived infractions, with pitchers throwing purposefully at batters or runners sliding hard into bases. Rather than recognizing these as beyond legal considerations, I think they capture the relevant sense of resolution and punishment in sport, so players should count as a kind of official. While legal theory does not expect individuals to take the law upon themselves, a theory of sport would be incomplete without recognizing how players often seek to do so and are successful at it. Although "punishments" of this sort are not officially sanctioned, they are considered responses to certain actions that share the same aims as punishment (e.g., retribution, deterrence, or education). Other theories have sought to explain these actions through appeal to unwritten rules, but such analysis proves challenging when these unwritten rules conflict with the written rules. By treating actions on the field as comparable to adjudication, these disputes gain a clearer status within sport.

The penalty of holding in football provides an example to illustrate predictivism in practice. Holding is an illegal form of blocking that involves grabbing an opposing player. It is often said that holding could be called on every play in a football game, and it is widely acknowledged that referees do not call holding precisely as the infraction is defined in the rulebook. This fact should be problematic for many other theories of sport, since it implies that the rules do not accurately describe how the game is played. Yet the players and coaches in the game are not worried by the discrepancy between rules and the game on the field. Instead, they want to know what kinds of actions will or won't be penalized. Their interest is entirely in the prediction of how future actions will be adjudicated on the field. Understanding football entails looking at how the game is played on the field, and how the set of individual rulings affects future behavior. Offensive players know that grabbing a player who is running in another direction will be visible to the referee, who is likely to call a penalty. Thus, offensive players seek to develop the most effective strategies that will not be penalized during the game, and coaches design plays in light of what is likely to be allowed or disallowed on the field. While the rules (and their interpretation) might be useful in making these predictions, the calls on the field are what actually matter.

Sport realism does not distinguish between the tasks of adjudication and legislation. Many sports openly combine the two tasks in one person or body, as in a golf rules committee that also evaluates infractions, or sport commissioners like Roger Goodell who wield tremendous power to punish and write rules. Even umpires and referees must act as legislators from time to time. Consider Dave Kingman's lost fly ball from Chapter 1. No rule covered the scenario, so umpires were forced to decide what the rule should be. This ruling will likely influence future decisions, along with any necessary changes to the rule. If we look carefully, we find that sport legislation of this sort is surprisingly routine. Furthermore, sport has no comparable distinction between legal and non-legal reasons to overcome. Sport realism acknowledges that decisions made by referees, leagues, players, and coaches are influenced by a variety of inputs, within and beyond sport. These include, among others, moral and political considerations, social or economic consequences, and subconscious influences. All of these influences must be taken into consideration in order to provide the best explanation of sport.

The realist view does not hold that sport is only prediction, since this would render the process of adjudication nonsense. An official deciding what to do would be essentially predicting her own behavior.[44] Instead, the predictive aspect of sport realism entails a search for patterns in different kinds of scenarios and disputes, or what was earlier termed situation types. The consideration of situation types can reveal or identify the kinds of reasons likely to determine how the case will be resolved. For instance, predicting a referee's decision in a hard case requires empirical consideration of that situation type (i.e., how this referee and others have dealt with similar disputes), along with relevant facts about consequences, possible biases, or unique features of the case that are most likely to influence the result. Together, these features should get us most of the way there. The law is complicated, but at least many legal systems have a lengthy history of decisions made at the highest court levels, and the judges themselves usually have a long paper trail. In sport, decisions can be made by inexperienced referees, a first-time coach, or a new commissioner. Furthermore, the institutional history of most sports is shorter than that of a legal system, with rules that are changed routinely. And sport decisions are made at many different levels, without the hierarchical structure of the law. All of these are hurdles to identifying patterns that aid prediction, but none are absolute barriers to the project.

We can use another of Holmes' legal resources to develop the idea of predictivism in sport. Holmes used his "bad man" thought experiment to show how his approach best captured the practical import of law, in contrast to its formal structure. The bad man interprets law in view of possible consequences for his behavior. In the realm of sport, the "bad athlete" is an individual who might receive penalty or punishment as a result of some action by a sport official of the sorts previously described. The "badness" here is not a moral claim but refers to undesirable consequences. A football player trying to block without getting called for holding, a coach who speaks out against a mistaken call in a press conference, or a baseball player who considers stealing a base when his team already has a big lead are all "bad athletes" in this sense. To them, sport is found in (the prediction of) what, if any, penalty their actions will accrue, whether that penalty is a game infraction, a fine, or a future pitch directed at his body.

The bad athlete comparison is limited because the resolution of a dispute does not always result in one side receiving a form of punishment. Also, it would be inappropriate to label an athlete as "bad" for merely trying to gain an edge in competition. So the bad athlete notion should not be conflated with the sport realist theory as a whole. Still, the thought experiment remains useful in reorienting our theory of sport with emphasis on studying how decision-makers actually act, along with the significance of these actions in particular contexts.

So what of idiosyncratic decision-makers? Obviously prediction cannot be perfect, and some outcomes will surprise—perhaps a referee sees something others didn't, a coach acts with an unforeseen bias, or a league decides a case based on some information that had been downplayed in the past. The goal of predicting outcomes is not undermined by exceptions and imperfections. There are at least two responses to this concern. First, so long as individuals seek to understand the reasons and their influences, realism remains the best theory to explain sport. That we can identify situation types and predict some, if not most, outcomes show that sport realism will fare better than competing theories in many hard cases. In the next section, I will offer additional case studies to support the explanatory power of sport realism.

Second, participants within sport always pursue predictability. In baseball, a common refrain holds that an umpire's consistency is far more important than accuracy. The idea is that a player will be less upset if, for example, a strike is called on a ball two inches off the plate so long as the umpire consistently calls that pitch a strike for both teams. I am skeptical of this conventional wisdom, insofar as I think players (and coaches) likely will be upset on such calls regardless of consistency. However, I agree that the statement contains an important insight. To gain their best chance to succeed, players, coaches, and other participants seek to understand and predict calls so that they may adjust their behavior accordingly. In sports like soccer or basketball, players adjust to how fouls are called. Behavior during or after games is modified in view of the perceived authority of coaches or leagues. And players avoid certain actions that are perceived to violate the conventions of sport as defined by other players or the media. Sport realism offers a framework acknowledging the importance of predicting outcomes, and that sports should be understood in the context of a profession.[45]

Advantages of Sport Realism

I have argued that sport realism provides an effective explanation of sport by conceptualizing it in terms of what occurs on the field or court, with focus on how various kinds of sport officials resolve disputes. In looking at these resolutions, we can better predict how decisions will be made in the future, which affects the manner in which sport is played. Beyond explaining sport, I find that sport realism has a number of additional virtues; here I will discuss some of note.

Legal realists argue that their theory is amenable to (or even a means of) legal reform in the pursuit of justice. I believe the same can be said for sport realism. For example, a realist account should result in a clearer recognition of biases or inequalities that influence sport. The search for patterns in decision-making allows us to identify ways that officials may exclude or limit other perspectives. Imagine we find that a sport has a discrepancy in how players are punished for certain acts. We may need to reexamine the fairness of these decisions. In the NFL, many have noted that players often are suspended longer for the use of illegal substances than they are for incidents of domestic violence. This has to do, at least in part, with how these suspensions are decided. Illegal substances are governed by the collective bargaining agreement, while domestic violence suspensions are within the purview of the commissioner. Perhaps the recognition of such procedures and imbalances will lead to future changes that treat domestic violence more seriously.

Sport realism by itself may appear a relatively conservative or pragmatic approach to sport, emphasizing the way it is currently played. However, the pursuit of justice in sport may be supported through more radical approaches that can be aligned with the realist framework. Sport realists may draw upon perceptions from later legal theories influenced by legal realism, such as CLS or CRT. Proponents of CLS aim to uncover the politics and power dynamics inherent to the legal system, while advocates of CRT investigate forms of discrimination and racial inequality that the law is built on or otherwise reinforces. By adopting these or similar models of inquiry into sport, realism becomes a more progressive theory that questions the implicit or explicit biases built into the current structures of sport.[46]

Sport realism provides essential flexibility. Different sports are played under disparate sets of rules, with wide variance in how officials resolve disputes. In order to develop the best explanation for each sport, we need to look at how decisions are made in it, even down to the level of particular leagues or officials. At the same time, the principles guiding realism are broad enough to apply to sport as a whole. So realism takes in the context of each sport without devolving into descriptions of each sport that are entirely relative to it.

The plasticity of realism might make it better suited to sport than to law. Today, most legal systems have a constitution or other founding documents that ground the law. Even when the interpretation of these documents itself is in question, at least they provide a common ground for discussion and debate.

Hence, many object to legal realism because the rules or foundational documents provide some framework in which the law must be adjudicated, marking a proper distinction between legal and non-legal reasons. Sports have no such common framework. Most sports have nothing like a constitution, and no overarching guidance beyond a rulebook. Aside from certain events like the Olympics, few sports claim any broader purpose or meaning. Thus, while legal scholars might appeal to implied principles or foundational aims, no clear framework exists for sports.

One could argue that sports ought to develop such a framework, or that they should seek guiding principles that officials could employ in making their decisions. I have no objection to any theory that makes this kind of argument, so long as it is solely normative rather than explanatory. In my view, this is precisely what sport interpretivism amounts to: the idea that sport would be better if it could be understood in terms of rules and implied principles that we can discover through interpretation. But I have argued that sports do not function this way in practice. Until they do, sport realism offers a better explanation of sport as it is played. Even if some set of rules were to gain this traction, the result would best approximate a form of rule-oriented realism, since the stability of the rules would depend on the practitioners.

Despite its plasticity, one might object that sport realism works best with sports that are organized in ways that resemble the legal system, including officials, hierarchies, and punishments. The challenge is not unique to sport realism; it applies to any theory that uses law as a model for sport. Sport realism is better positioned than other theories to address sports that have an informal or disorganized character. To show this, I need to develop the challenge.

Consider two examples: a pick-up basketball game at a university gym, and my weekly tennis match with my colleague Steve. Neither of these activities includes referees, umpires, or any other official to adjudicate disputes, and there are no mechanisms for review. The rules are unofficial, and few principles seem to govern the activities. In the pick-up game, the conventions of the game seem relatively static, in that rules might remain consistent over an entire afternoon even as different players take the court. My tennis match lacks even this consistency; we follow most standard tennis rules, though not all, and we make occasional changes, such as shortening a set when we get tired of playing in hot, muggy weather. This game looks little like organized tennis and even less like the law.[47]

Sport realism, as I have presented it, works most clearly when applied as an institutional view of sport. By institutional, I mean that an activity is considered a sport only when it achieves a degree of popularity and organization to guide or govern the activity. Many philosophers accept such a definition of sport. If I invent my own physical activity, performed only by myself, it's not clear that it is a sport, or at least one appropriate for philosophical study of sport. This stance strikes me as reasonable when concerning the development of theories to understand the activity.[48] And as I have suggested, I believe the competing theories of sport I have described also work most effectively when applied to institutional sports. Nevertheless, I do not want to limit sports only to those with official organizations or clear institutional structures. The aforementioned pick-up basketball and tennis match lack these, but I think it's obvious that they should be considered sports. A successful theory of sport ought to be able to explain or understand them.

Both formalism and interpretivism will struggle to explain these cases of amateur, informal, or unorganized sports. The formalist defines sport in terms of the rules. When the rules are unofficial or may be changed, it may seem to the formalist that no game is being played at all. Surely this is not the right conclusion, even for my tennis match with Steve. Meanwhile, the interpretivist imagines officials interpreting the rules in light of the implied principles of sport. In these cases, there are no officials designated with identifying and interpreting the principles that underlie the activity. One might respond that the amateur or pick-up athletes themselves perform this interpretation, but I am skeptical that they do so in a manner consistent with interpretivism. It might be that players joining a pick-up game develop an interpretation of the activity, but they would not be able to do so with any real understanding of the history or trajectory of it. Perhaps Steve and I have developed an interpretive understanding of our ongoing tennis matches, as might players of a longstanding pick-up basketball game. Although I think in most cases the perspectives are too limited to really aim at a best interpretation of the activity as a whole. So I cannot see how this theory proposes to deal with hard cases in unorganized or informal sports.

Sport realism can handle these sports that lack organization or institutions because it defines sport through the actions of its officials. While informal tennis matches are unlikely to have any sort of traditional official, we can again widen our notion of who counts as an official. If an official is someone who resolves disputes and issues sanctions or punishments, then we find that the players themselves perform these functions.[49] They may even develop informal procedures to aid in such cases. For instance, in my tennis matches with Steve, we resolve typical disputes regarding whether a ball was in or out by deferring to the player closest to where the ball landed. In rare cases where an important point is borderline, we may replay the point. Other tennis players may develop different strategies for dealing with similar cases. But what matters is that the activity is taken to be the one on the court, not the rules and procedures themselves, which are not always the deciding factors for whatever decision is made.

In a pick-up basketball game, one important feature is that (typically) players call their own fouls. On adjacent courts, players may call fouls using different criteria. On one court, players may call fouls on light contact, while on the other court players call only hard, shooting fouls. For the players involved, predictability is a paramount concern. A player will change her actions based on how other players are calling fouls. And, in my experience, players get most upset not with how fouls are called in general but when one player calls them differently than everyone else. A player who continually calls touch fouls in a rough game is likely to earn the scorn of fellow players for not picking up on the patterns of how decisions are being made in that particular game.

Some might attempt to explain the differences between these adjacent pick-up games in terms of unwritten rules or conventions, but sport realism better captures the changes in the game that occur due to the manner in which it is being called. An influx of new players, for instance, may lead to changes in how fouls are called, essentially modifying the nature of sport or creating a new situation type. In such games, I am not sure what the relevant unwritten rules or conventions would be. There is no obvious practice community or sense of purpose employed in determining how fouls should be called. It will prove difficult to understand and explain the sport at any time without emphasizing the resolution of disputes in the activity, which suggests the employment of a realist framework to explain what is going on.

SPORT REALISM IN PRACTICE

My aim for the remainder of this book is to provide further defense of sport realism as the most successful theory of sport in both its explanatory and normative capacities. My defense engages with three areas of sport covered by theory. First, I will examine a number of case studies, drawn from situations that have already happened, to show that sport realism can and does explain how disputes in sport are resolved. Second, I will argue that sport realism provides adequate means to grapple with conceptual and philosophical issues in sport, using cheating as an example. Third, I will consider the normative aspects of the theory, to show that sport realism has resources available to provide guidance in resolving disputes and addressing ethical issues in sport.

So far, I have emphasized how sport realism predicts future outcomes. Here, I investigate past cases because they are important to help us identify situation types and patterns of decision-making. The sport realist goal, before or in the midst of these cases, would be to anticipate their resolution. After the fact, we can use them to aid in identifying the facts and reasons that motivated the decisions made by sport officials. All the same, I will suggest that had we viewed these cases through a sport realist framework in the first place, we may have been less surprised by their outcomes.

Michael Pineda

I will start with the two cases that were the focus of Chapter 2, beginning with Michael Pineda. The first matter is to identify which officials were involved in adjudicating the dispute. Obviously the umpire and league played direct roles in determining how to handle Pineda's use of pine tar; the umpire ejected him from the game, and MLB officials suspended him. However, neither of these reflected a hard case that required philosophical analysis. Pineda's use of pine tar was blatant, making his ejection and subsequent suspension obvious and uncontroversial. The philosophical interest of his case comes from the decisions and actions rendered by coaches and other players.

It is worth reexamining why sport realism considers players and coaches to be sport officials. At least three features of the case are relevant. First, members of the Red Sox decided to bring Pineda's pine tar to the attention of the umpire. Had they not done so, it is unlikely that Pineda would have been ejected for its use. Second, the Red Sox could have employed other forms of retaliation against the Yankees. Traditionally, such actions might include throwing at other players on the team, since pitchers do not bat in the American League. Or they could have used photographic evidence after the game to shame Pineda, perhaps inspiring some subsequent, albeit less-certain, suspension from the league. Third, calling out Pineda's actions damaged his reputation. Within baseball, the effect might be that any future attempts to use pine tar are more likely to be discovered. Outside baseball, the reputation of being a cheater may have effects such as limiting his promotional opportunities. All of these fit within the broad framework of punishment or penalty.

The sport realist searches for patterns in decision-making. Here, the situation type is the repeated and obvious use of pine tar. Pineda blatantly used pine tar a previous time and did not change his behavior, or even try to better hide it the second time. Comments from the Red Sox indicated that they were motivated by some sense of tradition or unwritten rules of baseball. In their view, Pineda showed a disregard for the way baseball should be played, and specifically the manner in which pitchers are expected to conceal certain substances. The flagrant nature of Pineda's usage required some response, and alerting the umpire was the most straightforward way to bring consequences. That the Yankees' management seemed to agree with the thrust of Boston's charges suggests the response was expected and fit the parameters of the situation. We can assume that another motivating reason involved the protection of the Red Sox's own pitchers. Many speculate that teams are hesitant to call out others for the use of illegal substances, since it might increase focus on their own players who do the same. By waiting for Pineda to use pine tar a second time, blatantly, the Red Sox avoided bringing attention to their own pitchers.

Thus far, the sport realist explanation might sound like one given by a conventionalist. I don't doubt that sport realism and conventionalism offer similar analysis in cases where the decisive reasons include appeals to tradition and unwritten rules. Nevertheless, the sport realist approach to Pineda's case differs from conventionalism in at least two ways. First, the conventionalist argues that sport is constituted by its conventions or ethos. In contrast, the realist view holds that sport is found in the decisions made by officials within sport, with conventions being only partially predictive of these. Just as there are some cases that involve appeal to conventions, we have seen that many do not. For Pineda the actions of the umpire and league are best explained by the written rules and do not require further analysis. In other words, conventions and unwritten rules have a similar status to that of the written rules, although the written rules are likely more predictive in most cases.

Sport realist analysis of the situation type helps to discern which are more likely to influence a particular case. This offers an important contrast to both early conventionalism and Morgan's conventionalist theory. Using Morgan's account of conventions, we may be able to predict outcomes when decisions are made within a practice community, or when a group is committed to a clear conception of a sport's purpose. Social norms are more difficult to predict when no single view of sport is dominant. Rather than looking to purpose, I have argued that understanding all of the factors that influence decisions will be more successful in explaining and predicting sport. Sport realism recognizes how this can be done even when the conventions or social norms are not shared by all participants.

Second, while the conventionalist encounters difficulty making sense of changes in tradition and practice, sport realism has no such trouble. For example, improved technology has itself altered the way that pine tar is used. The Red Sox were aware of Pineda's pine tar use in the previous game because it was spotted by television cameras. A. J. Pierzynski argued that Pineda needed to be more creative in how he hides his pine tar usage, but a pitcher's ability to get away with such behavior is limited now that every game is televised from multiple camera angles. Perhaps in past years the pine tar on Pineda's neck would have gone unnoticed. We can compare this to an incident involving Kenny Rogers in the 2006 World Series. In the first inning of Game 2, cameras picked up on a brown smudge on his hand, which became a point of much discussion. When Rogers returned for the second inning, his hand was clean. Rogers insisted that the brown smudge was merely dirt mixed with rosin. However, one can easily imagine this being a technique for putting a substance on a ball that became ineffective with additional cameras.

These technological changes pose trouble for conventionalist analysis. As we saw in Chapter 1, many conventionalist appeals to tradition seem to require that the unwritten rules are stagnant; players and coaches ought to do what is traditionally done, since unwritten rules lack the procedures for change that apply to the written rules. But technological innovation, media focus, and social media discussion have unavoidable implications on future behavior. Previous conventions and traditions become untenable as new motives become more important. We cannot predict how such a case might be dealt with in thirty years. Nonetheless, we can expect that a similar situation next season will likely be addressed in a comparable manner by the players and coaches on the field.

Tiger Woods

For the 2013 Masters, the official in question is the rules committee that determined the appropriate penalty for Woods' drop. The situation type would initially seem to be relatively clear, following a tradition of disqualifying players who sign an incorrect scorecard. But the situation was changed by the recent implementation of Rule 33, which indicated a desire by golf officials to change the way that some penalties, including disqualification, are applied.

The matter is further complicated because the USGA provided its own explanation of why the Masters Rules Committee acted, although not until three weeks after the tournament. In its statement, the USGA sought to quell criticism that it acted arbitrarily by claiming that the Masters Rules Committee *did not* employ Rule 33 after all.[50] It explained that the penalty of disqualification was waived because the committee had initially talked to Woods about the situation, and if it had done so with the information that came out later, the situation would have been resolved before the scorecard was signed. Essentially, the committee argued that Rule 33 did not apply since the rule concerns only video replay. Instead, it invoked an exception that waived the penalty of disqualification due to the Committee's error.

This convoluted USGA statement smacks of revisionist history, offering a retroactive explanation to justify the decision upon realizing it had opened a can of worms. Sport realism embraces the fact that the underlying reasons behind decisions are not always those that a sport theorist might want them to be. Thus, to explain this case we must consider the applicable underlying motivations behind the decision to let Woods continue play in the first place, which I contend are similar to those behind the original changes to Rule 33. I find it more plausible that the rules committee did not act precisely as the later statement suggests. Surely one factor it considered, consistent with the Rule 33 changes, was how to handle challenges brought by media technology. With viewers calling in violations that went unnoticed on the course, golf officials were put in a tough position. While most other sports would prevent outsiders from influencing rules decisions, golf professionals around the country are qualified to spot violations. Moreover, the history of golf puts great emphasis on individual accountability for an accurate score. With no game clock and tournaments that extend for days, there is ample time for penalties to be applied. The Rule 33 changes suggest that the USGA was searching for a way to minimize these penalties, which can be seen as intrusive and unfair. The Masters committee may have seen these moves as a way to regain control of the tournament and its rules.

Also, we can assume that the committee felt pressure from the players and fans. Players do not want to be disqualified for penalties they are not aware of. Fans do not want the best players disqualified on a technicality rather than basing the outcome on their quality of play. Masters officials possibly had in mind the fiasco at the 2010 PGA Championship, in which Dustin Johnson was penalized for grounding his club in a bunker that looked nothing like a regular bunker. The penalty likely cost Johnson the championship. While everyone acknowledged that the rules of the course were clearly posted, many people believed this penalty marred the championship, hindering the goal of identifying athletic excellence. Concerns of players and fans may not fit neatly within other theories of sport, but we would be naïve to ignore their influence on sport officials.

That golf officials care about popular opinion is evident in recent modifications to the rules, including further changes to the content of Rule 33 (the rules have been reorganized and renumbered in the most recent rulebook). In March 2017, golf's governing bodies released proposed changes for a six month comment period, during which it received over thirty thousand comments.[51] Based on these comments, rules were modified concerning things like drops and relief areas. In making their changes, officials were guided by the principle that golfers should not be penalized for unintentional acts they do not benefit from. While it's not clear that this principle applies in Woods' case, since he dropped two yards back in what he considered a more favorable position, it does suggest that golf will change its rules and traditions to better match the interests of modern players. We can see that principle underlying many of its recent decisions, regardless of the technical explanations it provides. Although it does not appear evident that the principle was derived from a conception of sport, given the other elements at play. Sport realism is best suited to recognize how various influences and inputs factor into decisions of this nature.

Additional motivating factors likely played a role in allowing Woods to complete the tournament. In analyzing the decision, we cannot ignore Woods' popularity. I ended Chapter 2 with a tweet from Graeme McDowell highlighting Woods' singular impact on television ratings. I doubt this was the sole factor in not disqualifying Woods, although we often acknowledge that superstar players get special treatment. Officials would be unlikely to disqualify Woods unless it was clearly the only option. Similar discussion has surrounded star players at other tournaments. Consider the 2018 US Open, in which Phil Mickelson putted a moving ball on the green. After the round, he explained that he did so strategically, as the penalty would be better than letting the ball roll off the green. His actions and comments immediately afterward undercut his claim; a more plausible explanation is that he was frustrated and not thinking about the penalty. Again, the question emerged of which rule to apply. Officials applied the rule concerning striking a moving ball, which includes a two stroke penalty but not disqualification. However, critics contend that this rule is meant for cases in which the ball is accidentally struck while moving, and that doing so intentionally should entail disqualification.[52] Some speculated, in sport realist fashion, that Mickelson's popularity led officials to treat him differently than if a lesser-known player had acted similarly.[53] Regardless of whether that is the case, the sentiment suggests that officials are influenced by factors like player popularity and importance. Ultimately, they want their tournaments to be successful, and not overshadowed by disqualifications and complex rules debates. These may not be the only factors, but they do appear to influence some decisions made by rules officials, making them relevant considerations for understanding the nature of the sport.

Jesse James' Incompletion

In the 2018 National Football League's AFC Championship Game, the New England Patriots clung to a 27–24 lead over the Pittsburgh Steelers. With twenty-eight seconds left in the game, Steelers quarterback Ben Roethlisberger found his tight end Jesse James open near the goal line. James received the ball, and as he went down he turned and lunged for the end zone. The pass was ruled complete for a touchdown, and the Steelers took the lead. Then the catch went to replay review. As James worked toward the goal line, the ball hit the ground and jostled. The question became whether James had established possession prior to the ball hitting the ground. If so, it should be a catch. If the ball hit the ground as he was in the process of catching it, then it should be incomplete. James' dive to the end zone was the complicating factor. That he could grasp the ball, turn, and lunge suggested to many he had satisfactory control of the ball. Instead, the referee determined that James' catch did not "survive going to the ground," so the pass was ruled incomplete. The Patriots won by the same 27–24 score. After the game, players and coaches on both sides admitted confusion regarding the call.

Many observers of the NFL believed the wrong decision had been made on James' incompletion. As the play was being reviewed, the announcers believed the only question was whether James had been touched by a defender before crossing the goal line. Only after numerous replays did they recognize a question of whether the pass was complete in the first place, and they expressed surprise over the eventual reversal. Once again, theories of sport are challenged to explain what happened. At first glance, this might seem to be an easy case, since determining whether a ball is caught or not should be straightforward. But the NFL rules make this kind of catch into a hard case. In requiring referees to determine whether the receiver made a "football move" sufficient to establish possession, they are left to adjudicate a dispute concerning the rules.

Interpretivism is of little help in explaining this case. The referees did not interpret the rules in light of any unwritten principles, and their decision did not create anything like the next chapter of a chain novel. Similarly, conventionalism does not add much to our understanding of the case. There is no clear ethos or sense of purpose at play, nor does this dispute concerning a catch show a conflict of different communities or traditions. Sport realism makes the most sense given the context. The players, coaches, and fans want to know which actions do and do not count as receptions in football, so predictivism best captures how those involved are evaluating the situation at hand. Those involved look to classify the situation type and predict the outcome based on empirical evidence of identifiable patterns in prior decisions.

Recognizing the situation type for questionable receptions should be fairly direct, as there are many disputed calls each year that depend on claims of what constitutes "going to the ground" or a "football move." Predicting how referees will rule has proven difficult, as is evidenced by the announcers' surprise in this case. Still, this is the most reasonable approach to understanding such situations. There is no absolute determination of whether a certain play was a catch or incompletion, but simply chalking it up to official discretion is unhelpful. Players, coaches, and announcers will consider similar situations that have happened, perhaps even those with the same referees, to predict the likely outcome. This process of prediction resembles how players might determine whether or not a certain referee is likely to call penalties such as holding or pass interference in particular circumstances, only with disputed catches there are fewer past instances to look at. This makes them more difficult to predict ahead of time.

The situation type of uncertain receptions has been altered by replay review and rule changes. The ability to review plays prevents obvious mistakes; the referee can see that the ball hit the ground or the receiver was out of bounds when these were missed in real-time. But the introduction of replay review also brings to light actions that would have otherwise gone unseen.

With James' play, that the ball moved and hit the ground was evident to the referees and announcers only after additional views. Referees using replay can look for any ball movement that would indicate the receiver did not maintain complete control throughout the play. For current purposes, we need not evaluate whether replay review is appropriate or beneficial for football.[54] We only need to acknowledge that the referee now looks for small movement that previously would have been unnoticed. Therefore, previously unknown or irrelevant information is now essential to the situation type.

The dispute concerning James' incompletion is not unique in the annals of football. It seems like every season at least one game is decided on the basis of whether a pass is complete or incomplete. For the sport realist, the bigger issue is that players, coaches, fans, and media seem unable to predict the decision in any particular case. That no one has a consistent understanding of what constitutes a catch is, from the sport realist perspective, a significant problem for the profession of football, whether due to a poor rule, poor officiating, or something else. We expect some consistency or pattern to how a football catch is understood. Without this, the ruling might seem random or arbitrary, which inhibits those who need to predict the actions of officials from being most effective at their jobs. Thus, the sport realist advocates that the NFL work to clarify the rule and to get all interested parties on the same page. In fact, the NFL did modify the rule after the 2018 season. It remains to be seen whether these changes will be effective. Since each change limits the applicability of previous catches to the situation type, it may be some time before a determination can be made.

CONCLUSION

These case studies show that sport realism can explain how decisions have been made, with more success than competing theories. Yet they all share a potentially misleading feature—they derive from professional sports. Just as Holmes reimagined law as a profession, these examples may seem to make sport entirely into a profession, which would limit its explanatory power. But sport realism explains any number of cases outside professional sports, and my previous examples should serve as useful guideposts. My focus on these professional sports in this section is due to the widespread awareness and availability of commentary on the decision-making process.

Let's return to the pick-up basketball example. Consider the following scenario: a new player joins a pre-existing group of friends for a pick-up basketball game. The new player consistently calls opponents for blocking fouls, which are contested by the defense. The dispute seems to arise due to a disagreement of conventions. The new player brings a different understanding of the ethos of pick-up basketball. The conventionalist has little to offer, since neither set of conventions has preferred status over the other. Just because one set of players on that court has played one way does not entail that a new arrangement of players ought to do so. And I find no overriding excellence, purpose, or constitutive skill at stake in defining the difference between a charge and block. In a pick-up game, there is no rule or rulebook to interpret in the first place. From the sport realist perspective, the new player's actions and expectations have disrupted the situation type. The participants are no longer sure which precedents and previous actions will predict how fouls will be called going forward. Most likely, one set of players will adjust in the interest of consistency, or else the new player will not be invited to play again.

Sport realism captures sport as it is played, which directs attention to the sports officials who decide or adjudicate the activity. I have argued that sport realism succeeds by shifting our conception of sport to those directly involved in the game. As a result, we find no clear delineation between the sorts of reasons, motives, and influences that officials act on in practice. While any single decision may seem idiosyncratic, reflection on sport shows that these decisions fall into patterns and situation types that we can study and use to predict future outcomes. Sport realism provides a more accurate understanding of sport, and taking this approach adds a kind of flexibility that benefits sport in a variety of ways. Having shown that sport realism can explain how sport is played, I will explore next how it analyzes topics within the philosophy of sport.

NOTES

1. Others have used the term "realism" to describe theories of sport, although none of these realist views are similar to my sport realism. Nicholas Dixon embraces the label of realist. He uses "sporting realism" in reference to moral realism, so it covers his and Robert Simon's moral realist versions of interpretivism, supported by discourse ethics. Claudio Tamburrini defends a realist view of sport that bears similarity to conventionalism. His realism entails expanding our conception of ethos in sport to include conventions and other norms. And Randolph Feezell characterizes a realist as someone who believes the ultimate purpose of sport is to win. Feezell rejects realism on grounds that it removes any ethical point of view and renders any action permissible in pursuit of victory. Dixon, "Canadian Figure Skaters, French Judges, and Realism in Sport," *Journal of the Philosophy of Sport* 30, no. 2 (2003): 110–112; Tamburrini, "The 'Hand of God'?," in *The Ethics of Sport*, ed. Mike McNamee (London: Routledge, 2010), 136, 140; Feezell, "Baseball, Cheating, and Tradition: Would Kant Cork his Bat?," in *Baseball and Philosophy*, ed. Eric Bronson (Chicago: Open Court, 2004), 113–123; and Feezell, *Playing Games* (London: Routledge, 2017), 78–79.

2. When I discuss legal realism, I exclusively mean American rather than Scandinavian legal realism. American legal realism considered the manner in which the law is made and developed, with particular emphasis on appellate courts. As we will see, it sought to create an empirical, social scientific understanding of law and how it is made in practice. While American legal realism has its roots in pragmatism, Scandinavian legal realism emerged out of logical positivism. Its naturalist approach led to criticism and skepticism of metaphysical concepts and explanations that do not correspond with those that exist in the world. Accordingly, Scandinavian legal realism developed an interest in the sociology of law, investigating how the force of law is produced. For a concise discussion of Scandinavian legal realism and its differences with American legal realism, see Suri Ratnapala, *Jurisprudence*, 2nd ed. (Cambridge: Cambridge University Press, 2013), 119–130. Those seeking a more thorough discussion may look to Gregory S. Alexander, "Comparing the Two Legal Realisms—American and Scandinavian," *American Journal of Comparative Law* 50, no. 1 (2002) or Michael Martin, *Legal Realism: American and Scandinavian* (New York: Peter Lang Publishing, Inc., 1997).

3. Wouter de Been, *Legal Realism Regained* (Stanford, CA: Stanford University Press, 2008), 8.

4. Martin, *Legal Realism*, 29.

5. Brian Leiter, *Naturalizing Jurisprudence* (Oxford: Oxford University Press, 2007), 22. Leiter calls this the "core claim" of legal realism, and he uses this phrase referring to the stimulus of the facts throughout the book. However, he notes that legal realist Herman Oliphant used the same language, and other legal realists offered similar characterizations.

6. Examples include William W. Fisher III, Morton J. Horwitz, and Thomas A. Reed, "Introduction," in *American Legal Realism*, ed. William W. Fisher, Morton J. Horwitz, and Thomas A. Reed (Oxford: Oxford University Press, 1993), xiii–xiv and Leiter, *Jurisprudence*, 88.

7. Leiter, *Jurisprudence*, 24. See also Laura Kalman, *Legal Realism at Yale: 1927–1960* (Chapel Hill: University of North Carolina Press, 1986), 6–8.

8. Leiter, *Jurisprudence*, 25–26.

9. Kalman, *Legal Realism*, 3.

10. Leiter, *Jurisprudence*, 60. Michael Martin emphasizes that the legal realist project is pragmatic in nature. Rather than defining law, realists are presenting some ways that it might be useful to view or define law, for scientific purposes. Martin, *Legal Realism*, 69–76.

11. Leiter, *Jurisprudence*, 104.

12. That legal realism offers an account of legal adjudication is uncontroversial. Some legal scholars might object to the implication that legal realism itself offers a theory of law beyond adjudication. Of course, in order to develop a theory of adjudication, legal realists must presuppose some understanding of the nature of law. And we can locate legal realist commitments regarding the nature of law. For instance, legal realists were aware of positivism through early advocates like John Austin. Legal realists agree with positivists that the law should be understood as it is rather than as it ought to be, the implication being that morality and law have a relationship

that is merely contingent. The law can, and should, be studied without reference to moral principles, and the legitimacy of law does not require moral foundation. This places legal realism in contrast to Dworkin's interpretivism, even if realists did not intend a concept of law.

13. Holmes' views developed over time, so the positions he takes in "The Path of the Law" are not always the same as those he held earlier. G. Edward White provides a clear description of how Holmes' ideas progressed to that point in *Justice Oliver Wendell Holmes: Law and the Inner Self* (Oxford: Oxford University Press, 1993), 218–224.

14. Justin Zaremby, *Legal Realism and American Law* (New York: Bloomsbury, 2014), xviii and Frederic R. Kellogg, *Oliver Wendell Holmes, Jr., Legal Theory, and Judicial Restraint* (Cambridge: Cambridge University Press, 2007), 116.

15. White contends that Holmes' position in "The Path of the Law" maintains a positivist methodology at root. Holmes urges judges to expose the ends that have served to justify legal rules, modifying the rules when needed. Such analysis can leave the judge to choose between irreconcilable preferences. White, *Justice Oliver Wendell Holmes*, 221.

16. *Lochner v. New York*, 198 U.S. 45, 76 (1905).

17. Frederic Kellogg writes, "Holmes's initial formulation of common law rules, derived by the community-oriented process of 'successive approximation' and strikingly parallel to the process Peirce attributed to the development of scientific principles, prefigures Dewey's theory of democratic inquiry. The function of a community of inquirers was as central to the legal theory of Holmes as to the scientific and philosophical theory of Peirce." Kellogg, *Legal Theory*, 109.

18. Oliver Wendell Holmes, Jr., "The Path of the Law," *Harvard Law Review* 10 (1897): 457.

19. Ibid., 459.

20. Stephen Budiansky, *Oliver Wendell Holmes: A Life in War, Law, and Ideas* (New York: W. W. Norton & Company, 2019), 244–245.

21. Jack M. Balkin and Sanford Levinson, "The 'Bad Man,' the Good, and the Self-Reliant," *Boston University Law Review* 78, no. 3 (1998).

22. Fisher III, Horwitz, and Reed, "Introduction," xii.

23. Kalman, *Legal Realism,* 11.

24. De Been, *Legal Realism Regained*, 5.

25. Kalman, *Legal Realism*, 16.

26. Leiter reconstructs what he takes to be the insights of legal realist naturalism in light of later twentieth century philosophy. For his discussion of the naturalism of legal realism, see Leiter, *Jurisprudence*, 31–46.

27. Ibid., 39.

28. De Been, *Legal Realism Regained*, 7.

29. Leiter offers a useful distinction in rule skepticism, separating what he terms Conceptual Rule-Skepticism, which denies that previously enacted rules are laws, from Empirical Rule-Skepticism, which makes empirical claims about the causal role of rules in judicial decision-making. Leiter argues that most have understood legal realists as Conceptual Rule-Skeptics, following an interpretation provided by H. L.

A. Hart, but we can instead recognize them as Empirical Rule-Skeptics who make no claims about the concept of law. Leiter, *Jurisprudence*, pp. 68–69. See also De Been, *Legal Realism Regained*, 7–8.

30. Ratnapala, *Jurisprudence*, 114.

31. Kalman, *Legal Realism*, 6. See also Zaremby, *American Law*, 45.

32. Karl N. Llewellyn, *The Bramble Bush* (Oxford: Oxford University Press, [1930] 2008), 6.

33. Kalman, *Legal Realism*, 7. See also Martin, *Legal Realism*, 109–111.

34. Leiter, *Jurisprudence*, 62.

35. Fisher III, Horwitz, and Reed, "Introduction," xv.

36. De Been, *Legal Realism Regained*, 8.

37. Ratnapala, *Jurisprudence*, 113.

38. Zaremby, *American Law*, 1.

39. Llewellyn, *Bramble Bush*, 15.

40. Hanoch Dagan, *Reconstructing American Legal Realism & Rethinking Private Law Theory* (Oxford: Oxford University Press, 2013), 54.

41. Martin P. Golding, "Realism and Functionalism in the Legal Thought of Felix S. Cohen," *Cornell Law Review* 66, no. 5 (1981): 1051–1052.

42. The sense of functionalism employed by legal realists is not the same as that used today in the law and social sciences. For legal realists it refers to the survival of rules and concepts because of their having thrived or persisted in the system. Some endure regardless of whether or not they currently benefit society. For more on the legal realist understanding of functionalism, see De Been, *Legal Realism Regained*, 89–94.

43. Llewellyn, *Bramble Bush*, 5.

44. An oversimplified version of this criticism has also been made against legal realists. Leiter, *Jurisprudence*, 17–18.

45. I'm using the sense of profession broadly. An amateur athlete, for instance, views sport as a professional, even if she is not a professional at the sport in the strictest sense. She engages in relevant behaviors such as predicting calls and punishments meted out by whoever is functioning as a sports official in that context.

46. In Chapter 5 I explore the normative aspects of realism in more detail. The main questions of that chapter are whether and how realism provides guidance to resolve disputes in sport. But I will build on these themes of how theories of ethics or justice mesh with realism to improve sport itself.

47. We should acknowledge that law also goes beyond its more formal instantiations, and it is certainly found outside the court. In an intriguing appraisal of the law, Ratnapala compares the law to children and adults playing games for fun. He argues that these games could not exist without the rules, and the introduction of an official would not change the previous rules. Ratnapala, *Jurisprudence*, 112). I take issue with his comment on officials. The introduction of an official may not change all the rules; after all, I have argued that the players themselves function as a kind of official. But a new official, with a unique pattern of decision-making, will change the manner in which the game is played.

48. It could be that, as a limitation of the subject matter, sport theories apply primarily to sports that are institutional in nature, even if we accept that the definition of sport includes activities that lack popularity or organization. In other words, it might be that a theory of sport has little to say about individual, informal activities. Some might consider this an argument against any such theory, but as I will argue below, I am not convinced that this is a problem for theories of sport.

49. The practice of players calling their own lines in tennis happens at many levels, including many NCAA sanctioned tennis matches.

50. Emily Kay, "USGA, R&A Clarify Tiger Woods' Masters Ball-drop Ruling," *SBNation.com*, May 1, 2013, https://www.sbnation.com/golf/2013/5/1/4289788/tiger-woods-masters-ball-drop-ruling-usga-ra.

51. Josh Sens, "Final Version of New Rules of Golf Include Significant Changes that Affect Everyday Golfers," *Golf.com*, March 11, 2018, http://www.golf.com/tour-news/2018/03/11/usga-unveils-final-version-proposed-rules-golf-main-changes-affecting-everyday-golfer.

52. Ian O'Connor, "Why Phil Mickelson Should Apologize, Then Withdraw from the U. S. Open," *ESPN.com*, June 16, 2018, http://www.espn.com/golf/story/_/id/23815139/phil-mickelson-withdraw-us-open-bizarre-display-13th-hole-shinnecock-hills.

53. Mitchell Berman offers additional philosophical analysis of this case in "Why Sport Illuminates Law (and Vice Versa)," *New York Law School Law Review* 63, no. 2 (2019): 239–241.

54. In Chapter 5 I will explore the kinds of normative considerations that sport realism might bring to bear on cases like this concerning the kinds of rules and procedures a sport should have, including an exploration of replay review. Suffice it to say I don't think it particularly matters whether or not a sport employs replay review, so long as we recognize how its introduction (or removal) changes the way a sport is played and officiated. However, pragmatist ethics will provide additional considerations for this topic.

Chapter 4

Cheating

Cheating is the white whale of sport ethics. It is supposed to be a paradigmatic moral wrong in sport. A person unfamiliar with philosophical sport ethics would assume reasonably that cheating is defined clearly in the discipline. An examination of the literature shows that the situation is far more complicated. There is surface-level agreement about the basic features of cheating, but little convergence on the particulars; every proposed criterion or definition seems to admit of exceptions. Without a clear definition of cheating, its centrality to sport ethics has come under suspicion.

John Russell has raised a more troubling challenge. He finds that previous attempts to define cheating are either too narrow or too broad, but he takes these failures to indicate that there is likely "no distinctive conceptual core to the notion of cheating."[1] For Russell, the diversity and deficiency of the available definitions make it unlikely that a unitary conception of cheating can be agreed upon. Instead, cheating is used as a broad term to express moral disapprobation. It is not a technical term defining a distinct kind of wrong action.[2] If sport ethicists aim to identify improper or morally wrong actions, he doubts that anything in the concept of cheating will offer a precise account of wrongness. Thus, he advocates setting aside the concept of cheating in sport ethics.

It would be shocking if the concept of cheating, so intertwined with wrongs in sport, turns out to be useless. Still, Russell's challenge is serious, and I agree with him that tweaking available definitions is insufficient. As I see it, Russell's mistake is to depict cheating solely in moral terms. He assumes that the function of cheating in sport ethics can be replaced by some other ethical analysis, such as interpretivist theory. This view conflates the definition of cheating with its (moral) wrongness, as if this is the only meaning that cheating offers. To be fair, most of the literature assumes that cheating in sport is a specific instantiation of a general phenomenon. That is, many believe that cheating in sport is fundamentally the same kind of action as cheating in other contexts. I question the underlying assumption. I will argue that cheating in sport does not admit of the same meaning or definition as cheating in other contexts.

Russell, I believe, has thrown the baby out with the bath water in his analysis of the current definitions. Although we cannot make progress toward defining cheating in a useful manner without reconsidering the context in which cheating is applied, I hope to have supplied such a theoretical framework in previous chapters. I maintain that my realist theory of sport is able to successfully define and employ the concept of cheating in sport ethics, showing cheating to be a distinct kind of (wrong) action in sport. Just as the legal wrongness of an action can be distinct from its moral wrongness, the same can be true for actions in sport. Sport realism allows for the identification of a quasi-legal sort of wrongness that applies to cheating without reducing it to a question of morality. Before developing my account of cheating, I first need to work through briefly the most common approaches to cheating in the current literature. I will identify the most significant challenges and the reasons for why we need to look elsewhere to define cheating. After constructing my definition of cheating, I will show its application to philosophy of sport and philosophy of law, with the former including a discussion of strategic fouls.

SALVAGING THE VERY CONCEPT OF CHEATING

The Dominant Model of Cheating

There is no standard definition of cheating in the philosophy of sport literature. Most definitions cluster around key concepts, creating what Ken Kirkwood calls the "dominant model." I will use his term. According to the dominant model, cheating occurs in sport when a person intentionally breaks a rule in order to gain an advantage.[3] Defined this way, cheating amounts to a form of non-cooperative behavior, so long as the activity is otherwise fair and rule-governed. The advantage gained is unfair or illicit in that it creates inequalities or interferes with the conditions of competitive equality. Most scholars accept that cheating must be done intentionally; unintentional rule-breaking may prove problematic in sport, but it is generally seen as less wrong.

I will work through the two principal features of the dominant model—rule-breaking and unfair advantage—to illustrate the shortcomings in the available definitions. I will begin with the advantage gained. S. K. Wertz claims that cheating creates an unfair advantage because "the constitutive or regulative rules and conditions for winning a contest are (were) changed in favor of one side."[4] Similarly, Randolph Feezell contends that the core conception of cheating involves "altering certain conditions of competitive equality."[5] These representative definitions indicate that cheating is wrong simply in the attempt to make a purportedly fair activity weighted toward one of the competitors.

It might seem evident that attempts to gain an illicit advantage in sport are wrong. But the notion of unfair advantage has little conceptual connection to cheating. Unfair advantages exist for reasons other cheating. Moreover, many "unfair" advantages are acceptable in sports. Some teams might have better coaching or training equipment. More pressing inequalities pertain to financial resources or location (e.g., training at high altitude). Still further imbalances may have to do with an athlete's genetics or upbringing. All of these affect the competitive balance of sport, yet none involve cheating and few are seen as genuine threats to sport. An athlete who gains an advantage comparable to blood doping through high altitude training, altitude tents, or even genetic mutation is perhaps praised, and certainly not criticized, for the advantage. And while it might be that these inherent inequalities do not change the conditions of the activity, it's hard to see how disparities in financial resources or training technologies would not lead the sport to favor some over others.[6]

Given that such advantages are routinely praised in sport, some maintain that the problem is the manner in which the advantage is gained, not the unfair advantage itself. As Ashkan Atry, Mats Hansson, and Ulrik Kihlbom note, this is also a slippery claim. After all, the problem of unfairness would seem to entail that an athlete has avoided some obstacles inherent to the sport, but oftentimes we commend those who find shortcuts or easier means to accomplish the aims of a sport.[7] Consider the various ways technology allows for studying oneself or the opponent, reducing the effort required to improve performance or defeat others. And many pharmacological or dietary substances are seen as appropriate, even as other substances are ruled out for being performance-enhancing. The distinction between appropriate and inappropriate technologies and supplements is difficult to draw because none eliminate completely the effort intrinsic to athletic success.

Scholars such as Oliver Leaman and Brian Glenney push this line farther, arguing that advantages of this sort should be sought even when they constitute cheating. Leaman acknowledges that some instances of cheating ruin the game. However, those without such deleterious effects may make the sport more exciting or provide new challenges for opponents to overcome.[8] Glenney argues that sport requires subversive acts that disrupt the normal rules of play. While he initially distinguishes subversion from cheating, he later acknowledges that the difference is not so clear; real subversion may even "cheat cheating" and overwhelm any ethical considerations.[9] With these difficulties in defining unfairness or identifying which advantages are morally problematic, this component of the dominant model is not especially helpful in defining or applying the concept of cheating.

Perhaps the inappropriateness of cheating lies not in the advantage gained but in the rule-breaking of the action. Many argue that cheating is fundamentally wrong because it is a disrespectful form of non-cooperation; the precise nature of its inherent wrongness is unclear and a matter of debate. Some hold that cheating involves breaking an agreement, made either between the participants or to the practice itself upon the decision to play. On this view, participants make explicit or implicit commitments that create something akin to a contract, although the precise nature of this contract may be spelled out in different ways.[10] For instance, Sigmund Loland puts a Rawlsian spin on the idea of a contract, that entering any rule-governed practice gives rise to a tacit social contract with a moral obligation.[11] In sport, the content of a contract is supposed to be supplied by the rules of the game. Maartje Schermer includes unwritten rules as part of the contract, since the tacit agreement to join a game includes accepting these as conditions.[12] Feezell uses contract and promise-breaking language interchangeably to explain the violation of an implied agreement to play a game.[13] Similarly, Jan Vorstenbosch describes the promise as part of the contract, while suggesting that this promise is actually made to the sport's authority rather than to fellow participants.[14]

Not all concur that agreement, contract, and promise can be used in these overlapping ways. Wertz argues that the tacit agreement to play can be neither a contract nor a promise. Relations between participants and officials are nothing like a promise, which would be too rigid to explain the changing expectations of sport. And sport is not legalistic enough to make a contract anything more than metaphorical, since walking on to the court is nothing like signing a legal contract.[15] Of greater concern for this project, these claims about sport do not provide a satisfactory explanation or definition of cheating. Specifically, the proposed content of the agreement or contract is too imprecise to ground a definition of cheating.[16] Claudio Tamburrini adds that the vagueness of the content casts doubt on the validity of a contract. Furthermore, he emphasizes that participants routinely fail to act in ways that have been supposedly agreed upon, with the implication that the agreement or promise must be relatively weak.[17] To determine the expectations that define the contract or promise, we need to examine how the sport is actually played, which suggests that rule-breaking isn't the primary concern in defining the wrongness of the action.

The notion of agreement, contract, or promise could ground an argument that rule-breaking is morally wrong, but the focus on rule-breaking fails to provide a useful definition of cheating. I take cheating be a distinct kind of action that is wrong in the context of sport; defining it as violating a tacit agreement with others gets us no closer to understanding what cheating really means to the participants. Characterizing cheating in terms of rule-breaking has additional unintended consequences regarding the nature of sport. If we are worried that intentional rule-breaking undermines the activity and its implied agreements, then we might worry that accidental rule-violations have similar effects. These are especially prevalent in amateur sports but also present in professional sports.[18] For instance, a baseball player who accidentally runs out of the basepath or unwittingly pitches with a compromised baseball acts no differently from the cheater, aside from the intention. Even if there is a moral difference between the two, their effects on the sport or advantages gained would undermine the activity in either case. We should be hesitant to reach this conclusion.

Earlier I noted that Feezell is among those who treat cheating as breaking an agreement or promise. Still, he shares the concern that using rule-breaking to define cheating fails once we recognize that other kinds of rule-breaking affect sport in the same way. Paradigmatic instances of cheating differ from other actions due to the advantage gained, not the rule-breaking itself.[19] To go in this direction would take us back to the other part of the dominant model, which already proved ambiguous and unsatisfactory. Of course, none of the challenges I have presented here are definitive, but they point to serious pitfalls with each component of the dominant model held in much of the literature. It is worth pursuing accounts beyond the dominant model.

Unwritten Rules

The above considerations reveal that rule-breaking may not be essential to cheating, at least not as normally understood. This may be because, upon reflection, some instances of rule-breaking simply aren't seen as instances of cheating. Consider a batter wiping away the chalk with his cleats in order to stand outside the batter's box, or a sprinter who times her start to beat the gun and get ahead of the other runners. Both are examples of rule-violations intended to gain an edge which might be considered unfair, although many people either do not consider these to be cheating or find them to be minor infractions. At first glance, these examples might suggest a conventionalist theory, as discussed earlier, that defines sport by its ethos. Yet conventionalism does not provide a useful conception of cheating because it can define cheating only as a violation of the manner in which the game is played. Such a definition fails to capture the wrongness that many associate with cheating. More worrisome is that it doesn't shed any light on what cheating is in the first place.

Despite conventionalism providing an unsatisfactory response, we should take seriously the idea that the ethos of sport contributes to an improved definition of cheating. Feezell offers the most promising account of cheating along this line. On his view, the rules of a game create a "prescriptive atmosphere," which "defines an atmosphere of competitive expectations in which the participants may gain a competitive advantage, and perhaps win, only in the context of an underlying equality expressed in the rules."[20] More simply, the explicit rules play an important role in defining the atmosphere of a sport, but "latent agreements" including custom and unwritten rules also partially constitute it.[21] Feezell describes this atmosphere as prescriptive because it encourages or restrains specific actions in that particular sport. Cheating is defined in reference to this atmosphere, meaning that some rule-breaking acts are "part of the game" rather than forms of cheating.

An obvious worry about this view is that what counts as cheating might change as goes the ethos. Feezell allows that a sport's prescriptive atmosphere can change due to social and cultural pressures. He compares moral judgments about cheating to aesthetic judgments concerning the value of art. The explicit rules and traditions that govern the case will make some core cases of cheating obvious. While difficult cases will emerge around the margins of this prescriptive atmosphere, we should not conclude from such uncertainty that anything goes. On his view, the standards still provide a useful distinction between which actions comprise cheating and which are part of the game, requiring only good judgment in our assessment of these activities.[22]

Feezell avoids the significant problems of the rule-breaking aspect of the dominant model, providing a definition that better matches up with ordinary practice. He addresses a central concern in cheating, explaining why some actions are cheating while similar actions are not. Nonetheless, I am not convinced that Feezell's definition of cheating is suitable, with two challenges being most evident. First, in making clear his reasons for thinking cheating is morally wrong, he distinguishes his view from conventionalism. Yet relativism remains a worry. In the strict sense, Feezell is right that his view does not collapse into a form of relativism that precludes moral analysis of sport.[23] However, I think a wider concern about Feezell's view may stand. By allowing that the unwritten rules can essentially override the written rules in determining which actions are acceptable or unacceptable, it is difficult to locate any standard of evaluation beyond custom or tradition. Even if many actions are "core cases" around which there is little debate, such agreement does not entail anything beyond the unwritten rules. It will be difficult to explain or assess shifts in how the rules are interpreted or applied. If an action is considered cheating at one point but not at a later point, then this provides little moral analysis; in practice, the evaluation of the action will resemble conventionalism or relativism.

Second, Feezell faces a question of whether he makes cheating a useful concept for sport ethics. Russell argues that Feezell's account does not give moral or practical guidance. If features like rule-breaking are inessential to cheating, we may not be able to distinguish cheating from gamesmanship or other instances of poor sportsmanship.[24] As a result, the view may not explain why some borderline actions are morally problematic while others are not. Furthermore, the wrongness of an act may not depend on it being an instance of cheating, but rather some other moral analysis of it. If cheating is indistinguishable from other kinds of questionable actions, then it becomes a superfluous categorization. All of this suggests that while Feezell offers an intriguing way forward, defining cheating in terms of unwritten rules or prescriptive atmosphere does not provide a complete analysis of it in sport.

Russell's Critique

Having explored some inherent challenges to both the dominant model and ethos approach, Russell's reasons for moving past the concept of cheating are understandable. The concerns I have presented so far generally overlap with, or at least are consistent with, those he raises. In terms of the unfair advantage, Russell accepts that cheaters need not actually gain an advantage over others, with the example of a player who uses a corked bat but strikes out. To this, he adds that cheating may not require even the attempt to gain advantage over others. A golfer who keeps a handicap but regularly flouts the rules by improving her lie or taking mulligans seems to be cheating at golf without cheating others.[25] With respect to rule-breaking, he argues that our conception of the rules must include principles, drawing on Ronald Dworkin's analysis of *Riggs v. Palmer*.[26] Cheating may involve violating principles without violating the written rules. The above examples indicate to Russell that attempts to define cheating are typically too narrow, excluding plausible candidates for cheating because they don't fit a specific conception of rule-breaking. At the same time, he finds these accounts too broad in other aspects, each including cases that should not be understood as instances of cheating. Such actions might include attempts at deception committed by baseball pitchers which, while violating a written rule, are "widely regarded as part of a pitcher's toolbox."[27]

From these and similar challenges, Russell concludes that we are unlikely to agree upon a unitary conception of cheating. I believe he is right when it comes to the definitions of cheating offered in the literature thus far. The dominant model has trouble characterizing either the rule-breaking or unfair advantage that purportedly define cheating. With a more informal approach that defines its wrongness in terms of a prescriptive atmosphere or unwritten rules, we risk making cheating a moving target. Also, it cannot be easily distinguished from other kinds of improper or questionable actions in sport.

The question is how to move forward, which is really a matter of what is best for the field of sport ethics. Russell frames the debate as between two paths: continuing the search for a definition that offers a satisfactory distinction for what is or is not cheating, or setting aside the concept of cheating in lieu of moral evaluation of actions. He advocates the latter. I agree that fine-tuning definitions of cheating is unlikely to work. However, his alternative is unconvincing. He proposes that moral progress is more likely to come through interpretivism, which provides "a more coherent way of engaging in a critique of misbehavior in sport than the concept of cheating allows."[28] He acknowledges that the interpretivist approach needs further development, but he is more optimistic about developing interpretivism than defining cheating.[29] As I argued in Chapter 2, I do not believe that interpretivism provides the best explanation of sport. It faces a quandary in trying to both explain sport and provide adequate normative guidance based on its interpretation. The dilemma in developing an interpretation that is neither too general nor too specific, while maintaining elements of each, is reminiscent of Russell's concern that definitions of cheating are either too broad or too narrow. And this dilemma precludes interpretivism from offering a precise account of wrongness in many instances.

Furthermore, Russell is too quick to dismiss the role of ethos to clarify the nature of cheating. For instance, he criticizes Feezell's idea of prescriptive atmospheres as "unacceptably vague, and open to the criticism that it will make discussions about cheating follow prevailing conventions in an uncritical manner."[30] While I have indicated my own reservations about Feezell's view, Russell's challenges are unfair and, potentially, misguided. Russell seems to be arguing for more flexibility in how we account for cheating, so it is surprising when he criticizes a nuanced position for vagueness. More importantly, Feezell's position seems anything but uncritical, even if it does not provide the best definition of cheating. At minimum, the unwritten rules and context of sport influence how certain actions are adjudicated, which are important considerations for what cheating means in sport.

Luckily, we do not need to accept Russell's false dichotomy of either redefining the dominant model or setting cheating aside. Drawing on under-appreciated implications from legal positivism's separation of the legal and the moral, sport realism offers a third option. When law and morality are separated in theory, we allow that actions can be wrong in either sense. A parking violation may be legally wrong but not immoral, while lying to a friend precisely the opposite. Many actions are wrong in both ways, albeit for different reasons. In sport, analysis of cheating has explored whether and how it is morally wrong, but it has not considered whether the concept of cheating might be a useful way to capture an action that is wrong in the quasi-legal manner. Thus, while moral assessment is certainly appropriate in sport, it is not the only alternative strategy available. Russell misses this by collapsing the entirety of cheating into a moral concept.

A REALIST ACCOUNT OF CHEATING IN SPORT

Preliminaries

Most accounts of cheating in sport ethics aim to identify the core features of it. Typically, they start with a general conception of cheating, expecting that cheating in sport is fundamentally the same as cheating in other aspects of life.[31] Many accounts, such as with Feezell and Vorstenbosch, begin with examples outside sports to illuminate the concept or wrongness of cheating.[32] But why should we assume a core conception through all of these instances? Perhaps cheating on one's taxes, diet, spouse/partner, and poker are distinct kinds of behavior. Even if we should set aside those forms of cheating that are more metaphorical in nature (e.g., the diet), I see no reason to expect that the core notion of cheating remains the same in each category. If cheating is connected in some way to rule-breaking, we must recognize that the nature of rules is not consistent across activities or forms of life. And some instances of cheating don't relate to any sense of unfair advantage gained. In general, we might think that the status of rules, or breaking the rules, takes on different meaning in sports, since they are constructed competitions. So I argue that we should treat sport as a distinct setting in which cheating occurs.[33]

Sport realism is broadly functionalist in nature, defining sport through consideration of what decision-makers in sport will actually do. This entails examination of how disputes will be resolved and what sorts of punishment will be meted out by sports officials. We take the perspective of the athlete who wishes to know whether (and which) consequences might accrue to a certain action she may perform. Most athletes and coaches, I argue, do not want to know how cheating is defined; they want to know what it *means*—whether any proposed actions will be treated as cheating, and if so, what sanctions will apply.

Participants of sport are not inquiring into the morality of their actions so much as their liability for them. Earlier I termed this sense of wrongness quasi-legal; in both law and sport we can identify wrong actions as distinct from moral wrongs. Those involved in sport often see themselves as beholden to it, just as many feel toward the law in general. Atry et al. explore this commitment to the practice of sport. They argue that cheating is not a stand-alone ethical concept, but instead functions as part of the "strategic structure and logic of sports competitions."[34] They understand sports as rule-governed joint activities (or social practices) that require some degree of mutual cooperation among athletes, referees, coaches, spectators, organizations, the media, etc. Consequently, they argue that the relevant ethical considerations in sport are our concrete responses to others engaged in joint social activities, which they find in P. F. Strawson's account of reactive attitudes. According to Strawson, attitudes like resentment and gratitude only make sense through our relationships with others, given a system or practice of mutual demands and entitlements. Atry et al. conclude that cheating can be understood as a possible target of reactive attitudes like resentment, blame, and indignation, directed at the cheater's attitude and will toward us, not at the rule-breaking or competitive advantage per se.[35] More simply, cheating is an appropriate target of our reactive attitudes because it represents a failure to show goodwill to the others involved in sport.

Atry et al. capture something essential about cheating connected to the mutual relations of a practice, even though I do not suggest any role for reactive attitudes within sport realism. As I see it, the mutual relationships of sport practice partially explain the need for a predictive theory of sport. The groups that Atry et al. describe as having mutual relationships—including athletes, coaches, referees, and institutions—are the same ones that I identified earlier as sport officials. And the expectations (and attitudes) that form between these constituencies ground the expectations for what responses and sanctions will apply to different kinds of actions, including cheating. In other words, the social practice of sport resembles a legal system, making possible a distinct way that actions can be "wrong" in that context without appeal to morality or reactive attitudes.

Also, the sport realist approach shows why the attention paid to rule-breaking in the dominant model is misguided. The rules of the game often prove useful in predicting how some particular case or dispute will be decided, yet they provide at best a partial explanation of these. Other factors influence outcomes, including the context and consequences of the actions, precedent, and social or political considerations. The written rules matter because the violation of some rules, in certain contexts, will likely trigger sanctions that may be unwanted or undesirable to the participants. Hence, a definition of cheating that aims to define which kind of rule-violations comprise cheating is necessarily incomplete without a predictive component concerning the wrongness of cheating within the activity.

Constructing a Definition of Cheating

Sport realists predict outcomes by examining situation types. A situation type is a set of cases or scenarios that share key features, allowing for the identification of patterns in decision-making. Recognition of a situation type reveals the sorts of reasons and influences likely to determine how the dispute is resolved. Cheating is too broad of a category to comprise a situation type. Purported examples of cheating across sports occur in many different ways, and they are not always similar enough to identify patterns in how they are treated. Imagine comparing pine tar pitching cases to strategic fouls in basketball as if they are adjudicated with similar features. No clear pattern is going to emerge. Nevertheless, the notion of situation types illuminates the sport realist strategy, for which cheating is an identifiable category of action within sport. Numerous kinds of disputes emerge within sport, and actions that are treated as cheating comprise a distinct kind or subset of these disputes. My claim is parallel to Karl Llewellyn's view of law, as he argues that crimes are a subset of a larger category of disputes.[36] Analogously, cheating constitutes a much narrower class of sport disputes.

According to Oliver Wendell Holmes, Jr. we find the law once we identify which actions will, in fact, trigger sanction by a court. Sport realism defines cheating in similar terms. For an initial definition, I propose that cheating in sport is an action that will, in fact, prompt sanction by a sport official. Cheating can occur with reference to sanction provided by any sport official, keeping in mind that sport officials have been defined widely to include individuals and institutions that perform the actions of resolving disputes and meting out punishment.[37] An obvious challenge to this initial definition arises because cheaters are not always caught. By defining cheating as an action that will, in fact, trigger sanction from sport officials, we risk concluding that anyone who didn't receive sanction didn't cheat. This conclusion is unacceptable, so long as we hold that cheating is a subset or class of dispute. Accordingly, we can modify the definition into a counterfactual: cheating is an action that would be sanctioned, if identified by a sport official.

This definition still needs further refinement. The rest of the section aims to do so. In particular, cheating is not the only kind of action in sport that receives a penalty or triggers sanction. I will develop more precisely what I take to be the core features of cheating in sport in order to differentiate it from other such actions. On my account, cheating appears to require rule-breaking. If an action does not break a rule, it is unlikely to be treated as cheating by officials or other interested parties. For example, consider the unique strategy employed by Bill Belichick's New England Patriots in a January 2015 playoff game against the Baltimore Ravens, discussed previously in Chapter 2. Many responded immediately by claiming that the plays were illegal, or "tricks," though in the following days it became clear that the Patriots had followed the rules. The accusations of cheating and trickery subsided once it was accepted that no rules were broken.

Perhaps it is obvious that cheating usually involves breaking the written rules. We need to examine whether or not violations of the unwritten rules can be (or are) treated as cheating in a comparable manner.[38] Consider tennis players who take long restroom breaks or ask for unnecessary treatment to throw off the opponent's rhythm, which some consider to be "unsportsmanlike gamesmanship" instead of cheating.[39] Stefanos Tsitsipas found himself in the middle of two such controversies during the 2021 season. At the Western

& Southern Open in Cincinnati, he took long breaks and brought his equipment with him, leading some to speculate that he was receiving illegal coaching via his phone. At the U.S. Open, he took two lengthy restroom breaks and received medical treatment during the course of a five set victory over Andy Murray. The maximum time allotted for restroom breaks is not specified in the Official Grand Slam Rule Book.[40] However, breaks are expected to be timely, with a line umpire ensuring that no other activities are occurring. And, of course, medical treatments are supposed to concern genuine health matters.

Sanctions are not given often for illicit restroom breaks or injuries due to the difficulty in determining whether or not these are legitimate instances. Even so, I believe such actions would likely be sanctioned by sport officials, if practicable. This makes them, effectively, forms of cheating. The same is true in other sports where players may fake or embellish injuries in order to slow down the opponent's tempo or to disrupt rhythm. These should be considered acts of cheating, despite the difficulties in penalizing them as such. Compare these injury embellishments to the case of Ben Davis, a catcher for the San Diego Padres who bunted in the 8th inning to break up Curt Schilling's perfect game in 2001. This was clearly a violation of the unwritten rules, according to which it is inappropriate to break up a no-hitter with a bunt. But few in baseball, if any, treated it as an act of cheating. Davis became the target of "punishments" from others, including name-calling and the threat of a future beanball. But these are not the same kinds of sanctions generally applied to acts of cheating, which I will examine shortly. So even though I'm willing to allow that violations of unwritten rules can amount to cheating, I think such cases are rare.[41]

While violations of the written (and occasionally unwritten) rules are a necessary precondition for cheating, not all violations comprise cheating. Loland provides support for this conclusion, noting that different social and cultural settings influence how we understand rule-violations. He offers Maradona's famous "hand of God" goal that was seen by some as a paradigmatic instance of cheating, yet by others as an "act of courage and heroism."[42] This kind of explanation fits well with sport realism, which is unsurprising given some parallels with legal realism and legal theory. In the law, we find that which laws are enforced and how they are enforced depend on the social context. I have argued that similar influences and reasons play important roles in resolving sport disputes. Which actions are treated as cheating depends on the broader context such as the relevant situation types or kinds of action in question.

The unwritten rules play a critical role in defining this social context. If a rule-violation is likely to be ignored, for the purposes of the participants it simply isn't an instance of cheating. Whereas Feezell argues that the unwritten rules create a prescriptive atmosphere, I contend that they provide something akin to non-legal reasons. Routinely sport officials take them into account and are influenced by them in how they decide cases. These expectations can change, but that doesn't prevent us from predicting outcomes at any given time. For example, the expectation that baseball pitchers are allowed to manipulate the ball with foreign substances has been limited in recent years, evident through both rule changes and the gradual augmentation of punishments.

Thus far, I have argued that rule-breaking is a necessary but not sufficient condition for cheating. Now we must distinguish the kind of sanction warranted by cheating from those appropriate to violations of sport etiquette or other disputes. Beyond breaking the rules, cheating also seems to violate some notion of fairness, which is why so much of the literature has sought to connect cheating to unfair advantage despite the problems of doing so that I discussed previously. The basic motivation is right, even if others conflate the unfair advantage of cheating with its more basic wrongness. An adequate account of cheating should be able to explain why these actions trigger sanction. Yet the matter is complicated because I have argued that sanction and punishment in sport must be defined broadly such that they can be meted out by the array of sport officials.

Instances of cheating warrant sanction because they reflect a certain sense of unfairness—they change the conditions of the activity. In particular, they alter conditions of competitive equality or otherwise result in a contest that favors one side.[43] Tamburrini suggests that sanctions are appropriate responses for two aims: they may seek to annul the unfair conditions that result from cheating, or they may aim to restore competitive balance between players or teams.[44] Thus, cheating is a kind of action that warrants sanction, based on both the predictive context of the activity and interest in maintaining some degree of competitive equality. Though sanction cannot return the activity to its state prior to cheating, the sanction attempts to restore the prior condition of the activity to the greatest (reasonable) extent possible, once the cheating act is recognized by officials.

The same kind of explanation should be given for a sanction applied to the above examples of extended restroom breaks and fake injuries. These warrant a sanction aimed at restoring competitive balance, which confirms that these cases are best understood as forms of cheating, even though these penalties are rarely given in practice. While other kinds of actions receive or deserve sanction, generally it is for other reasons. If we return to Ben Davis' breach of baseball etiquette, the claim that he deserves a penalty cannot be rooted in an argument of competitive equality. A better explanation is that others see his bunt as a form of promise-breaking. I have argued that cheating is not the violation of a contract or a promise, but it seems evident that other kinds of actions are routinely sanctioned on these terms. Given these considerations, we can now identify a considered definition of cheating: an action constitutes cheating when an instance of rule-breaking warrants a restorative sanction given by sport officials, and we would expect such sanction to be given if the action is caught.

Sport and Law

My realist account of cheating has further advantages over other views. In Chapter 3, I argued that sport realism better deals with disputes that arise in informal or disorganized sports, like pick-up games. Definitions that focus on rule-breaking will face difficulty in sports that lack formal rules or have nothing like a contract or promise among participants. On my account, these informal sports still have people who function as sport officials, which provides a framework for identification of cheating; even without institutions or an official rulebook we can still predict what sorts of actions are likely to earn sanction for altering the conditions of competitive equality.

One might worry that my account begs the question. At first glance, it may seem that I have defined cheating in terms of what actions will be treated as cheating. Hopefully it is evident by now that this is not my view. I have sought to define cheating through an investigation of the conditions under which a sanction should be expected for rule-breaking. Again, a comparison to law is instructive. Just as a lawyer looks to both the written laws and the situation type in order to understand how the law will be applied, participants in sport consider cheating in terms of rules, precedents, and patterns in decision-making. Cheating is not simply an ethos that depends on conventions and current practices. Rather, analysis of cheating is a study of how future actions are likely to be understood or interpreted, with an eye toward the punishment or penalty likely to be given out in response to cheating behavior.

Others might worry that my position is relativist, since assessment of cheating depends on the specific demands of the sport community and its unwritten rules. I resist this characterization. The sport realist readily identifies standards of assessment beyond mere convention or practice. Cheating is a certain kind of rule-breaking, with distinct reasons for punishment, rooted in precedent and situation types. Even though these expectations may change based on new rules or altered social conditions, we can still identify the basic requirements and expectations that define cheating. An example from Craig Lehman further illustrates my point. In Chapter 2, I argued that Japanese and American baseball differ in their conceptions of the relevant skills of baseball, which cannot be captured by a single interpretation of the sport. Lehman notes that Japanese and American baseball have very similar rules. It seems that we can imagine similar rules giving rise to what are essentially different sports, based on divergent attitudes toward certain rules in each culture.[45]

On my view, the explanation for why these activities become different sports is that they are, in practice, different "legal" systems. Comparably, countries may have similar constitutions and written laws but legal systems that come to different conceptions of the law. With different situation types and precedents, the participants might develop diverse expectations of which rule-violations will or should be treated as acts of cheating that warrant sanction.[46] It is possible that similar actions might turn out to be cheating in one sport and not in another, just as parallel actions might be legal in one jurisdiction and illegal in another. Yet there are still standards for these violations, and the actions can be criticized for their wrongness. And, importantly, the basic sport realist definition of cheating would apply across sports.

Another aspect of legal theory suggests an additional response to any relativist concerns.[47] Imagine we want to define negligence in philosophy of law. We can study the basic requirements that constitute negligence or differentiate it from other kinds of legal liability, such as recklessness. These concepts can be analyzed philosophically. However, for a lawyer the analysis of negligence cannot end here because the issue isn't abstract. Instead, the meaning of negligence constitutes a practical determination of whether some particular action (or omission) will be treated as negligence in the legal system, and whether a client will likely be held liable. This definition of negligence requires exploration of the precedents, jurisdiction, and standards to be applied to the case. In other words, the meaning of negligence only becomes fully realized once it is translated into the situation type. At the same time, we have no trouble acknowledging that just what constitutes negligence or legal liability might change from one jurisdiction to another, or change over time. For instance, localities differ in the adoption of specific subjective or objective (i.e., reasonable person) tests for negligence. Likewise, I have sought to offer a philosophical characterization of sport cheating and its distinct sanction, which cannot be separated from the participants' interest in knowing which kinds of actions are likely to receive sanction. All the same, we can clarify philosophically the concept of cheating while accepting that its application or meaning of cheating varies from one jurisdiction to another.

The analogy between cheating and negligence provides additional insight into the wrongness of cheating. We can acknowledge that negligence is a moral wrong. However, the immorality of negligence is a concern distinct from legal (and philosophy of law) analysis of it and its sanction. Its moral wrongness and legal wrongness are separate considerations. Similarly, cheating might be morally wrong for some of the reasons presented earlier. It might break a promise or contract, or be a proper target for reactive attitudes like blame or resentment. It might be unsportsmanlike, or be inconsistent with some other moral theory. Yet to conclude as Russell does that this is all we have to say about cheating misses an important component of its wrongness, which includes quasi-legal liability and sanction that deserve recognition given their importance to sport participants. Sport realism allows for philosophical investigation of *how* cheating ought to be defined, without limiting us to a purely moral perspective. All told, cheating means a certain form of wrong action, requiring rule-breaking, that warrants a certain kind of sanction relating to competitive balance, when we would expect such sanction to be given by officials.

DECEPTION AND INTENTION

In the previous section I laid out the necessary components of cheating. Other features commonly associated with cheating are incidental to the concept. Of these, deception needs specific mention. Cheating usually involves deception, which some believe contributes to or enhances the wrongness of cheating. Even so, most scholars agree that deception is not a core feature of cheating.[48] After all, cheating can be done openly, even brazenly. To define cheating in terms of deception conflates the definition with "the hope that one will not be called for, or detected, openly violating a rule."[49] Deception is usually employed because the cheater anticipates some kind of sanction or negative response from others. But the wrongdoing itself is separate from any attempt to disguise the action from others.

The role of intention is more complicated. The prevailing view is that cheating must be an intentional action, done "knowingly and willingly."[50] Kirkwood remarks that no "disciplined use of the word" cheating can be construed to include unintentional rule-breaking.[51] This is predicated on a moral distinction between intentional and unintentional rule-breaking, perhaps comparable to the difference between lying and making an unwitting falsehood. Not all instances of rule-breaking deserve the same degree of disapprobation. A cheater is morally blameworthy in breaking the rules and seeking an advantage in a manner distinct from someone who breaks a rule through ignorance or accident.[52] Unintentional rule-breaking may be morally blameworthy in some cases, but not to the same degree as an act of cheating.[53]

I disagree with the prevailing view. Sport realism is consistent with using cheating in the "undisciplined" manner that Kirkwood opposes, at least in certain kinds of cases. My claim here is not that all unintentional rule-breaking counts as cheating, only that unintentional rule-breaking in sport is sometimes treated in a manner indistinct from cheating.[54] From the perspective of participants, there may be no difference in their expectations for intentional and unintentional rule-breaking, making them part of the same situation type.

Three reasons support the position that the concept of cheating in sport includes some unintentional actions. First, a number of different examples show that intention can be irrelevant to whether an action is treated as cheating. Many considered Tiger Woods' drop to be cheating even if he was not he was aware of the rule. A sprinter who tests positive for an illegal substance faces an almost insurmountable task of avoiding suspension. A baseball player who uses an illegal bat, such as a corked bat, will be punished the same regardless of his awareness of it. And a cross country runner who cuts part of the course will be disqualified no matter the explanation. Second, in some cases a previous intention may be sufficient. Imagine a player or team punished earlier for an instance of cheating, such as a team that tries to illegally substitute in a basketball player for a technical foul free throw without getting noticed. Any subsequent violations are likely to be treated as intentional, with corresponding restorative sanction, no matter the cause.

One might object that the above cases are not really unintentional actions because in penalizing the athletes we are assuming the intention must have been present. Perhaps if we could be absolutely certain of intentions we would, in fact, treat these cases differently. This response might work in some scenarios. For instance, if we had evidence that the sprinter's substance was planted by someone else, or the baseball player's bat was unwittingly swapped out for a corked bat, we would think of the situations differently. But I don't find this response entirely convincing. The new evidence might change what we personally think of those involved, or inform our moral assessment of them, but I expect the result would be the same in practice. Equipment and substances ingested are often sanctioned on what is effectively a strict liability standard, with penalty based on the act rather than intention. The competitive balance is altered in such a way that the result cannot be undone, and this takes precedence over intention in predicting the outcome. The same is true for the cross country runner who goes outside the course. She is not going to be let back into the race, as there is no other way to restore fairness to the race.

For a third reason, consider the famous "fifth down" game. In a 1990 NCAA football game between Colorado and Missouri, referees mistakenly gave Colorado an extra play, having failed to record one earlier in the sequence. Colorado scored a touchdown on the last play of the game. Colorado seemed unaware of the extra down, leading Robert Simon, Cesar Torres, and Peter Hager to conclude that they did not cheat.[55] I argue that this example, in practice, is no different from a case of cheating in how we expect it to be addressed. To some, it may not seem fair that the same sanction is applied to the unknowing fifth down as it would to a team that gained a fifth down through trickery or manipulation. But to those involved in the game, the wrongness of both actions is clear. And if noticed at the time, I do not believe intentional or unintentional fifth downs would be treated differently on the field. Colorado won the game via a rule-violation, which was discovered after the fact and at a point when the officials did not believe they could go back and overturn it. However, had it been discovered at the time, I believe that a restorative sanction—the same one to be given *if* Colorado had knowingly taken an extra down—would have been appropriate.

If we limit our definition of cheating to intentional actions, the narrower concept does not match the practice of sport. Participants are interested in their liability for actions. This includes predicting what kinds of actions will likely receive sanction, along with the kind of penalty or punishment it will be. And I have shown that expectations pertaining to cheating likely include some unintentional rule-breaking. My claim is that participants of sport already think this way. For example, sprinters and distance runners expect to be sanctioned if they test positive for performance-enhancing substances regardless of the particular circumstances. Through further study, we might find that the situation type of cheating includes unintentional rule-violations pertaining to equipment and illegal substances more commonly than other accidental or unintentional violations, in part due to the effects these have on the competitive balance of sport.

STRATEGIC FOULS

Definitions of cheating in sport are often applied to the question of strategic fouls. Strategic (or tactical) fouls are deliberate rule-violations in which the participant expects the action to be penalized but prefers this to the alternatives. The most commonly discussed example involves a losing team fouling at the end of a basketball game. The team that commits the foul hopes its opponent will miss the free throws, and it chooses to take this risk rather than letting the clock run down. The problem is that strategic fouls are intentional rule-violations and would seem to qualify as instances of cheating on many definitions. Some believe this intuition is obvious, or find no way around the conclusion that cheating and strategic fouling are indistinguishable means of gaining an advantage.[56] Nevertheless, most consider strategic fouls to be acceptable, akin to myriad other tactics employed in the pursuit of victory.

I will offer no definitive statement on the appropriateness of strategic fouls, but I want to show what sport realism can contribute to the philosophical discussion. Some have proposed that the distinction between constitutive and regulative rules clarifies the matter if we can identify which type of rule is broken in instances of cheating. However, this approach does not seem satisfactory, since breaking either type of rule can amount to cheating.[57] Simon, Torres, and Hager offer a different distinction, separating actions that warrant a sanction or penalty from those for which some price is paid. They provide the example of a golfer moving a ball from an unplayable lie at the cost of a penalty stroke. They suggest that the penalty stroke is just the price paid to take this option.[58] Strategic fouls might be understood similarly as offering a price that a player or team is willing to pay in return for some course of action. A price differs from a penalty because the price serves to make something permissible, whereas the act which receives a sanction is supposed to remain a wrong or impermissible action.

The distinction between penalty and price fits nicely with the definition of cheating I provide in this chapter. Both price and penalty might be seen as kinds of sanction that apply to different situation types. Still, this distinction is not wholly satisfactory, for at least two reasons. First, Russell points out that the distinction of whether something is a price or a sanction is distinct from the question of rule-breaking. Since rule-breaking is a necessary condition for cheating on my view, this difference suggests the price/penalty distinction may not illuminate all cases.[59] Second, Warren Fraleigh notes that some actions that seem like strategic fouls are reexamined and given greater penalties to establish that they are impermissible, such as a reckless plays in soccer that now draw immediate red cards.[60] This undermines the possibility of locating a definite difference in kind between price and penalty; perception of the action may depend on the context, or an action may shift from one category to another based on other considerations.

The sport realist definition of cheating might elucidate the price/penalty distinction through examination of the sanction, which is connected to the situation type.[61] Cheating warrants a sanction because it aims to diminish the fundamental competitive equity of the activity. The sanction seeks to annul the advantage or restore the previous condition to the extent possible. The same explanation often does not work for strategic fouls, when free throws are given in response to a late-game foul. Plausibly, these are a different kind of sanction, which is reasonably called a price.[62] However, this answer is unlikely to hold for all strategic fouls. For instance, if a soccer player performs an illegal handball in order to prevent a goal, the resulting penalty kick provides a sanction that aims at annulment or restoration, although a corresponding red card adds a different kind of penalty into the mix. Still, the predictive aim of sport realism allows us to investigate how such cases have been treated in the past so we can identify how certain infractions are likely to be received the next time.

Should the price/penalty approach prove unconvincing, the sport realist has available another reply. Although Fraleigh finds strategic fouls to be morally problematic, he suggests they may not meet his stipulative definition of cheating—the cheater tries to avoid penalty while the strategic fouler expects a penalty, making them different actions.[63] Sport realism cannot accept Fraleigh's stipulative claim. I argued earlier that intention may not be essential to defining cheating, so determining the motivation behind the foul may not completely decide the matter. Still, the sport realist might attempt a maneuver comparable to Fraleigh. On my definition, an action constitutes cheating because we expect that it would be treated as such if recognized. We simply don't treat strategic fouls as cheating, so for practical purposes they aren't cheating. They are not included in what we mean by the concept of cheating.

This response might seem too arbitrary to some, but I think another comparison to the law shows that this attitude is reasonable and consistent. Consider a law in the West Virginia Code, repealed only in 2010, which banned the wearing of hats or bonnets in theaters.[64] Despite it being illegal, by rule, to wear hats in these locations, I suspect no one in recent memory took this law into account or considered theater hat-wearing to be illegal. The fact that the law existed had no influence on how people acted. Therefore, I argue that this rule wasn't included in any reasonable construal of what the law really meant. Someone reminded of the law would likely respond with a shrug of the shoulders.[65] The law would be unlikely to take on a new meaning unless authorities began enforcing it regularly. Similarly, strategic fouls are not treated as cheating, and this will not change without some modification in sanction. The sanction here would have to be some additional negative response from other players, coaches, or members of the community that shows a deeper opposition to the action to supplement the sanction already anticipated for the foul.

Some examples of strategic fouls show what this development might look like. Consider the 2010 FIFA World Cup, in which Ghana played Uruguay in a quarterfinal match. Late in extra time, Ghana had a shot that looked destined for the winning goal. Uruguay's Luis Suárez reached out with his hand and prevented the goal. Suárez was sent off with a red card, but Ghana missed the subsequent penalty kick. Uruguay won the game in the eventual penalty kick tiebreaker. Suárez's handball was a strategic foul, albeit one that many more people are inclined to treat as cheating than is the case for strategic fouls in basketball. This incident emphasizes that we cannot understand cheating and related actions without some recognition of what we expect to be treated as cheating and sanctioned accordingly. Analysis of the concepts alone does not illuminate how the sport is actually played.

I have provided two approaches to strategic fouls in order to represent what sport realism offers for the examination of cheating. It might connect the action and sanction to a situation type, or it may investigate how the action is likely to be treated in future situations. According to the latter, strategic fouls might be considered a relatively insignificant action, like wearing a bonnet in a theater. If the action in question were something more toxic—perhaps rampant doping or widespread use of illegal equipment—some might not want to accept that these simply don't mean cheating based on the situation type. Nonetheless, I maintain that this is the appropriate response. Sport realism doesn't preclude moral analysis even as it tries to offer a unique perspective on wrongness in sport. In a case of widespread cheating, it may turn out that sport realism has less to offer than a moral theory, and I expect the same is true of a condition with widespread illegal action. I do not see this as a limitation on sport realism.

I have argued in this chapter that sport realism is advantageous in allowing for distinct ways in which sport actions can be wrong. Should we find a situation type in which widespread cheating is currently accepted, we can still consider whether the action in question violates the norms of some ethical theory, like Kantianism or utilitarianism. Or we might examine whether the action constitutes bad sportsmanship. These conversations are generally separate from a theory that explains the practice of sport. In the same way, our moral analysis of negligence might differ from a consideration of its legal wrongness. However, I do not believe that sport realism is entirely separate from ethics such that it should be set aside when moral questions are asked. Sport realism allows for some kinds of moral analysis. In the next chapter I will explore in more detail the extent to which sport realism incorporates ethical analysis of sport disputes.

NOTES

1. J.S. Russell, "Is There a Normatively Distinct Concept of Cheating in Sport (or Anywhere Else)?," *Journal of the Philosophy of Sport* 41, no. 3 (2014): 304.

2. Ibid., 303–304. See also Stuart P. Green, "Cheating," *Law and Philosophy* 23, no. 2 (2004): 139.

3. For some representative examples of the dominant model of cheating, see Edwin J. Delattre, "Some Reflections on Success and Failure in Competitive Athletics," *Journal of the Philosophy of Sport* 2, no. 1 (1975); S. K. Wertz, "The Varieties of Cheating," *Journal of the Philosophy of Sport* 8, no. 1 (1981); Kathleen M. Pearson, "Deception, Sportsmanship, and Ethics," in *Sport Ethics: An Anthology*, ed. Jan Boxill (Malden, MA: Blackwell Publishing, 2003); and Ken Kirkwood, "What Do You Mean I Wasn't Cheating? Testing the Concept of Cheating Through a Case of Failed Doping," *Sport, Ethics and Philosophy* 8, no. 1 (2014). Wertz differs from the other accounts in allowing that unintentional actions can constitute cheating in addition to intentional actions.

4. Wertz, "Varieties," 26.

5. Randolph Feezell, "On the Wrongness of Cheating and Why Cheaters Can't Play the Game," *Journal of the Philosophy of Sport* 15, no. 1 (1988): 59.

6. For further discussion, see Roger Gardner, "On Performance-Enhancing Substances and the Unfair Advantage Argument," *Journal of the Philosophy of Sport* 16, no. 1 (1989).

7. Ashkan Atry, Mats G. Hansson, and Ulrik Kihlbom, "Cheating is the Nature of the Game—Conventional Cheating Arguments Fail to Articulate Moral Responses to Doping," *Physical Cultures and Sport. Studies and Research* 59, no. 1 (2013): 24–25.

8. Oliver Leaman, "Cheating and Fair Play in Sport," in *Ethics in Sport*, 2nd ed., ed. William J. Morgan (Champaign, IL: Human Kinetics, 2007), 204–205.

9. Brian Glenney, "Skateboarding, Sport, and Spontaneity: Toward a Subversive Definition of Sport," in *Defining Sport*, ed. Shawn E. Klein (Lanham, MD: Lexington Books, 2016), 155.

10. Examples include Wertz, "Varieties," 20, 24 and Jan Vorstenbosch, "Doping and Cheating," *Journal of the Philosophy of Sport* 37, no. 2 (2010): 168–169.

11. Sigmund Loland, "Fair Play: Historical Anachronism or Topical Ideal?," in *Ethics and Sport*, ed. Mike McNamee and Jim Parry (London: E & FN Spon, 1998), 85, 92.

12. Maartje Schermer, "On the Argument that Enhancement is 'Cheating,'" *Journal of Medical Ethics* 34, no. 2 (2008): 85.

13. Randolph Feezell, "Sportsmanship," *Journal of the Philosophy of Sport* 13, no. 1 (1986): 2.

14. Vorstenbosch, "Doping," 172–173.

15. Wertz, "Varieties," 23–24. Simon Easson also raises concerns about the social contract analogy to sport, finding it at best a partial fit in "Games, Rules, and Contracts," in *Ethics and Sport*, ed. Mike McNamee and Jim Parry (London: E & FN Spon, 1998).

16. Robert Butcher and Angela Schneider, "Fair Play as Respect for the Game," *Journal of the Philosophy of Sport* 25, no. 1 (1998): 5 and Robert L. Simon, Cesar R. Torres, and Peter F. Hager, *Fair Play: The Ethics of Sport*, 4th ed. (Boulder, CO: Westview Press, 2015), 60.

17. Claudio Tamburrini, "The 'Hand of God'?," in *The Ethics of Sport*, ed. Mike McNamee (London: Routledge, 2010), 136.

18. Craig K. Lehman, "Can Cheaters Play the Game?," *Journal of the Philosophy of Sport* 8, no. 1 (1981): 42–43.

19. Randolph Feezell, *Playing Games* (London: Routledge, 2017), 71–72.

20. Feezell, "Wrongness," 60.

21. Ibid., 62.

22. Ibid., 61.

23. Elsewhere, Feezell suggests that his view cannot be a form of moral relativism because he characterizes cheating as a form of unfairness or injustice, which makes it wrong in all cases. Feezell, *Playing Games*, 75.

24. Russell, "Cheating," 317.

25. Ibid., 314.

26. For a discussion of *Riggs v. Palmer*, see Chapter 1 section "Legal and Philosophical Foundations of Interpretivism."

27. Russell, "Cheating," 312.

28. Ibid., 319.

29. Russell finds that the biggest challenge to interpretivism in the context of cheating pertains to the argument that some types of cheating actually improve sport. If seen as part of the game, some forms of cheating may make sport more interesting, dramatic, or challenging. Ibid., 319–320.

30. Ibid., 319.

31. For instance, Stuart Green develops his conception of cheating with examples from business, war, politics, and sport, although he is writing primarily for the philosophy of law. Green, "Cheating," 138.

32. Feezell, "Wrongness," 58 and Vorstenbosch, "Doping," 167–168.

33. I am not the first to suggest that sport provides a lens through which we must interpret the concept of cheating. Definitions of cheating put in terms of an ethos use a framework specific to sport. And Craig Lehman argues that determining whether actions qualify of cheating requires the application of social custom or a notion of utility and convenience. Lehman, "Cheaters," 43–44. I agree with the sentiment that undergirds these views. However, I intend to show that my sport realist theory provides a more successful framework.

34. Atry, Hansson, and Kihlbom, "Cheating," 26.

35. Ibid., 29.

36. Karl N. Llewellyn, *The Bramble Bush* (Oxford: Oxford University Press [1930] 2008), 8.

37. On the surface my position here might appear to resemble one staked out by Tamburrini, but a closer inspection reveals that the two views are very different. He argues that the ethos of sport is too often defined in terms of sport officials and authorities, leaving out the perspective of "game practitioners." So an adequate theory of sport must take into account these multiple ethoses. Tamburrini, "The 'Hand of God'?," 136. I agree with Tamburrini that the perspective of the practitioners is essential to understanding sport, but I am also arguing that we must broaden our sense of who or what counts as a sport official. And my definition of cheating relies on a framework analogous to a legal perspective, not ethos.

38. I am hesitant to accept Russell's argument that breaking principles can also count as cheating. He argues that instances of breaking principles often, in practice, amount to exploiting loopholes. Russell, "Cheating," 310–311. I disagree that the baseball examples he provides of watering down basepaths or "selling" calls to umpires should be treated as cheating (or at least they typically aren't). Nonetheless, should we identify violations of principles in sport that are clearly taken as cheating, I believe my view can accommodate them.

39. Feezell, *Playing Games*, 69.

40. Jackie Spiegel, "Stefanos Tsitsipas and Bathroom Breaks: Explaining 2021 US Open's Biggest Controversy," *Sporting News*, September 2, 2021, https://www.sportingnews.com/us/tennis/news/stefanos-tsitsipas-bathroom-breaks-explaining-2021-us-opens-controversy/djk9ak3td65h1wzrunwkp4swt.

41. Another reason that unwritten rule violations infrequently count as cheating is because they are often used for the opposite effect. The unwritten rules sometimes justify actions that should not be allowed by the letter of the law. For example, the

unwritten rules allow baseball pitchers to use scuffed balls, or professional basketball players to get away with traveling. Violations of this kind of unwritten rule have no association with cheating.

42. Sigmund Loland, "The Varieties of Cheating—Comments on Ethical Analyses in Sport," *Sport in Society* 8, no. 1 (2005): 12.

43. This idea is present in many discussions of cheating, but it is made most directly in Wertz, "Varieties," 26–27; Feezell, "Wrongness," 59; and Feezell, *Playing Games*, 70–71.

44. Tamburrini, "The 'Hand of God'?," 135.

45. Lehman, "Cheaters," 44.

46. I reject Kathleen Pearson's argument that two games with identical rules must be the same game, since the rules define the activity. Pearson, "Deception," 81–82. I think it's clear that differences in sport officials and expectations result in very different practices and rule-applications.

47. In Chapter 5, I will develop and respond to a related concern about moral relativism.

48. Examples include Leaman, "Cheating," 202; Schermer, "Enhancement," 85; and Simon, Torres, and Hager, *Fair Play*, 60–61.

49. Russell, "Cheating," 306.

50. Vorstenbosch, "Doping," 168. For additional representative definitions, see Pearson, "Deception," 82–83 and Schermer, "Enhancement," 85.

51. Kirkwood, "Cheating," 59.

52. Leaman, "Cheating," 202 and Simon, Torres, and Hager, *Fair Play*, 60–61.

53. Most who push against the necessity of intention primarily seek to clarify what is meant by intentional action. For instance, Tamburrini argues that cheating need not require an intention to break a rule, but he holds that cheating involves an intention to gain an advantage. Wertz goes further in allowing that cheating can be unintentional, though he excludes accidental rule-violations from this category. He uses unintentional to include acts that a person has awareness of, such as when an act is informed by a person's experiences or position. Tamburrini, "The 'Hand of God'?," 133 and Wertz, "Varieties," 30–32.

54. Many note that, in practice, the same penalties are often given for intention and unintentional actions. Examples include Green, "Cheating," 156 and Loland, "Varieties," 13.

55. Simon, Torres, and Hager, *Fair Play*, 74–76.

56. Examples include Loland, "Varieties," 14; Tamburrini, "The 'Hand of God'?," 133; and Russell, "Cheating," 306–307.

57. Green, "Cheating," 149–150. Although, as Green notes, a player who repeatedly breaks constitutive rules actually may be playing a different game, in effect, and not cheating.

58. Simon, Torres, and Hager, *Fair Play*, 67.

59. Russell, "Cheating," 308–309.

60. Warren P. Fraleigh, "Intentional Rules Violations—One More Time," *Journal of the Philosophy of Sport* 30, no. 1 (2003): 172.

61. Simon, Torres, and Hager respond to such concerns by proposing that we might seek to develop a fair price for an action in *Fair Play*, 67–68. This strategy works for interpretivism but is not open to sport realism, which denies any such thing.

62. One implication of my proposal is that the same response might be considered a penalty in some instances and a price in others. If a basketball player is fouled while shooting a lay-up, we might interpret the resulting free throws as attempting to annul an advantage or restore a previous condition. At the same time, we likely do not want to consider common fouls to be cheating either. Setting aside the question of whether a foul constitutes intentional rule-breaking, we can accept simply that a common foul is a completely different situation type.

63. Fraleigh, "Intentional," 168–169. Another way to look at it is that the cheater does not want her action emulated, while the strategic foul conforms to general practice. Simon, Torres, and Hager, *Fair Play*, 65–66.

64. West Virginia Code §61–6–16: "No person attending any performance at any theater, hall or opera house, or any such building where theatrical or other performances are given, when an admission fee is charged, shall wear upon his or her head any hat, bonnet or covering for the head which may obstruct the view of any person or persons during the performance in such theater, hall, opera house or other building where such performance is given; and if any person wear upon his or her head any hat, bonnet or other covering for the head which may obstruct the view of any person or persons, and refuse or fail to remove the same at the request of any person or persons whose view may be obstructed, he or she shall be guilty of a misdemeanor, and, upon conviction, shall be fined not less than two nor more than ten dollars."

65. This is consistent with the fact that a person might be motivated by other reasons to take off a hat in a theater, such as etiquette, consideration of other audience members, etc.

Chapter 5

Sport Realism and Ethics

Over the last two chapters I have defended a realist theory of sport that explains sport as it is actually played. Sport realism locates the meaning of sport with the interests and needs of the participants themselves. It defines sport in terms of the decisions and resolutions made by sport officials, which are irreducible to written rules, principles, unwritten rules, or other elements. I have argued that sport realism offers numerous benefits over other theories. In Chapter 3, I provided case studies to show that it provides the best explanation of decision-making procedures based on situation types, illuminating the kinds of reasons that motivate decisions by sports officials. In Chapter 4, I argued that it presents a better approach to conceptual work in philosophy of sport. Thus, sport realism stands to best explain both how sport is played and the philosophical framework that sport exists within.

In Chapter 1, I accepted the widespread view that a successful theory of sport should offer both an explanation of and normative guidance for sport. This chapter addresses the latter, exploring sport realist ethical analysis. That I do so takes on added importance given my criticisms of other theories. I have argued formalist and conventionalist theories are unable to provide normative assessment of rules and rule changes. And I have made the case that interpretivism offers limited normative guidance for many sport dilemmas, given the tension between its general principles and specific practices in sport. I don't deny that interpretivism provides effective ethical analysis in some cases, but I have found that it is frequently inadequate.

In the field of sport ethics, one might envision a theory that clearly delineates what actions are right or wrong, sportsmanlike or unsportsmanlike. Most decisions are rarely so clear-cut in practice, and black-and-white ethical analysis is seldom available. Sport realism moves focus to the decision-making process. It provides normative guidance through investigation of the parameters and features of good decision-making in sport, whether by sports officials, participants, philosophers, or other interested parties.

Through this framework it analyzes what a person should do or how rules might be changed.

I begin my argument in this chapter by delving into two related challenges to the very idea of normativity within sport realism. These objections are that realism comprises either a conventionalist or relativist theory of sport, either of which would be unable to provide a critical perspective. After contextualizing these objections, I incorporate features of two ethical approaches that are not only consistent with sport realism but more closely tied to it such that they are seemingly entangled with the theory itself, due to shared assumptions. The first of these is a form of pragmatist ethics, inspired by the connection made by early legal realists to pragmatist methodology. The second applies recent work in virtue jurisprudence to sport officiating.

TWO OBJECTIONS TO SPORT REALISM

In turning to normative considerations, I anticipate a cluster of overlapping concerns surrounding whether my realist theory of sport is in position to offer any ethical analysis. I envision two specific forms of this objection. The first pertains to conventionalism. Recall from Chapter 1 that traditional forms of conventionalism define sport in terms of its practices or ethos. I argued that conventionalism cannot address the normative requirement of a theory of sport. Simply put, if conventionalism defines sport by how it is played, it doesn't seem able to show why it should be otherwise. My sport realism might seem to fail likewise. After all, I also define sport "as it is" instead of through its formal features, and the expectations of a sport community play an outsized role in determining how an action will be treated by sport officials. Yet I hope I have made it clear how the sport realist perspective differs from this kind of conventionalism. The predictive nature of realism considers what sport means to those involved, which is unlike the view that sport simply *is* the conventions of how it is played. Additionally, the sport realist examines the conditions or situation types in which certain actions occur in order to explain them. This kind of analysis, which treats sport akin to a profession for those involved, is distinct from a conventionalist appeal to a sport's ethos.

The second objection is a worry that sport realism amounts to a form of moral relativism. By moral relativism, I have in mind the general claim that morality is relative to some person or group, with the implication that someone outside the relative community cannot provide moral analysis of actions within it. If sport realism is relativist, then external criticism of strategies, rules, or procedures may prove impossible. The result could be an "anything goes" view of sport in which all actions are allowed in the pursuit of victory. Fortunately, sport realism clearly does not constitute a form of moral relativism. First, as I argued in the previous chapter, sport realism offers analysis separate from moral considerations. While moral relativists reject non-relativistic moral theories, sport realism need not take a position on the status of particular moral theories. Second, sport realism has no trouble accepting that some actions within sport can be wrong beyond the acceptance of the community. For instance, the previous chapter examined the conditions under which an action would be considered cheating, which is a form of wrongdoing. Sport realism does not accept that any action is right merely as a means to win in sport.

Although sport realism is not reducible to a form of conventionalism or relativism, I believe these concerns express a broader worry that deserves examination. By characterizing sport in terms of how it is actually played and likely to be officiated, it might seem that sport realism does not have room for a critical perspective or independent moral assessment of how sport ought to be played. Some philosophers worry that sport is already treated in this way. In *Why Sports Morally Matter* William Morgan argues that contemporary society emphasizes individuality, with many today unable or unwilling to think about sports in moral terms. Morgan begins his book with a memorable example of students responding skeptically to an example of apparent sportsmanship, which portends a cynical view.[1] Sport realism, through features like predictivism and the "bad athlete" thought experiment, might be thought to contribute to this amoral thinking. Moreover, the term "realism" has had similar associations in the philosophy of sport, which portray ethics as anathema to realism. For example, Randolph Feezell uses realism to represent a philosophical position that ignores ethics and accepts whatever action is required to achieve victory.[2] And Claudio Tamburrini embraces what he calls realism, which accepts that sport practices are sanctioned by the way they are played. So an action that everyone performs does not violate a breach of contract, even if it is against the rules.[3]

If sport realism explains sport yet abdicates our ability to identify actions or rules that are wrong or ought to be changed, the theory would be of little use. A theory of sport needs to be able to identify wrong actions, ineffective practices, or toxic attitudes that are harmful and ought to be otherwise. I do not believe sport realism falls prey to these worries. In fact, I maintain that sport realism can ground a robust ethical view. I provided an initial rejoinder to the relativist concern in my discussion of cheating in Chapter 4. Through philosophy of law we can find actions and rules wrong in various ways. Sport realism, akin to legal realism, accepts quasi-legal forms of wrongdoing. Moreover, I argue that it improves our understanding of transgression in sport. Of course, sport realism offers a theory of sport, not of morality itself. But nothing about sport realism precludes additional ethical analysis. One can explain sport through realism yet maintain that people should be Kantians or Aristotelians or anything else.

While external ethical analysis remains available to sport realism, to leave it there would not satisfy the standard that a theory of sport should itself offer normative guidance. I will argue further that sport realism is closely tied to specific ethical views of sport. The theory informs ethical approaches to sport, which contribute the critical perspective that sport realism might seem to lack. This claim that certain ethical perspectives are closely connected with realism might be unexpected since I have advocated for a distinction between sport and morality, just as various philosophies of law separate law and morality. In what sense can ethics be intertwined with sport realism? I propose that the ethics associated with sport realism most directly apply to the ethical considerations that inform decision-making in sport. In particular, we can elucidate the kinds of considerations that characterize good reasoning in sport. The focus should be on deliberation because, in most cases, there will not be a single, evident right action; sport realism does not suggest a universal moral code.

Sport realists accept that ethical reasons are not the only ones that motivate decisions; all sorts of reasons and other motivating factors may influence behavior. Nevertheless, we can identify ethical considerations that are appropriate to incorporate as reasons, even if they are not decisive. Development of these reasons and values does not require a commitment to some account of rightness or shared conception of purpose or excellence. I contend that sport realism leads us to recognize certain moral sensitivities as uniquely complementary to its framework. Specifically, some elements of pragmatist ethics and virtue jurisprudence have a natural fit with sport realism. These viewpoints share some key explanatory and methodological assumptions with sport realism that allows each to draw from the other. This does not mean that a sport realist must adhere to either ethical position. Important differences suggest that these views cannot be fully integrated. Rather, sport realism can draw upon and develop insights from these other positions in order to provide some kinds of normative guidance and ethical constraint in sport, suited to the subject matter.

PRAGMATIST ETHICS

Fundamentals of Pragmatist Ethics

Sport realism draws inspiration from legal realism, and the relationship between legal realism and pragmatism is as much historical as it is philosophical in nature; I noted some historical connections previously in Chapter

3. Notably, future Supreme Court justice and legal realism forerunner Oliver Wendell Holmes, Jr. was a founding member of "The Metaphysical Club," along with notable pragmatists C. S. Peirce and William James. Members of the club discussed their emerging philosophical viewpoints, which came to share a number of basic assumptions. The realist and pragmatist views that these thinkers developed are considered by many to be the first distinctively American contributions to the fields of law and philosophy. We should keep in mind that pragmatism here refers to a distinctive philosophical method and set of commitments, not to the connotation it has accrued as referring to what is useful or convenient. I will argue that pragmatist ethics neatly fit with my realist theory of sport, with the qualification that there is no "pragmatist ethics" as such. Pragmatist philosophers defend a variety of ethical positions. Nevertheless, I will identify some characteristic features of pragmatist ethics with application to sport and sport realism.

Pragmatism has emerged in recent years as a philosophy of sport on its own. I am not the first to employ pragmatism as a response to relativist concerns, as some conventionalists have also done so. As I noted in Chapter 2, Morgan has routinely drawn upon Richard Rorty's pragmatist work to ground a conception of practical rationality and to provide the basis of his critique of interpretivism's abstract principles.[4] Meanwhile, others have sought to extend conventionalism by amplifying its pragmatist underpinnings. On Morgan's view, disagreements rooted in different conceptions of sport may be intractable. Tim Elcombe and Alun Hardman argue that a pragmatic conventionalism has means to overcome or move beyond such disputes. Specifically, they argue that their pragmatism provides for a more open dialogue and a range of possible resolutions, including new or alternative conventions.[5]

Though my position shares some strategies with pragmatic conventionalists and other pragmatist philosophies of sport, my use of pragmatism differs in a few key ways. Among them are the following considerations. I have argued that conventionalist theories, including Morgan's, prove unsatisfactory in their explanation of sport and description of rational inquiry. Extending conventionalism in a pragmatist direction does not resolve the underlying issues. Unlike other pragmatist views, my sport realism foregrounds predictivism as an important feature of sport. The perspective of the participants provides the best framework for pragmatist analysis of sport. Additionally, the analogy to legal realism, and to philosophy of law more generally, places sport realism in better position to address matters of injustice in sport through pragmatist ethics. I hope to offer clearer standards for use in sport decision-making.

Both realists and pragmatists emphasize human embeddedness in the world. Humans examine the world from within it, which introduces unavoidable biases, perspectives, and assumptions. Acknowledging the lack of naïve objectivity does not preclude realist theories from studying the world.[6]

Working from within the system, while recognizing this position, might even aid scientific and philosophical endeavors. Moreover, since humans are within and not mere observers of society, both legal realists and pragmatists argue that we must participate in shaping and remaking the world. As Justin Zaremby puts it, both (legal) realists and pragmatists recognize the possibility of "harnessing the ability of the human mind to affect the world around the scientist."[7] They both overcome outdated theories, assumptions, and doctrines, with the idea that their philosophies benefit society by being more responsive to the times.

Most philosophers understand pragmatism as a method for doing philosophy, not a philosophical theory or set of beliefs. Pragmatists take all reasoning to be prudential, meaning that it aims at producing or accomplishing some action. Beliefs are not abstractions but tendencies to act.[8] In ethics, this places focus on methods of philosophical inquiry and deliberation. Pragmatist ethicists take special interest in human action, eschewing theory for a philosophy rooted in practice. As Colin Koopman writes, "The point of pragmatist moral theory is not to develop rules of morality that must be followed in practice but rather to develop tools for inquiry that we can employ within experience in order to improve it."[9]

Some have thought that its focus on human action reduces pragmatic ethics to matters of utility, but this is not the case. For instance, John Dewey defends an ethic concerning modes of inquiry, often with no obvious role for a concept of utility. James offers a pragmatist ethic of meliorism for which individual interests take center stage. However, James rejects any sort of value monism that would underlie an account of utility. In other words, even though he considers human satisfaction to be a guiding ethical consideration, he does not accept any single way of capturing what satisfaction is. Likewise, I see pragmatist ethics as defined by its pluralism.[10] We will find no foundational principle to guide our ethical deliberation. Conflicts between values and goods may prove incommensurable, forcing a choice in the absence of an overarching theory or principle. James argues that results will often be tragic, meaning that whatever choice is made we will incur some moral loss.[11] I think this holds for other pragmatist and pluralist ethics.

Rather than utility, pragmatist ethicists are especially interested in examining what makes for (more) successful human action. This is the guiding idea of pragmatism that I draw upon for sport realism. The notion of successful human action is obviously slippery, but developing it will help the realist think through the ethics of sport and offer normative guidance. The success of an action includes goal attainment, but it is not limited to whether the action accomplishes its intended purpose. Roughly, the question is of whether or not an action makes sense given the situation, goals, and consequences of the action. I'll begin my elucidation of successful human action by modifying an example from Jeremy Randel Koons. Consider rules against goaltending in basketball. In previous decades when the game was played below the rim, goaltending was not a problem. The emergence of players with size and ability like Wilt Chamberlain changed the game. Players on the offensive or defensive end could more readily interfere with shots. A team with such a player on defense might make it nearly impossible for the other team to score; a team with such a player on offense might not be stopped. For subsequent discussion, I will focus on the defensive player. The interpretivist might begin by identifying the purpose or relevant excellences and skills of basketball. However, basketball has excellences on both offense and defense. I see no reason for an interpretivist to prefer one side over the other, resulting in a conflict.[12] Meanwhile, the conventionalist is faced with a novel action, so the practice community may have no clear expectation. Nevertheless, when one team cannot score a basket, we should recognize that this is a problem that needs a resolution.

I argue that it was reasonable for the NBA to eliminate certain kinds of goaltending because on some level it just doesn't make sense to allow one player to stand at the basket and block every shot. Successful action is inhibited to a significant degree. The game becomes too frustrating, difficult, unenjoyable, or even pointless. This is not to say that other theories could not reach this same conclusion about goaltending, but I think the pragmatic sport realist approach is simplest and provides the clearest answer. No conception of purpose or excellence is needed to recognize how basketball is undermined by rampant goaltending, or to invoke some change in the rules. Instead, we can identify actions like goaltending as wrong in some sense given the basic framework of the game, even though the practice is arbitrary. The arbitrary rules provide a sort of rationale.[13] Of course, none of this is to say that the NBA absolutely needed a rule against defensive goaltending. The game could be played in some fashion even if goaltending were allowed, but it would likely become a very different sort of game with little success at scoring baskets.

The development of new techniques and technologies continually change sport, and these should provoke further reflection on what bolsters or inhibits successful action. The line between similar cases can be fuzzy. Consider two comparable technological developments in baseball, the introduction of bats made of different kinds of wood and bats made of metal. Metal bats are allowed at most lower level leagues in the U.S., in part due to their cheaper cost. Wood bats break and are often replaced, whereas metal bats typically last for longer periods of time. However, higher levels of baseball in the U.S. and around the world generally disallow metal bats. I argue that this is based on a sense of successful action. Metal bats risk significantly inhibiting successful action by the defensive team, as even poorly hit balls may travel far. NCAA baseball faced this problem in the late 1990s, with the prevalence of what was called “Gorilla Ball.” NCAA baseball was dominated by home runs and huge offensive performances. This form of college baseball reached its apex during the 1998 College World Series, when USC defeated Arizona State in the final by the score 21–14. Most did not consider this good or desirable baseball. Afterward, the NCAA worked with bat companies to change the way that metal bats function in order to reduce the impact of powerful offenses.

I include injury risk within the realm of successful action. In the hands of professionals, metal bats might reasonably be deemed too dangerous. These kinds of assessments are subjective in that there is no clear measurement of when pitching has become too frustrating a task or the sport too dangerous for those on the field. Yet I believe these are the appropriate criteria. What kind of bat should be used is not likely to be decided by a conception of the sport’s purpose or excellences. It is better suited as a question for how the participants want to play the game, or what features they think make the most sense for the game to be effective and enjoyable. This should not be construed as an appeal to the beliefs or values of a specific community. The question of successful action focuses on whether the game can be played in a sensible manner, not whether this is in accord with some understanding of the game’s purpose.

I have focused on examples where successful action is inhibited, but this standard also helps us recognize cases where action has become too easy. Sport is defined by unnecessary challenges. Without obstacles, the activities of sport mean nothing. If technological changes remove the obstacles of sport, then it is unlikely to be enjoyable to the participants. So thinking about successful action also leads us to consider how difficult we want sports to be. This is not about identifying the aims of a sport, but calibrating an activity to the interests of those involved so the game seems worth playing.

We can widen this benchmark of successful action by looking again to legal realists, who sought to make action in law successful by examining the function of the law. They advocated for reform when legal rules proved impractical or inefficient in order to keep the law updated with needs of society. For some legal realists, successful law also meant changing the law to avoid or repair injustices, especially those that resulted from the formal jurisprudence that preceded the realist movement.[14] Beyond legal theory, thinking of successful action in the law leads us to the perspective of public policy, since our decisions, actions, and rules affect others we live with in society. The applicability of such considerations to sport should be evident. Sports regularly change rules to better their products, and a notion of successful action provides insight into how and why this is done. We can evaluate whether sport rules or practices need modification to make them more effective or to remove unfairness or injustice that results from them. None of these modifications or guidelines require any reference to an interpretation of sport, its principles, telos, or conceptions of purpose.

In defining successful action, typically we begin with our own experiences and observations. We refine these ideas over time and in different contexts, and continually reexamine any potential conclusions through what Elcombe and Hardman call working resolutions.[15] From a pragmatist perspective, there is a degree of acceptable circularity in this reasoning. Koons provides a useful example to underscore why a kind of circularity is permissible.[16] Participants in soccer may decide that some specific rule, such as offsides, is frustrating the aim of scoring goals. They might choose to modify the rule by appealing to the aim of scoring goals. But this is not chosen in terms of sport excellence. In this case, the aim of scoring goals is justified (partly) by the rules, and this is then used to justify some further rule within the game. Ultimately, a rule change to foster goal-scoring justifies some practice or set of rules, though the goal itself is justified by the arbitrary rules of the practice. The decision is made based on a pragmatic understanding of successful action, and that the offsides rules as it was applied was inconsistent with this. The upshot is that the rules of the practice mesh with claims about successful action as potential rule changes are discussed.

Justice and Pragmatist Values

Injustices in sport merit examination. In Chapter 3 I described how many legal realists were motivated to address injustices created by outdated laws or inflexible adherence to legal rules. Similarly, sport realism seeks to improve sports rather than adhering to outmoded views. A standard of successful action helps to identify injustices caused by impractical or inflexible rules. For example, recent research has exposed the serious nature of head injuries and concussions. Yet many athletes report reluctance to inform coaches or trainers about injuries. Some teams seem hesitant to take action, possibly because they do not want to lose players for an extended period of time. Obviously, players should not be put in positions where they feel a need to risk debilitating injury. Outdated rules contribute to the problem by inhibiting players and teams from making the decisions for the long-term benefit of all involved. In 2011 Major League Baseball implemented a 7-day injured list for players diagnosed with a concussion. In being shorter than the usual injured list, it reduces the "penalty" for those who have suffered head injuries. This kind of response is in line with those that a sport realist and pragmatist might advocate. Other sports should pursue new strategies to ensure that concussions are diagnosed and treated in all possible cases.

Not all injustices are directly related to the rules. For instance, some inequalities of opportunity and participation in sport pertain to gender or race. Or locker rooms can have toxic atmospheres, where certain players experience discrimination and harassment from others. The pragmatic realist can recognize both unequal opportunity and discrimination as failures of successful action, where actions within sport fail to harmonize with stated goals. Of course, these sorts of injustices are not purely about action, and they do not typically call for compromise as a resolution. Pragmatist values provide additional guidance for individual deliberation or the promotion of preferable alternatives.

Self-cultivation is a core pragmatist value. For most pragmatists, the self is not viewed as something that underlies or stands behind human experience. Instead, they view the self as "the byproduct of an unending process driven toward the actualization of human potential."[17] The self is established and remade by human action through its interactions in the world, so we ought to pay close attention to how these selves are made. Self-cultivation has a straightforward application to the pragmatist concern with successful action. Richard Lally provides the example of successful action for endurance athletes.[18] Here, self-cultivation means essentially improved performance, which he calls "self-measurement."[19] This is not just the ability to achieve a personal best. Rather, it is a more holistic conception of the person being directed toward a goal and organizing one's efforts around it. Accordingly, we can distinguish actions that contribute to self-improvement of an endurance athlete, such as dedication to a workout regimen, from those that do not, such as cutting the course during a marathon in order to cross the finish line at an earlier time.

Self-cultivation is not limited to athletic improvement. It applies to longer-term interplay between our activities and goals, and whether our goals are realized in action. Lally offers the example of a triathlete who engages in intense physical activity for months or years. Improved self-measurement is unlikely to sustain such intensity over long periods of time. Lally contends that sustaining this action requires the athlete to feel connected to a wider world that is itself rich in meaning. The result would be something of an "unfolding," a process by which the individual has moments of meaningfulness that in time foster a new perspective.[20] The athlete will be able to look back at previous versions of herself to see how she has improved and developed, which amounts to a process of self-realization. The triathlete might find a meaningful arc in her life as she looks at her accomplishments and dedication, along with other activities and goals that have come to define her. In this way, the guideline of successful action directs us to considerations of unity and harmony that allow for self-realization.[21]

Loyalty is also a value appropriate for sport realist and pragmatic deliberation. Matthew Foust argues that the value of loyalty is closely associated with the need in sport for fair play and community. His essay is motivated by the question of player loyalty, illustrated when LeBron James chose to leave his hometown Cleveland Cavaliers for the Miami Heat in 2010. Foust draws on pragmatist philosophy to understand loyalty as devotion to a cause, which includes devotion to a person, institution, or ideal.[22] This devotion must be sustained over time. Importantly, loyalty cannot be directed toward just any cause. Loyalty to an unworthy cause only undermines loyalty in general. In Foust's example, a referee who accepts bribes is complicit in undermining loyalty for refereeing and rule-following more generally. There is no absolute distinction between worthy and unworthy causes in sport, even though the language of sport suggests differentiation. We speak of being a good teammate who is on the same page as fellow team members, or a loyal trainer who improves and ensures the health of the players.[23] On Foust's view, pragmatist deliberation aids decisions by inquiring into which loyalties are thoroughgoing and which might improve loyalty in general.[24] At the very least, such deliberation is likely to rule out certain choices as disloyal, while illuminating the best options that remain available.

Pineda Redux

I will now sketch the application of a pragmatic realist ethic to specific situations. The first is a case study that further illuminates pragmatist deliberation by participants and sport officials. The second is a philosophical dispute concerning the rules of sport. For the first I will return to the Michael Pineda situation. Recall that Pineda was ejected from a game for blatant use of pine tar, and he was subsequently suspended for ten games by MLB. The reactions from many in the baseball community were pragmatic in nature. For instance, Red Sox manager John Farrell and catcher A. J. Pierzynski adjusted their expectations to fit the situation. They indicated no objection to a pitcher using pine tar in cold weather to get a better grip on the ball. If the pitcher cannot grip the ball, his wild pitches would prove risky to batters who might get hit. Their reasoning seems to employ a standard akin to successful action. If the pitcher cannot control the ball, everyone in the game is worse off. Criticism of Pineda was directed toward the sloppy manner in which he applied pine tar. As a result, we might consider rule modification regarding substance usage to ensure that pitchers can pitch safely in cold weather.

Other pragmatic values may apply as well. In examining loyalty, we found that a pragmatist approach required clarification about how specific actions contribute to or undermine loyalty more generally. With Pineda, the value of respect among participants can be treated similarly. The manner in which Pineda applied pine tar was seen as disrespectful; whether using pine tar in the first place is disrespectful seems more debatable. At a minimum, the pragmatist encourages players to be judicious in terms of both whether and how substances like pine tar might be used. Again, rule clarification, including perhaps allowing pine tar to be used in cold weather, seems appropriate.

The pragmatist value of self-cultivation suggests a holistic look at self-measurement rather than accepting shortcuts to short term improvement. When Pineda was caught with pine tar, it seemed that he was using it, at least more visibly, after a rough first inning. If so, this might be viewed as a scheme to avoid the requisite effort and dedication to the goal. To explore this, the pragmatic realist should inquire into the actual effects of pine tar rather than rejecting the kind of action in question. Consider an imagined substance, Clemenstine, that when used by pitchers makes the ball move in a pronounced and unpredictable manner. We likely have good reason to ban this substance on grounds that it simply makes hitting a baseball too difficult. It also might be a pitching shortcut, comparable to the marathoner who cuts the course. Note that there is no absolute standard to answer these questions. How difficult it should be to hit a baseball is inherently subjective, involving factors like whether the sport can be successfully played and what makes it challenging and enjoyable. Yet this subjectivity does not preclude making such assessments, just as we must do with any technological innovation in sport. The rules still need a rationale, even if the framework is arbitrary.

Our reasoning about Clemenstine is similar to the previous discussions of goaltending in basketball or goal-scoring in soccer. By studying the actual effects of pine tar in different conditions, we can compare its effects to the imagined Clemenstine. Research might show that pine tar has limited effect on movement of the ball, at least under certain conditions. With little benefit to be gained, there is no reason to ban pitchers from using pine tar to improve their grip. On the other hand, if empirical study shows that pine tar has a substantial effect on ball movement, then it is reasonable to proscribe its usage.

Finally, a pragmatic sport realist should examine whether the use of pine tar creates injustice. Deception is routinely considered an acceptable strategy in sport, although some instances of deception are seen as unfair to the opponent. It is difficult to draw a line between acceptable and unacceptable deception, although the notion of successful action may prove useful in doing so. Typically, we accept that participants must use equipment that meets certain standards, with both teams aware of what is being used. If deception concerning the use of pine tar provides a significant advantage to the pitcher, then we ought to keep the current ban in place. If deception offers little measurable advantage, then the rules might warrant change. Once again, there is a role for empirical study. To determine how we should respond to pine tar usage, we need some sense of how it changes the game. To be clear, this does not require an interpretivist appeal to constitutive skills or a sense of how the game ought to be played. It only requires an assessment of whether some action or rule inhibits to too great a degree some action that we prefer, on whatever grounds we prefer them. No matter what we decide concerning pitchers using pine tar, the pragmatic sport realist acknowledges that something is likely to be lost. No answer is obviously the best and able to satisfy all concerns.

Video Replay in Sport

Video replay is now a part of many high-level professional sports. The aim of replay is to get calls right. Incorrect calls can be a problem, especially for those who hold that sports are intended to make manifest the best individual or team. Incorrect calls undermine successful action either by precluding effective actions or by allowing unsuccessful actions to be effective. Arguably, incorrect calls also create unfairness; while they can happen to either team, they may advantage or disadvantage one side over the other in any particular sporting contest.[25] And Seth Bordner shows how certain bad calls clearly play outsized roles in deciding the outcome of the competition, which raises concerns about justice.[26]

Given these problems with incorrect calls, replay might seem an effective means to promote successful action. However, there are at least two reasons to think that replay review actually undermines successful action: it disrupts the flow of the game and is time consuming. The pragmatic sport realist might aim for a balance between competing values, allowing for replays that can be done quickly or infrequently so as to avoid interrupting the game. However, this strategy fails to achieve the values on either side of the debate—it still interferes with the game yet it doesn't get all of the calls right. Even so, we might conclude that limited replay is the preferable option. It addresses the concerns of sport by promoting successful action and avoiding injustices, with relatively minimal costs. Application of limited replay should vary by sport. In some sports, we might decide to place more value on getting the call correct, which would support more intrusive replay reviews. In other sports, we might place more value on continued action, leading to limited replay and the acceptance of occasional bad calls.[27] Again, there is no absolute way to decide how much interruption is too much, and no specific skill or interpretation of sport will provide the best answer. The interests of all involved are considered, with the aim of losing as little as possible for all of the participants.[28]

Philosophical inquiry into replay benefits from experience and empirical data when possible. We should look to current forms of replay to see what lessons we can learn. The Hawk-Eye system used in tennis is arguably the most effective form of replay, although it is more simulation than televised replay. Harry Collins has termed it a "Reconstructed Track Device" that constructs an image based on calculations.[29] Hawk-Eye reviews happen quickly, only delaying points a few seconds. Players are given a set number of challenges, limiting the distraction. Players and fans appear to have bought into the system, likely due in part to its limited intrusiveness. In contrast, the VAR system recently implemented in various soccer leagues and tournaments has been widely criticized. It is time-consuming in a sport that values continuous action. Moreover, many argue that the kinds of infractions identified through VAR would go unnoticed without it. In other words, VAR creates new infractions beyond just catching obvious infractions that were missed by officials on the field. For these reasons, VAR is more disruptive to soccer action on the field.

From a realist perspective, the biggest problem caused by VAR is that infractions are less predictable. Players, coaches, and fans no longer know what to expect when the referee goes to replay review. This situation is similar to the Jesse James catch discussed in Chapter 3. Perhaps this problem with VAR will resolve itself as we experience more replays and can identify new situation types. Still, an unpredictable replay system is a serious threat to successful action in sport. This is not necessarily an argument against the use of replay, although it calls for a slower and more limited introduction of replay into sport. Against Bordner and others who advocate more immediate and all-encompassing technological solutions, I hold that significant changes to sports officiating create chaos or unpredictability and, ultimately, a messier game.

VIRTUE JURISPRUDENCE

Fundamentals of Virtue Jurisprudence

Sport realism defines sport with an eye to the decisions made by officials. I contend that it contributes to our understanding of not only what sports officials do but also what it takes to do the job well. This idea might seem in tension with the basic idea of sport realism, which I defined as a study of sport as it is, not as it ought to be. Yet I see no reason to preclude a realist from examining the role and identifying preferred qualities or characteristics of sports officials, so long as analysis of what happens on the field remains central to understanding what sport is. More to the point, sports officials themselves think the job can be done well or poorly, since they routinely appeal to specific values or traits in explaining how they make decisions.

I argue that sport realism aids in the recognition of some virtues of sports officiating. In making this argument, I draw upon work in virtue jurisprudence concerning virtues constitutive of good (law) judges. Virtue jurisprudence is a legal theory which holds that the final end of law is to promote human flourishing or to enable humans to live excellent lives. Accordingly, virtue and excellence should be the fundamental concepts of legal theory instead of traditional legal concepts like autonomy, equality, rights, or privileges.[30] Adherents to this theory seek improvement in law and legal institutions by selecting judges who possess judicial virtues.

The legal approach of virtue jurisprudence, on the whole, is at odds with the kind of realist theory I have pursued. In fact, defenders of virtue jurisprudence have pitched it as an alternative to legal theories drawn from realist or neorealist theories, including legal realism, critical legal studies, and legal pragmatism.[31] The differences are manifest. Most notably, virtue jurisprudence requires a conception of human excellence. Sport may contribute to human excellence, but I have argued that no unified account of excellence can be located in sport. Consequently, I will not argue that sport realism and virtue jurisprudence have a number of shared assumptions, as was the case with pragmatist ethics. When I suggest that some elements of virtue jurisprudence fit with sport realism, I only mean to utilize certain insights that I do not believe are limited to that framework. For instance, as I noted above, sports officials do appeal to values or characteristics of good officiating in their own descriptions of what they do. I doubt that these explanations depend on working out some view of flourishing or human excellence, or imagining virtues as constitutive of these.

That being said, sport realism and virtue jurisprudence share some notions about good judging. Both are motivated by resistance to formalist adjudication. Neither judging nor officiating should be understood as formulaic. So both accounts maintain, as Feezell puts it, that "good judgment is possible."[32] Feezell directs us to consider the role of practical wisdom in sports officiating.[33] He uses this phrase in a broadly Aristotelian sense, which is more amenable to virtue jurisprudence. However, many legal realists also suggest a need for practical wisdom in their accounts of legal adjudication. For instance, Zaremby encapsulates Holmes' approach to law as one emphasizing "logic mixed with a bit of judicial experience, judicial creativity, and a great deal of serendipity."[34] Meanwhile, Karl Llewellyn advocates that judges need a "situation sense," with which they consider the facts in their context "coupled with whatever the judge or court brings and adds to the evidence, in the way of knowledge and experience and values to see with, and to judge with."[35] Effective judges are able to recognize the relevant features of the situation and the significance of the facts in order to resolve a given case. They may explore the implications of a case by seeing it as an example of a broader situation or identify the means by which to accomplish some goal. This situation sense brings Llewellyn close to views that incorporate practical reason or prudence.[36] If legal realists can make room to examine judicial technique or character traits as essential to the study of law as it is, then sport realism should have no trouble incorporating some sense of practical wisdom for sports officials.[37]

We do not need a robust account of human flourishing in order to locate some virtues of sports officiating. We might think of virtues more like regulative ideals than traits constitutive of flourishing, allowing that they can be understood from different perspectives with other background assumptions about human excellence. To this end, I view the virtues of sports officiating as, in part, a development of the pragmatist ethic I described in the previous section; we can examine virtues in the context of successful action in sport. If sports officials lack the appropriate virtues, or worse yet act in vicious ways, then we can expect that effective or predictable action likely will be inhibited.

Lawrence Solum has been one of the main proponents of virtue jurisprudence, and much of his work is inconsistent with realism at a theoretical level. However, at times he explores the virtues of good judging without "Aristotelian baggage." In his essay "A Tournament of Virtue," Solum investigates how we should select judges or otherwise identify the best or most excellent judges. Admittedly, he defines virtues as "a dispositional quality of mind or characteristic that is constitutive of human excellence."[38] But the rest of his argument does not appear to rely on any conception of human excellence. Rather, he offers an account of judicial virtue derived from widely accepted beliefs about good judging, human nature, and society.[39] In another work, he describes this strategy as theorizing virtues that are based on "uncontroversial assumptions about what counts as good judging."[40] His strategy of locating judicial virtues through widely-shared notions of good and bad judging applies equally well to the virtues of sports officiating. More importantly, this strategy is available to the realist.

Solum begins his investigation of virtue in "A Tournament of Virtue" by cataloging judicial vices, observing that there is near-consensus regarding judicial vices and the worst judges. Judicial virtues would aim to correct these. While there are obvious differences between judging and officiating, the initial vices Solum describes—corruption (greed), intemperance, cowardice, hot temperedness, partiality, laziness, carelessness, and ignorance—all seem pertinent to sports officiating. Incorruptibility and good temper, for instance, are clearly traits that we expect an official to exhibit. If an official acts through greed or anger, this inhibits successful action in sport and undermines its predictability. Likewise, we expect officials to be diligent and careful in their decision-making, since the details are typically what matter in hard cases.

Other judicial virtues seem applicable to sport officiating, with caveats. Solum characterizes a virtue of impartiality, that we want judges to be neutral arbitrators. We expect that "a judge should be open to the law and evidence and not be biased in favor of one side or another," so long as this doesn't amount to indifference.[41] Sport realists can embrace the first component of Solum's description, since they, like legal realists, hold that decisions should be made based on the evidence and facts of the case. And anyone would accept that an official should not be in the pocket of one player or team. However, sport realists take a different attitude toward bias, since realism is predicated upon understanding the biases and non-legal reasons that influence decisions. We cannot remove all biases or realistically constrain the kinds of motives, reasons, or influences that sport officials act upon. Impartiality risks severing officiating from the context and consequences in which decisions are made. We should circumscribe the virtue of impartiality to mean that no side of the contest is given preference.

Judicial courage also applies to sport, with qualification. For Solum, courage means not cowing to threats or consequences, like loss of reputation and social standing. When the best decision is manifest, correctness should be the overriding consideration, even when it is unpopular. Yet the decision is not likely to be clear in hard cases. Sport realism acknowledges that social consequences are part of the decision-making process, while trying to identify which of these are most likely to influence decisions. Of course, collectively we might decide that we want to minimize certain kinds of external influences. For example, we should agree that it's wrong to threaten officials with violence. But the realist does not expect that these sorts of influences can be eliminated, or that we can expect a judge simply to ignore them in all cases. To rule out various external influences risks defining sport as one believes it ought to be, and I have shown that such explanations of sport are inadequate.

Solum's list of virtues is only a starting point. We can identify other virtues pertaining to officiating analysis or technique. Following Justice Holmes, we can recognize a virtue of judicial creativity. Drawing on pragmatism, we find a virtue of imagination. Dewey argues that deliberation about effective action benefits from imagination in moving forward from experience and observation. For Dewey, imagination has two features.[42] Empathy allows us to treat others' interests and aspirations as our own; seeing the possibilities of a situation provides a means to overcome habit and adjust to the future. Steven Fesmire connects the imagination to dramatic rehearsal, through which a person develops and refines the identification of new possibilities and her own valuation of them.[43] In approaching situations with imagination, we are best able to see what actions are possible and which are likely to be most successful at that time.

Both the virtues of creativity and imagination highlight the need for officials to be inventive and resourceful when facing hard cases or situations not readily covered by rules and precedents. The virtues also help to address matters of injustice or unfairness, especially when they result from outdated or habitual thinking. These often require new ways of thinking or innovative solutions. Also, the sport realist advocates virtues of consistency and transparency. This is not to say that consistency overrides other features of a case, but that the need to predict sport outcomes is aided by officials who reason in a foreseeable and open manner. Many of the problems realists identify in competing theories of law and sport result from reality not matching an ideal. Accepting and explaining unacknowledged reasons or motives, akin to non-legal reasons, allows for a more accurate understanding of sports officiating, to the benefit of the participants.

Sport realism breaks from virtue theory on whether law can be grounded in virtue. The disagreement becomes clear when examining the role of practical wisdom. Solum defines practical wisdom, or *phronesis*, as "the virtue that enables one to make good choices in particular circumstances."[44] Solum contends that this virtue is little different from Llewellyn's notion of situation sense, as they share the basic idea that a judge must know how to accomplish goals in particular cases. Practical wisdom is necessary because theoretical wisdom does not guarantee reliable judging. So far so good. Solum's critique fits with realist complaints about formalism in judging and officiating, and the sport realist might accept a broad virtue of this sort. Even so, I question the centrality some give to the virtue of practical wisdom. The moral vision associated with practical wisdom might be adequately captured by other virtues like creativity.

At other times, Solum suggests a more robust conception of practical wisdom that is central to both virtue and law. He claims that "the *phronimos* can do equity because she grasps the point of legal rules and discerns the legally and morally salient features of particular fact situations."[45] Again, he compares this to Llewellyn's situation sense, although the connection here seems more tenuous. For sport, Solum's account is problematic because his appeal to the point of legal rules requires an interpretation of the rules and their teloi, reintroducing the problems of interpretivism. Elsewhere, Solum goes further, defining lawfulness in terms of virtue. He writes, "A *lawful decision* is a decision that would characteristically be made by a virtuous judge in the circumstances that are relevant to the decision."[46] On this view, lawfulness requires *phronesis*, or virtuous reasoning is necessary for lawful and correct decisions. The sport realist cannot accept making virtue prior to the law or rules of sport. Even though some difficult decisions may involve virtue or discernment, this does not require defining either law or sport in terms of virtue.[47] We would not expect a judge or official to justify a decision in a hard case in terms of virtue, as this account of *phronesis* indicates.[48] Moreover, *phronesis* is not required to determine whether some action is reasonable.[49] So for the sport realist, practical wisdom may comprise a virtue of sports officiating, but we should not identify a good (or lawful) official with the *phronimos*.

Woods Redux

To outline how the insights of virtue jurisprudence work with sport realism in specific situations, I will follow the same approach as I did with pragmatist ethics. The first is a case study that works through deliberation by participants and sport officials, and the second a philosophical dispute concerning the nature of sport and its officiating. I will begin with the Tiger Woods case that I introduced in Chapter 2.[50] Recall that Woods admitted to dropping in a preferred location two yards from his initial divot. That Woods was not disqualified led some to speculate that he was given preferential treatment due to his popularity and power. If these were the primary factors, we might conclude that the committee failed to act impartially. However, I argued in Chapter 3 that there is no clear evidence for this conclusion. It may well be that these factors influenced the decision, but I doubt these were the sole considerations.

The influence of virtue jurisprudence leads the sport realist to examine how the USGA proceeded in making its decision. The virtues most evident here are those of creativity and imagination. The committee might have been tempted to oversimplify the case by making one feature of it the overriding consideration. For instance, it could have stood by its initial statement as entirely satisfactory, or instead immediately disqualified Woods based on the incorrect scorecard. Instead, the committee appears to have grappled directly with the many complicating features of the case in the moment. They were resourceful in analyzing the various possible applications or meanings of the rules, including new rules that hadn't been tested yet.

The committee did not endorse a specific interpretation when considering possible rulings. Their deliberations allowed that the sport might admit of competing excellences, including integrity and the desire to have the tournament decided on the course rather than through disqualification. They sought to balance various concerns, precedents, and interests of those involved. Accordingly, the decision seems to have involved practical wisdom, or something comparable to Llewellyn's situation sense, by which officials identify a goal and determine how it is best attained. While we cannot know precisely how the conversations went, we can hope that the fundamental question was what is best for the game of golf in all its facets, for the participants, fans, and the sport itself, with an eye toward how the precedent might be employed in the future.

The USGA displayed some judicial virtues in adjudicating Woods' case, but it should be faulted for its vices as well. The most significant vices are lack of transparency and clarity in its rule applications. Initially, the USGA seemed to employ its new Rule 33 in allowing Woods to remain in the tournament. Its later statement indicated that Rule 33 was not used after all. In Chapter 3, I argued that the subsequent USGA statement was revisionist history, making the decision-making process appear more straightforward than it really was. The USGA needed to be more transparent in the moment, regardless of the accuracy of the later statement, as their approach gave the appearance of carelessness. Furthermore, the unique nature of this case raises questions of consistency. Some argued that tradition required Woods to be disqualified. The USGA need not remain wedded to all of its traditions, but we now face ambiguity regarding what kinds of actions will require disqualification in the future. Clearer explanations and procedures are appropriate.

The sport realist might find that the USGA decision in Woods' case was justifiable and reflected some judicial virtues, and that its later statement was well-intentioned but problematic. Nevertheless, we should resist concluding that this was obviously the correct outcome. Drawing on virtue jurisprudence does not mean all virtuous officials will rule the same way. The committee could have reasonably concluded that Woods' comments showed a disregard or misunderstanding of the rules to a degree that warranted disqualification. The critical point is that virtuous adjudication need not aim at some overriding excellence embedded in the telos of either sport or humanity. Ultimately, I think it sensible to conclude that the USGA acted in what it thought was a fair manner, in that it discussed the incident with Woods and applied a significant penalty that participants would understand. In such cases, we must simply ask that sport officials identify the most important features of a case along with the most relevant judicial virtues, and then act accordingly.

Makeup Calls

Sports officials make mistakes. Sometimes officials realize that they have made a mistake, raising a question of how they should proceed. Many believe that officials respond with makeup calls. A makeup call is an attempt to compensate for a mistake by making a proportional call against the team that benefitted from the initial call. Makeup calls are sometimes made subconsciously or unintentionally. Given that sport realism aims to understand how officials are likely to act, it is well-positioned to explain subconscious or unintentional makeup calls. Studying these is little different from investigating whether officials are influenced by a home crowd or other factors. Intentional makeup calls are more philosophically intriguing, and elements of virtue are useful in explicating the realist position on them.

There is an evident justification for intentional makeup calls—if a mistake is made, officials should seek to restore the situation or remove any unwarranted advantage gained through it. Yet Mark Hamilton offers a number of compelling arguments against the use of intentional makeup calls. Three concerns are of particular significance for my purposes here. First, if an official looks to issue a makeup call, she becomes partial to one side of the contest. As Hamilton puts it, such an official would have to be "ignoring what one 'sees'" in giving the makeup call.[51] Generally, we disapprove of an official who violates the rules or otherwise acts dishonestly in an attempt to compensate for her mistake. Such attitudes do not exemplify any virtues of good officiating. Second, it is not clear that a makeup call can attain a just result. There is no way to gauge proportionality, and a proportional call still changes the nature of the contest. Some even consider the makeup call an act of injustice that only serves to perpetuate further injustice.[52] Third, there is a conceptual puzzle with makeup calls because the official must be aware of the mistake. But if aware, then the call should not have been made in the first place. Therefore, if a call is mistaken, it seems we should demand it be overturned or reversed in the moment, otherwise the contest should continue as is.

Despite these forceful arguments, I believe sport realism carves out some legitimate usage of makeup calls. These are limited to situations where the call could not have been overturned in the first place.[53] Imagine two scenarios. In the first, a basketball official calls the ball out of bounds off of Smith, which she believes is the correct call. Shortly thereafter she sees a replay shown on the arena jumbotron that shows the ball was, in fact, out of bounds off of Jones. In the second, a softball umpire calls a pitch a strike, but by the time he realizes he has erred, the pitcher has the ball and is on the rubber. In these and similar cases the original call could not be reversed, whether due to new information, time constraints, or other considerations.[54] The question is how to decide the best course of action going forward, perhaps as forms of restorative or corrective justice. Hamilton argues they are not restorative because they cannot bring together the victim and the victimizer (official), but instead risk fraying the relationship with the other team.[55] Corrective justice aims to restore through compensation for harm done, restoring the social order and relationships in the process. Hamilton sees corrective justice as the best defense of makeup calls, when the official tries to see the contest as a whole in which individual plays are interconnected. Yet he remains opposed to makeup calls on grounds that they distort the game and improperly use participants as means to an end.

We should be more open to the possibility of makeup calls. From the sport realist perspective, we should not view one incorrect call as a clear deviation from an otherwise formal practice. There is no perfect outcome to be gained. With any such decision, the official should consider which course of action best reflects the interests of all participants. At times, this may involve a makeup call that compensates one team. I propose two criteria to specify when makeup calls might be appropriate. First, as with the scenarios described above, it must be a situation when the initial call could not be overturned or reversed. Second, the official must be reasonably confident that the initial call was mistaken, such as through the presence of new information.

The basketball and softball cases I described meet these criteria, although this does not mean a makeup call must be made. Beyond these two criteria, we cannot specify when makeup calls are appropriate. Instead, we can appeal to virtues of officiating. Here, practical wisdom is central. Hamilton proposes that we might seek makeup calls as part of the "internal justice" or "evolving ethos" of a sport.[56] Similarly, the sport realist might view makeup calls as an expected practice to pursue balance in response to evident mistakes. Sports officials use practical wisdom to identify an appropriate time and approximate proportion in doing so. They also need other virtues like imagination or creativity to envision how compensation might be given within a contest. Officials should be transparent and honest about the mistake and subsequent attempts to compensate, yet courageous in standing by the course of action she perceives as best. Even if we accept the theoretical legitimacy of makeup calls, officials should proceed with caution in order to maintain the predictability of the adjudication.

A special kind of mistaken call deserves further examination. Sometimes bad calls are (or could be) the final call of a game, where if the call were changed the other team would win. We have already explored one such case—George Brett's pine tar incident—where the game was played under protest and restarted at a later date after the call was reversed. Another MLB example occurred in 2010, when Armando Galarraga of the Detroit Tigers was denied a perfect game because umpire Jim Joyce wrongly called a runner safe at first base. It is generally accepted that these decisions cannot be changed after the fact. I disagree. We might worry about the procedures by which such decisions are made, but I do not see a problem with correcting mistaken calls of this sort. In fact, I believe that doing so is less problematic than other forms of makeup calls, since there is no further disruption to the contest. Again, the identification of relevant virtues and practical reasoning may provide guidance as to when game-deciding calls should be reversed after the fact.

CONCLUSION

I have proposed and defended sport realism as alternative theory of sport. It provides the best explanation of sport, allowing us to understand what sport is, and it provides normative guidance for philosophical disputes in sport. Some may worry that sport realism risks an unpalatable form of conventionalism or relativism of sport. In response, I have argued that two ethical views fit tightly with sport realism, showing that it need not be committed to any unacceptable normative conclusions. By drawing on pragmatist ethics, sport realism can employ ethical standards pertaining to successful action, emphasizing certain related values and modes of deliberation. By developing some ideas from virtue jurisprudence, we can explore the qualities appropriate to sport officials, who play a central role in defining sport from a realist perspective.

Through sketches of both ethical approaches, we see how sport realism informs the decision-making process of sport officials, helping us to understand what it means to be a good official. Yet realism implies pluralism in sport. Many difficult cases, if not most, lack an obvious right answer. This is unsurprising given that sports are human inventions, often with arbitrary developmental histories. We might hope to identify some overriding ethical consideration, but most often we are left to choose the course of action we find best with respect to various aims, interests, and participants. The sport realist approach suggests we interrogate how and why such decisions are made, in order to facilitate clear and predictable decisions and procedures in the future. None of this precludes the pursuit of the best answer, even if there is not always only one right answer.

NOTES

1. William J. Morgan, *Why Sports Morally Matter* (New York: Routledge, 2006), xii–xiii.

2. Randolph Feezell, "Baseball, Cheating, and Tradition: Would Kant Cork his Bat?," in *Baseball and Philosophy*, ed. Eric Bronson (Chicago: Open Court, 2004), 113–123 and *Playing Games* (London: Routledge, 2017), 77–79.

3. Claudio Tamburrini, "The 'Hand of God'?," in *The Ethics of Sport*, ed. Mike McNamee (London: Routledge, 2010), 136.

4. William Morgan, "Conventionalism Defended: A Reply to Moore," *Journal of the Philosophy of Sport* 46, no. 1 (2019): 103–104.

5. Tim L. Elcombe and Alun R. Hardman, "Pragmatic Conventionalism and Sport Normativity in the Face of Intractable Dilemmas," *Journal of the Philosophy of Sport* 47, no. 1 (2020): 20–28.

6. Wouter de Been, *Legal Realism Regained* (Stanford, CA: Stanford University Press, 2008), 20–22.

7. Justin Zaremby, *Legal Realism and American Law* (New York: Bloomsbury, 2014), 17.

8. Steven Fesmire, *John Dewey and Moral Imagination* (Bloomington: Indiana University Press, 2003), 28.

9. Colin Koopman, *Pragmatism as Transition* (New York: Columbia University Press, 2009), 149.

10. Traditionally, pluralism has been understood as a hallmark of pragmatist ethics. Recent work by Scott Aikin and Robert Talisse challenges whether pragmatists can or should be pluralist. For example, see Scott F. Aikin and Robert B. Talisse,

Pragmatism, Pluralism, and the Nature of Philosophy (New York: Routledge, 2018), 167–178. My view avoids this problem for at least two reasons. First, my position, at root, is realist and not pragmatist. From the realist perspective, I have argued here and elsewhere that many debates in sport ethics are incommensurable due to the lack of a clear purpose or notion of athletic excellence. Second, I accept the dominant view that pragmatists can accept a plurality of values, leading to conflicts lacking rational resolution, without undermining their emphasis on effective deliberation. Elcombe and Hardman reach a similar conclusion that pragmatist thinking in sport should encourage a plurality of new possibilities. Elcombe and Hardman, "Pragmatic Conventionalism," 27–28.

11. Aikin and Talisse, *Pluralism*, 80–81.

12. Sinclair MacRae makes a similar point. He argues that excellences pertaining to different roles in sport preclude interpretivism from offering an overarching ethical standpoint. MacRae, "Toward a Shallow Interpretivist Model of Sport," *Journal of the Philosophy of Sport* 44, no. 3 (2017): 294–295. However, MacRae responds with a modified view he calls shallow interpretivism, which locates a plurality of values in sport. His interpretivism view faces the same challenges I outlined for other versions in Chapter 2.

13. Jeremy Randel Koons, *Pragmatic Reasons* (London: Palgrave Macmillan, 2009), 107.

14. Zaremby, *American Law*, 19.

15. Elcombe and Hardman, "Pragmatic Conventionalism," 26.

16. Koons, *Pragmatic Reasons*, 144–145.

17. Richard Lally, "Deweyan Pragmatism and Self-Cultivation," in *Pragmatism and the Philosophy of Sport*, ed. Richard Lally, Douglas Anderson, and John Kaag (Lanham, MD: Lexington Books, 2013), 177.

18. Douglas Hochstetler and Peter Hopsicker offer a similar analysis of endurance athletes, which they put in terms of growth rather than self-cultivation. Hochstetler and Hopsicker, "The Heights of Humanity: Endurance Sport and the Strenuous Mood," *Journal of the Philosophy of Sport* 39, no. 1 (2012): 126–128.

19. Lally, "Self-Cultivation," 181.

20. Ibid. See also Douglas R. Hochstetler, "Process and the Sport Experience," in *Pragmatism and the Philosophy of Sport*, ed. Richard Lally, Douglas Anderson, and John Kaag (Lanham, MD: Lexington Books, 2013), 28–30.

21. Koopman connects these themes in pragmatist ethics to those of perfectionism and transformation of self and others in *Pragmatism*, 146–156. While I do not explore this perfectionist angle in detail, it seems available to sport realism.

22. Mathew A. Foust, "Where Should LeBron's Loyalty Lie? Where Should Ours?," in *Pragmatism and the Philosophy of Sport*, ed. Richard Lally, Douglas Anderson, and John Kaag (Lanham, MD: Lexington Books, 2013), 80.

23. Ibid., 82.

24. Ibid., 86–87.

25. Seth Bordner also notes that referees exhibit various biases, such as toward home teams and against a team that has been called for fewer fouls so far in a game. So we cannot say that bad calls are entirely unplanned. Furthermore, even if all

participants are affected, they may not be affected to the same degree. Bordner, "Call 'Em as they are: What's Wrong with Blown Calls and What to do about them," *Journal of the Philosophy of Sport* 42, no. 1 (2015): 107–108.

26. Ibid., 102, 109–110.

27. Bordner rejects considerations like the flow of the game. He argues that sports are fundamentally contests, and that we should not consider other factors when deciding how to implement replay. Ibid., 112–113. As I have defended throughout this book, such influences play a role in defining sport and determining how disputes are adjudicated. It is inaccurate and unrealistic to imagine sport is otherwise. We might wish sports were played as Bordner wants, but they are not, which is why these discussions must begin with an accurate conception of what sport is.

28. Some argue against replay on grounds that bad calls are part of the game. One might think that sport realism is committed to this idea, based on its attempt to define sport as it is actually played. However, sport realism is not committed in this way. While it is true that bad calls will always occur in sport, by itself this provides no compelling reason to leave things as they are. I have suggested that the communities around sports will likely differ in how they weigh various factors in considering replay or other means of correcting bad calls.

29. Harry Collins, "The Philosophy of Umpiring and the Introduction of Decision-Aid Technology," *Journal of the Philosophy of Sport* 37, no. 2 (2010): 140. Collins goes on to argue against the use of Reconstructed Track Devices on the basis that they create a false sense of precision regarding in/out calls. I don't disagree with Collins that officiating is more about justice than accuracy, but I suspect the potential consequences of this false transparency are relatively insignificant. Perhaps the problem can be mitigated by publicizing the margin of error to emphasize that we should not expect complete accuracy even with replay or RTDs.

30. Colin Farrelly and Lawrence B. Solum, "An Introduction to Aretaic Theories of Law," in *Virtue Jurisprudence*, ed. Colin Farrelly and Lawrence B. Solum (London: Palgrave Macmillan, 2008), 2–3.

31. Farrelly and Solum, "Aretaic Theories," 1.

32. Randolph Feezell, "On the Wrongness of Cheating and Why Cheaters Can't Play the Game," *Journal of the Philosophy of Sport* 15, no. 1 (1988): 61.

33. Ibid., 66.

34. Zaremby, *American Law*, xix.

35. Karl Llewellyn, *The Common Law Tradition: Deciding Appeals* (Boston: Little, Brown and Company, 1960), 60.

36. Daniel A. Farber, "The Inevitability of Practical Reason: Statutes, Formalism, and the Rule of Law," *Vanderbilt Law Review* 45, no. 3 (1992): 536–538.

37. Given my definition of sports officials in Chapter 3, we need not limit investigation of judicial virtues to judges in the strict sense. For instance, Hock Lai Ho investigates virtues that apply to jurors related to tasks like fact-finding and deliberation. These virtues seem applicable to sports officials as well. See Ho, "Virtuous Deliberation on the Criminal Verdict," in *Law, Virtue and Justice*, ed. Amalia Amaya and Hock Lai Ho (Oxford: Hart Publishing, 2013).

38. Lawrence B. Solum, "A Tournament of Virtue," *Florida State University Law Review* 32, no. 4 (2005): 1368.
39. Ibid., 1368–1369.
40. Farrelly and Solum, "Aretaic Theories," 7.
41. Solum, "Tournament," 1373.
42. Fesmire, *Dewey*, 65.
43. Ibid., 70.
44. Lawrence B. Solum, "The Aretaic Turn in Constitutional Theory," *Brooklyn Law Review* 70, no. 2 (2005): 510. See also Lawrence B. Solum, "Virtue Jurisprudence: A Virtue-Centered Theory of Judging," *Metaphilosophy* 34, no. 1/2 (2003): 192–194.
45. Solum, "Tournament," 1385.
46. Solum, "Virtue-Centered," 198. See also Lawrence B. Solum, "Natural Justice: An Aretaic Account of the Virtue of Lawfulness," in *Virtue Jurisprudence*, ed. Colin Farrelly and Lawrence B. Solum (London: Palgrave Macmillan, 2008), 180.
47. Claudio Michelon advocates a conception of practical wisdom that addresses the gap between universals and particulars. But he cautions, "It is clear that legal decision-making is not simply to be subsumed under general practical wisdom. Any conception of law and legal decision-making that is of any use to us must acknowledge the fact of positive law." Michelon, "Practical Wisdom in Legal Decision-Making," in *Law, Virtue and Justice*, ed. Amalia Amaya and Hock Lai Ho (Oxford: Hart Publishing, 2013), 48.
48. R. A. Duff, "The Limits of Virtue Jurisprudence," *Metaphilosophy* 34, no. 1/2 (2003): 221–222.
49. Antony Duff, "Virtue, Vice, and Criminal Liability," in *Virtue Jurisprudence*, ed. Colin Farrelly and Lawrence B. Solum (London: Palgrave Macmillan, 2008), 208–209.
50. One might approach the rules applied in Woods' case in a pragmatist manner similar to that I sketched concerning video replay review. By allowing television viewers to call in infractions, the USGA created a chaotic, unpredictable system. That unknowable penalties could be applied after the round precludes players from understanding their actions or making appropriate redress, hindering their ability to act effectively. Nevertheless, this recognition would not entirely resolve the complications surrounding the adjudication of the Woods' situation, since it does not address how the committee reached its decision. So we should consider what good judging might look like in such a case.
51. Mark Hamilton, "The Moral Ambiguity of the Makeup Call," *Journal of the Philosophy of Sport* 38, no. 2 (2011): 218.
52. Ibid.
53. Hamilton offers some psychological reasons that calls do not get overturned, such as that officials do not want to look inept or amateurish. Ibid., 215. The virtues of judging suggest that an official should overcome pride in order to make the best available call.
54. Sometimes the label of makeup call is applied to 50/50 cases, and it is suggested that if the official gives the benefit of the doubt to one team, the next time the

official should lean the other way. I don't consider these to be makeup calls because the official does not know whether or not she erred in the first place. Moreover, I find nothing wrong with alternating 50/50 calls, just as many basketball leagues alternate possession rather than employing jump balls.

55. Hamilton, "Makeup Call," 222.

56. Ibid., 224.

Conclusion

The interference call on Trea Turner in the 2019 World Series underscored a number of philosophical questions about the nature of sport, the contribution of elements like rules and traditions of sport, the interpretation and enforcement of rules, and how to explain the practice of sport while keeping an eye toward how it ought to be played. In the process of developing and defending sport realism as a new theory of sport, I hope to have provided some answers along with meaningful contributions to the ongoing discussion of these and similar questions. Sport realism draws upon aspects of legal theory to characterize sport in terms of its operations, with particular focus on how sport officials adjudicate disputes. A quick sketch of how sport realism analyzes the Turner call will highlight some key features of my theory.

Explanation of the interference call begins with identification of the situation type. Players regularly run to first without remaining entirely in the runner's lane, and this rarely gets noticed. It becomes a problem only when a subsequent action brings attention to the runner's location, such as when a throw hits the runner or, as in this case, the first baseman fails to catch the ball. Therefore, the relevant situation type involves these occurrences where fielders do not make the play successfully. Here we must acknowledge that an umpire has a more detailed understanding of the situation type based on their recognition of past situations. The sport realist may consider whether being in the World Series changes the situation type—those involved with sport sometimes insist that games are called differently when the stakes are more important, such as late in a game or during playoffs. I suspect there is little evidence of this in baseball. Nonetheless, the main point is that participants want to identify patterns in order to predict what calls will be made, so they can act accordingly. To do so, they will consider all plausible influences.

In the Introduction I noted various complications to the baserunning and interference rules, such as the requirement that the runner step back toward the field while stretching for the base. Still, interference seems to be the call made most often in this kind of situation. I argue that this is not rooted in any unwritten rule or convention. Instead, through sport realist analysis, it is based on a recognition of what facts umpires actually respond to. When the runner is not in the runner's lane and the ball does not make it into the first baseman's glove, we can predict that interference will be the most likely call. For players, coaches, and fans, this is the most important consideration, as they need to know how future instances of this kind of dispute will be addressed in order to modify behavior and act accordingly.

Sport realism can apply the ethical considerations outlined in Chapter 5 for normative analysis of the Turner play. On a pragmatist standard of what constitutes successful action, it is evident that changes are needed. It is confusing that a runner cannot take the most direct route to first base, with a right-handed batter needing to move into the runner's lane. Runners then swerve back toward fair territory as they reach the base, with the runner and fielder needing to occupy the same space. This problem may be minimized with larger bases or a different configuration. For example, current MLB player Kyle Schwarber tweeted a suggestion to add another part of first base in foul territory, as is often done in youth baseball and softball, to "make it clear where to touch the bag in FOUL territory."[1] In some instances, umpires might gain clarity through replay. Currently interference is a judgment call, so umpires are not allowed to review what happened. Earlier I advised that increased usage of replay might make sport less predictable. Yet surely there are some cases where clarity is gained by watching the play again. Since many umpire rulings require judgment, it seems curious to restrict the tool of replay based on a fuzzy notion of judgment.

Some circumstances surrounding the Turner call are simply odd. The umpires spent significant time on the phone to New York, which is how replays are usually performed. Since the play was not reviewable, the conversation was described as a consultation with officials, though the umpires should have already known the relevant rules. Meanwhile, chief baseball officer Joe Torre was sitting in the stands nearby. He was not called on for consultation, and his subsequent statement was unclear. None of this was a good look for MLB. Additional transparency is critical for future MLB decisions, so that participants may better predict how decisions will be made by all relevant sport officials.

I have maintained that this desire of participants to understand how sport is played should reorient theories toward the operation of sports. The written rules, unwritten rules, and conventions of sport are important features, but sport cannot be wholly defined by any of these. A theory of sport needs to examine sport as it is actually played, with the recognition that decisions made by officials sometimes deviate from rules and conventions in particular situations and depending on the facts of the case. Sport realists are skeptical of rules and other formal features of sport, but only in pursuit of patterns of decision-making. Reasoning done by sports officials has other inputs or influences, akin to non-legal reasons, which must be accounted for. Moreover, it is unlikely that officials decide most hard cases through a principled sense of integrity or a conception of the sport.

Sport realism focuses on how sport officials make decisions, resolve disputes, and mete out punishments. Even sports without institutions have individuals who function as officials. Therefore, sport realism is applicable to sports of all kinds at different levels, professional to amateur, well-organized to pick-up game. Against any connotation some may find between realism and cynicism or relativism, I have shown how sport realism can provide normative standards and direction. If anything, sport realism provides a clearer account of wrong action in sport by showing how wrongness is not always coextensive with immorality. By exploring which actions would be given certain kinds of sanctions, we come to better understand the sport activity. Finally, sport realism promotes reform of sport in the pursuit of justice, especially when rules are outdated or stagnant, just as was the interest of many legal realists in reforming the law.

My defense of sport realism examined three contexts in which sport realism meets the needs of a theory of sport: case studies, conceptual analysis, and normative guidance. I argued that sport realism best explains an array of hard cases that other theories struggle with, it provides a valuable framework for investigation of important philosophical concepts like cheating, and it has the resources to provide paths forward in challenging situations. I intend the theory to stand on its own accomplishments. Additionally, I have demonstrated various ways my theory supersedes other theories in hard cases and philosophical analysis, giving it further appeal. Interpretivism, conventionalism, and formalism are all broad frameworks that have been defended and adapted by many philosophers of sport. Though these have attractive features, I find that all fall short on their merits, and that sport realism is comparatively advantageous to each.

To make clear the relative success of sport realism as a theory of sport, I want to revisit Eliud Kipchoge's run at the INEOS 1:59 Challenge. In 2019 Kipchoge ran 26.2 miles in 1:59:40, which would be a world record for the marathon. The record time was not accepted by World Athletics due to the unprecedented organization and support that Kipchoge received during the run. I claimed that a theory of sport is essential for cases like this as we sort through our own attitudes. At the end of Chapter 1, I suggested that traditional versions of formalism and conventionalism provide only surface-level analysis of the event. Interpretivism offers a deeper justification for discounting Kipchoge's run, grounded in a conception of the spirit or purpose of a marathon. However, the interpretivist answer faces familiar questions about identifying the purpose and excellences of the activity, while navigating the tension between general and particular interpretations. Kipchoge's 1:59:40 seemingly reflects many excellences of the marathon. Despite the extra work put into arranging the race and providing support, the physical accomplishment was largely his own. He did not avoid the primary obstacles of the activity. In general, breaking records in distance running is largely a matter of choosing an event at a desirable place and time, then building up to the attempt; they are rarely organic occurrences.

Sport realism looks at the question of Kipchoge's run as a practical problem. We are not likely to find a definitive set of standards to delineate between official and unofficial records. The excellences of the sport are matters of debate, and they have changed over the last few decades. Even the fact that Kipchoge had no official competitor may not be a reason to discount his time. After all, the challenge of running sub-2:00 over 26.2 miles does not necessarily become easier due to no other entrants. Thus, we should not look for a single feature to provide an easy answer. Rather, we should investigate the reasons and stimuli that led officials to make their assessment. Officials may have acted on some understanding of the written rules or principles, but it might be that other contextual factors such as economic considerations or worries about future consequences were influential. Among these are that officials likely wanted to avoid opening up a can of worms with new events outside the usual calendar of international marathons, which would make it even more difficult for World Athletics to keep track of which records are "official."

Kipchoge and other marathoners want to predict decisions so they can adjust accordingly. They are in the position of the "bad athlete," an example I made that is analogous to Oliver Wendell Holmes, Jr.'s "bad man." This is not to say they are doing anything wrong in assessing the conditions that will or won't count as record-breaking. But they do want to know whether they will be credited or held liable for their work. To this end, I don't consider Kipchoge's run an instance of cheating or a wrong action, even though it was outside the regulations of World Athletics. There is no expected sanction for the event; the run just doesn't count in their official records.

Since a goal is to anticipate how officials will view future runs, we can use Kipchoge as a data point in looking for a pattern or delineating the situation type. We would be best served by reaching some pragmatic agreement regarding the allowable conditions and organization, acknowledging that these factors are not entirely internal to sport. For now, World Athletics has indicated that official records must be run in an event with other runners and minimal pacing. The schedule must be set in advance, and not shifted for the main purpose of record-breaking performance. If event times are shifted due to other concerns, such as athlete safety, they may be treated differently. This happened at the 2020 U.S. Olympic Trials for track and field in Eugene, Oregon, where some events were moved due to conditions of extreme heat.[2]

The legitimacy of the trials was not questioned. Perhaps events like the INEOS 1:59 Challenge are rare enough that they do not disrupt the ability of runners to identify official or unofficial conditions. But if more events like this are created, and sport officials do not provide consistent adjudication, successful action in the context of the marathon will be undermined.

Hard cases like Kipchoge's run occur often in sport, and they can be viewed usefully through a theoretical framework. My hope is that this book advances our understanding of sport, including the nature of officiating and accounts of wrongness that are integral to sport. I utilized core ideas in sport and legal realism to construct a more appropriate way to think about how sport is actually played, with an eye to relevant similarities between sport and law. I have advocated for a reexamination of how we conceive of good decisions and judgments in the context of sport. And I have emphasized the importance of transparency in how rules officials make decisions, which promotes coherence in action and should aid attempts to resolve injustices. Sport realism should not be taken to preclude other attitudes that participants of sport may have. Those involved in sport likely find it meaningful for all sorts of reasons beyond those described here. But sport realism, in my view, provides the most efficacious framework to explain sport and guide its development, so as to not lose touch with sport as it is.

NOTES

1. Shanna McCarriston, "World Series 2019: Kate Upton, Kyle Schwarber, Others React to Bizarre Interference Call in Game 6," *CBSSports.com*, October 30, 2019, https://www.cbssports.com/mlb/news/world-series-2019-kate-upton-kyle-schwarber-others-react-to-bizarre-interference-call-in-game-6/.

2. The 2020 U.S. Olympic Trials in track and field took place June 18–27, 2021, since the 2020 Olympics were delayed for a year due to the COVID-19 pandemic.

Bibliography

Aikin, Scott F., and Robert B. Talisse. *Pragmatism, Pluralism, and the Nature of Philosophy*. New York: Routledge, 2018.

Alexander, Gregory S. "Comparing Two Legal Realisms—American and Scandinavian." *American Journal of Comparative Law* 50, no. 1 (2002): 131–174.

Anderson, R. J. "World Series: What MLB Rulebook Says about Bizarre Interference Call Against Nationals' Trea Turner." *CBSSports.com*, October 30, 2019. https://www.cbssports.com/mlb/news/world-series-what-mlb-rulebook-says-about-bizarre-interference-call-against-nationals-trea-turner/.

Atry, Ashkan, Hansson, Mats G., and Ulrik Kihlbom. "Cheating is the Name of the Game—Conventional Cheating Arguments Fail to Articulate Moral Response to Doping." *Physical Cultures and Sport. Studies and Research* 59, no. 1 (2013): 21–32.

Bale, John. "How Much of a Hero? The Fractured Image of Roger Bannister." In *The Four-Minute Mile*, edited by John Bale and P. David Howe, 45–57. London: Routledge, 2008.

Bale, John, and P. David Howe. "Introduction: The Sporting Barrier: Historical and Cultural Interpretations of the Four-Minute Mile." In *The Four-Minute Mile*, edited by John Bale and P. David Howe, 1–6. London: Routledge, 2008.

Balkin, Jack M., and Sanford Levinson. "The 'Bad Man,' the Good, and the Self-Reliant." *Boston University Law Review* 78, no. 3 (1998): 885–902.

Barnwell, Bill. "Divisional Wrap-Up: A Crop of Classics." *Grantland*, January 12, 2015. https://grantland.com/the-triangle/nfl-divisional-cowboys-packers-panthers-seahawks-colts-broncos-patriots-ravens/.

Bascomb, Neal. *The Perfect Mile*. Boston: Houghton Mifflin, 2004.

Baumann, Michael. "The Trea Turner Interference Call Didn't Sway Game 6—but It Will Go Down As the Defining, Bewildering Image of the 2019 World Series." *The Ringer*, October 30, 2019. https://www.theringer.com/mlb-playoffs/2019/10/30/20939580/washington-nationals-houston-astros-world-series-trea-turner-interference-call.

Berg, Adam. "The Ethos of Excellence." *Journal of the Philosophy of Sport* 42, no. 2 (2015): 233–249.

Berg, Ted. "Pine Tar Still isn't a Big Deal, but Michael Pineda Deserves his Suspension." *USA Today*, April 24, 2014. https://ftw.usatoday.com/2014/04/michael-pineda-pine-tar-suspension-new-york-yankees-mlb.

Berman, Mitchell N. "On Interpretivism and Formalism in Sports Officiating: From General to Particular Jurisprudence." *Journal of the Philosophy of Sport* 38, no. 2 (2011): 177–196.

———. "Why Sport Illuminates Law (and Vice Versa)." *New York Law School Law Review* 63, no. 2 (2019): 235–248.

Bisceglio, Paul. "The Greatest, Fakest World Record." *The Atlantic*, October 13, 2019. https://www.theatlantic.com/health/archive/2019/10/kipchoges-sub-two-hour-marathon-how-legitimate-it/599974/.

Blake, William D. "Pine Tar and the Infield Fly Rule: An Umpire's Perspective on the Hart-Dworkin Jurisprudential Debate." In *The Cooperstown Symposium on Baseball and American Culture: 2013–2014*, edited by William J. Simons, 244–257. Jefferson City, NC: McFarland, 2015.

Bordner, S. Seth. "Call 'Em as they are: What's Wrong with Blown Calls and What to do about them." *Journal of the Philosophy of Sport* 42, no. 1 (2015): 101–120.

Boren, Cindy. "Michael Pineda Ejected for Pine Tar, Leaving Yankees with a Sticky Situation." *Washington Post*, April 24, 2014. https://www.washingtonpost.com/news/early-lead/wp/2014/04/24/michael-pineda-ejected-for-pine-tar-leaving-yankees-with-a-mess/.

Boswell, Thomas. "Tiger Woods Deserved Penalty, Not Disqualification, at 2013 Masters." *Washington Post*, April 13, 2013. https://www.washingtonpost.com/sports/othersports/tiger-woods-deserved-penalty-not-disqualificiation-at-2013-masters/2013/04/13/539c180c-a486-11e2-be47-b44febada3a8_story.html.

Budiansky, Stephen. *Oliver Wendell Holmes: A Life in War, Law, and Ideas*. New York: W. W. Norton & Company, 2019.

Butcher, Robert, and Angela Schneider. "Fair Play as Respect for the Game." *Journal of the Philosophy of Sport* 25, no. 1 (1998): 1–22.

Ciomaga, Bogdan. "Conventionalism Revisited." *Sport, Ethics and Philosophy* 6, no. 4 (2012): 410–422.

Collins, Harry. "The Philosophy of Umpiring and the Introduction of Decision-Aid Technology." *Journal of the Philosophy of Sport* 37, no. 2 (2010): 135–146.

D'Agostino, Fred. "The Ethos of Games." *Journal of the Philosophy of Sport* 8, no. 1 (1981): 7–18.

Dagan, Hanoch. *Reconstructing American Legal Realism & Rethinking Private Law Theory*. Oxford: Oxford University Press, 2013.

De Been, Wouter. *Legal Realism Regained*. Stanford, CA: Stanford University Press, 2008.

Delattre, Edwin J. "Some Reflections on Success and Failure in Competitive Athletics." *Journal of the Philosophy of Sport* 2, no. 1 (1975): 133–139.

Dixon, Nicholas. "Canadian Figure Skaters, French Judges, and Realism in Sport." *Journal of the Philosophy of Sport* 30, no. 2 (2003): 103–116.

Duff, R. A. "The Limits of Virtue Jurisprudence." *Metaphilosophy* 34, no. 1/2 (2003): 214–224.

———. "Virtue, Vice, and Criminal Liability." In *Virtue Jurisprudence*, edited by Colin Farrelly and Lawrence B. Solum, 193–213. London: Palgrave Macmillan, 2008.

Dworkin, Ronald. *Law's Empire*. Cambridge, MA: Harvard University Press, 1986.

———. *A Matter of Principle*. Cambridge, MA: Harvard University Press, 1985.

———. *Taking Rights Seriously*. Cambridge, MA: Harvard University Press, 1977.

Easson, Simon. "Games, Rules, and Contracts." In *Ethics and Sport*, edited by Mike McNamee and Jim Parry, 57–78. London: E & FN Spon, 1998.

Elcombe, Tim L., and Alun R. Hardman. "Pragmatic Conventionalism and Sport Normativity in the Face of Intractable Dilemmas." *Journal of the Philosophy of Sport* 47, no. 1 (2020): 14–32.

Farber, Daniel A. "The Inevitability of Practical Reason: Statutes, Formalism, and the Rule of Law." *Vanderbilt Law Review* 45, no. 3 (1992): 533–559.

Farrelly, Colin, and Lawrence B. Solum. "An Introduction to Aretaic Theories of Law." In *Virtue Jurisprudence*, edited by Colin Farrelly and Lawrence B. Solum, 1–23. London: Palgrave Macmillan, 2008.

Feezell, Randolph. "Baseball, Cheating, and Tradition: Would Kant Cork His Bat?" In *Baseball and Philosophy*, edited by Eric Bronson, 109–125. Chicago: Open Court, 2004.

———. "On the Wrongness of Cheating and Why Cheaters Can't Play the Game." *Journal of the Philosophy of Sport* 15, no. 1 (1988): 57–68.

———. *Playing Games*. London: Routledge, 2017.

———. "Sportsmanship." *Journal of the Philosophy of Sport* 13, no. 1 (1986): 1–13.

Fesmire, Steven. *John Dewey and Moral Imagination*. Bloomington: Indiana University Press, 2003.

Fisher, William W. III, Morton J. Horwitz, and Thomas A. Reed. "Introduction." In *American Legal Realism*, edited by William W. Fisher III, Morton J. Horwitz, and Thomas A. Reed, xi–xv. Oxford: Oxford University Press, 1993.

Foust, Mathew A. "Where Should LeBron's Loyalty Lie? Where Should Ours?" In *Pragmatism and the Philosophy of Sport*, edited by Richard Lally, Douglas Anderson, and John Kaag, 77–88. Lanham, MD: Lexington Books, 2013.

Fraleigh, Warren P. "Intentional Rules Violation—One More Time." *Journal of the Philosophy of Sport* 30, no. 2 (2003): 166–176.

Gardner, Roger. "On Performance-Enhancing Substances and the Unfair Advantage Argument." *Journal of the Philosophy of Sport* 16, no. 1 (1989): 59–73.

Gasper, Christopher L. "What a Foolish Mistake by Michael Pineda." *The Boston Globe*, April 24, 2014. http://www.bostonglobe.com/sports/2014/04/23/yankees-pitcher-michael-pineda-ejected-what-sticky-situation/bi1m0aruFUrLekQTeaFy7L/story.html.

Glenney, Brian. "Skateboarding, Sport, and Spontaneity: Toward a Subversive Definition of Sport." In *Defining Sport*, edited by Shawn E. Klein, 147–158. Lanham, MD: Lexington Books, 2016.

Golding, Martin P. "Realism and Functionalism in the Legal Thought of Felix S. Cohen." *Cornell Law Review* 66, no. 5 (1981): 1032–1057.

Green, Stuart P. "Cheating." *Law and Philosophy* 23, no. 2 (2004): 137–185.

Guinness World Records. "Eliud Kipchoge." *GuinnessWorldRecords.com*. Accessed November 28, 2021. https://www.guinnessworldrecords.com/records/hall-of-fame/eliud-kipchoge-fastest-marathon-distance-male.

Hamilton, Mark. "The Moral Ambiguity of the Makeup Call." *Journal of the Philosophy of Sport* 38, no. 2 (2011): 212–228.

Harper, Aaron. "'You're the Best Around': An Argument for Playoffs and Tournaments." *Journal of the Philosophy of Sport* 43, no. 2 (2016): 295–309.

Hart, H. L. A. *The Concept of Law*. 3rd ed. Oxford: Oxford University Press, 2012.

Ho, Hock Lai. "Virtuous Deliberation on the Criminal Verdict." In *Law, Virtue and Justice*, edited by Amalia Amaya and Hock Lai Ho, 241–263. Oxford: Hart Publishing, 2013.

Hoch, Bryan. "Pineda Gets 10-game Suspension for Pine Tar on Neck." *MLB.com*, April 24, 2014. https://www.mlb.com/news/yankees-michael-pineda-gets-10-game-suspension-for-using-pine-tar/c-73202466.

Hochstetler, Douglas R. "Process and the Sport Experience." In *Pragmatism and the Philosophy of Sport*, edited by Richard Lally, Douglas Anderson, and John Kaag, 17–31. Lanham, MD: Lexington Books, 2013.

Hochstetler, Douglas, and Peter Matthew Hopsicker. "The Heights of Humanity: Endurance Sport and the Strenuous Mood." *Journal of the Philosophy of Sport* 39, no. 1 (2012): 117–135.

Holmes, Oliver Wendell, Jr. "The Path of the Law." *Harvard Law Review* 10, no. 8 (1897): 457–478.

Holowchak, M. Andrew, and Heather L. Reid. *Aretism*. Lanham, MD: Lexington Books, 2011.

Howe, Leslie. "Gamesmanship." *Journal of the Philosophy of Sport* 31, no. 2 (2004): 212–225.

Jones, Carwyn. "Doping in Cycling: Realism, Antirealism and Ethical Deliberation." *Journal of the Philosophy of Sport* 37, no. 1 (2010): 88–101.

Kalman, Laura. *Legal Realism at Yale: 1927–1960*. Chapel Hill: University of North Carolina Press, 1986.

Kay, Emily. "USGA, R&A Clarify Tiger Woods' Masters Ball-drop Ruling." *SBNation.com*, May 1, 2013. https://www.sbnation.com/golf/2013/5/1/4289788/tiger-woods-masters-ball-drop-ruling-usga-ra.

Kellogg, Frederic R. *Oliver Wendell Holmes, Jr., Legal Theory, and Judicial Restraint*. Cambridge: Cambridge University Press, 2007.

Kirkwood, Ken. "What Do You Mean I Wasn't Cheating? Testing the Concept of Cheating Through a Case of Failed Doping." *Sports, Ethics and Philosophy* 8, no. 1 (2014): 57–64.

Koons, Jeremy Randel. *Pragmatic Reasons*. London: Palgrave Macmillan, 2009.

Koopman, Colin. *Pragmatism as Transition*. New York: Columbia University Press, 2009.

Kretchmar, Scott. "Pluralistic Internalism." *Journal of the Philosophy of Sport* 42, no. 1 (2015): 83–100.

Lally, Richard. "Deweyan Pragmatism and Self-Cultivation." In *Pragmatism and the Philosophy of Sport*, edited by Richard Lally, Douglas Anderson, and John Kaag, 175–198. Lanham, MD: Lexington Books, 2013.

Lauber, Scott. "Nieves: Red Sox Pitchers 'Don't Have to Worry' About Being Accused of Using Illegal Substances." *Boston Herald*, April 24, 2014. https://www.bostonherald.com/2014/04/24/nieves-red-sox-pitchers-dont-have-to-worry-about-being-accused-of-using-illegal-substances/.

Leaman, Oliver. "Cheating and Fair Play in Sport." In *Ethics in Sport*. 2nd ed., edited by William J. Morgan, 201–207. Champaign, IL: Human Kinetics, 2007.

Lehman, Craig K. "Can Cheaters Play the Game?" *Journal of the Philosophy of Sport* 8, no. 1 (1981): 41–46.

Leiter, Brian. *Naturalizing Jurisprudence*. Oxford: Oxford University Press, 2007.

Lengel, David. "Tar for the Course." *The Guardian*, April 24, 2014. https://www.theguardian.com/sport/blog/2014/apr/24/pine-tar-for-the-course-yankees-pitcher-michael-pineda-busted-for-using-foreign-substance.

Lenta, Patrick, and Simon Beck. "A Sporting Dilemma and Its Jurisprudence." *Journal of the Philosophy of Sport* 33, no. 2 (2006): 125–143.

Llewellyn, Karl N. *The Bramble Bush*. Oxford: Oxford University Press, (1930) 2008.

———. *The Common Law Tradition: Deciding Appeals*. Boston: Little, Brown and Company, 1960.

Lochner v. New York, 198 U.S. 45 (1905).

Loland, Sigmund. "Fair Play: Historical Anachronism or Topical Ideal?" In *Ethics and Sport*, edited by Mike McNamee and Jim Parry, 79–103. London: E & FN Spon, 1998.

———. "The Varieties of Cheating—Comments on Ethical Analyses in Sport." *Sport in Society* 8, no. 1 (2005): 11–26.

López Frías, Francisco Javier. "Broad Internalism and Interpretation: A Plurality of Interpretivist Approaches." In *Defining Sport*, edited by Shawn E. Klein, 22–44. Lanham, MD: Lexington Books, 2016.

MacRae, Sinclair. "Toward a Shallow Interpretivist Model of Sport." *Journal of the Philosophy of Sport* 44, no. 3 (2017): 285–299.

Martin, Michael. *Legal Realism: American and Scandinavian*. New York: Peter Lang Publishing, Inc., 1997.

"Masters 2013: Tiger Woods Given Two-shot Masters Penalty." *BBC.com*, April 13, 2013. http://www.bbc.com/sport/golf/22134938.

McCarriston, Shanna. "World Series 2019: Kate Upton, Kyle Schwarber, Others React to Bizarre Interference Call in Game 6." *CBSSports.com*, October 30, 2019. https://www.cbssports.com/mlb/news/world-series-2019-kate-upton-kyle-schwarber-others-react-to-bizarre-interference-call-in-game-6/.

McGuire, Bernie. "Padraig Harrington Disqualified Over Marker Incident." *Reuters*, January 21, 2011. https://www.reuters.com/article/us-golf-european-harrington/padraig-harrington-disqualified-over-marker-incident-idUSTRE70K1LS20110121.

Meier, Klaus V. "Triad Trickery: Playing With Sport and Games." *Journal of the Philosophy of Sport* 15, no. 1 (1988): 11–30.

Michelon, Claudio. "Practical Wisdom in Legal Decision-Making." In *Law, Virtue and Justice*, edited by Amalia Amaya and Hock Lai Ho, 29–49. Oxford: Hart Publishing, 2013.

Moore, Eric. "Against Deep Conventionalism." *Journal of the Philosophy of Sport* 45, no. 3 (2018): 228–240.

Moore, Kristina. "Box Score: Calling 'Balls and Strikes' at Sotomayor's Confirmation Hearing." *SCOTUSBlog*, July 13, 2009. https://www.scotusblog.com/2009/07/box-score-calling-balls-and-strikes-at-sotomayors-confirmation-hearing/.

Morgan, William J. "Broad Internalism, Deep Conventions, Moral Entrepreneurs, and Sport." *Journal of the Philosophy of Sport* 39, no. 1 (2012): 65–100.

———. "Conventionalism Defended: A Reply to Moore." *Journal of the Philosophy of Sport* 46, no. 1 (2019): 98–107.

———. "Interpretivism, Conventionalism, and the Ethical Coach." In *The Ethics of Coaching Sports*, edited by Robert L. Simon, 61–77. Boulder, CO: Westview Press, 2013.

———. "The Logical Incompatibility Thesis and Rules: A Reconsideration of Formalism as an Account of Games." *Journal of the Philosophy of Sport* 14, no. 1 (1987): 1–20.

———. "Moral Antirealism, Internalism, and Sport." *Journal of the Philosophy of Sport* 31, no. 2 (2004): 161–183.

———. "The Normativity of Sport: A Historicist Take on Broad Internalism." *Journal of the Philosophy of Sport* 43, no. 1 (2016): 27–39.

———. *Sport and Moral Conflict*. Philadelphia: Temple University Press, 2020.

———. *Why Sports Morally Matter*. New York: Routledge, 2006.

Muskat, Carrie. "Dave Kingman Proved What Goes Up Does Not Necessarily. . . . " *United Press International*, May 5, 1984. http://www.upi.com/Archives/1984/05/05/Dave-Kingman-proved-what-goes-up-does-not-necessarily/4771452577600/.

Noë, Alva. *Infinite Baseball*. Oxford: Oxford University Press, 2019.

O'Connor, Ian. "Why Phil Mickelson Should Apologize, Then Withdraw from the U. S. Open." *ESPN.com*, June 16, 2018. http://www.espn.com/golf/story/_/id/23815139/phil-mickelson-withdraw-us-open-bizarre-display-13th-hole-shinnecock-hills.

Office of the Commissioner of Baseball. *Official Baseball Rulebook*. Major League Baseball 2014 Edition. http://mlb.mlb.com/mlb/downloads/y2014/official_baseball_rules.pdf.

———. *Official Baseball Rules*. Major League Baseball 2019 Edition. https://content.mlb.com/documents/2/2/4/305750224/2019_Official_Baseball_Rules_FINAL_.pdf.

Papineau, David. *Knowing the Score*. New York: Basic Books, 2017.

Passan, Jeff. "Houston Astros' AJ Hinch Sides with Washington Nationals' Trea Turner on Controversial Game 6 Call." *ESPN.com*, October 30, 2019. https://www.espn.com/mlb/story/_/id/27968971/houston-astros-aj-hinch-sides-washington-nationals-trea-turner-controversial-game-6-call.

Pearson, Kathleen M. "Deception, Sportsmanship, and Ethics." In *Sport Ethics: An Anthology*, edited by Jan Boxill, 81–83. Malden, MA: Blackwell Publishing, 2003.

Ratnapala, Suri. *Jurisprudence*. 2nd ed. Cambridge: Cambridge University Press, 2013.

Riggs v. Palmer, 115 N.Y. 506, 22 N.E. 188 (1889).

Roan, Dan. "Nike Vaporfly Shoes are Not Banned but Kipchoge's Are." *BBC.com*, January 31, 2021. https://www.bbc.com/sport/athletics/51324991.

Russell, J.S. "Are Rules All an Umpire Has to Work With?" *Journal of the Philosophy of Sport* 26, no. 1 (1999): 27–49.

———. "Broad Internalism and the Moral Foundations of Sport." In *Ethics in Sport*. 2nd ed., edited by William J. Morgan, 51–66. Champaign, IL: Human Kinetics, 2007.

———. "A Critique of Conventionalist Broad Internalism." *Sport, Ethics and Philosophy* 12, no. 4 (2018): 453–467.

———. "Is There a Normatively Distinct Concept of Cheating in Sport (or Anywhere Else)?" *Journal of the Philosophy of Sport* 41, no. 3 (2014): 303–323.

———. "Limitations of the Sport-Law Comparison." *Journal of the Philosophy of Sport* 38, no. 2 (2011): 254–272.

———. "Moral Realism in Sport." *Journal of the Philosophy of Sport* 31, no. 2 (2004): 142–160.

Schermer, Maartje. "On the Argument that Enhancement is 'Cheating.'" *Journal of Medical Ethics* 34, no. 2 (2008): 85–88.

Schwartz, Nick. "World Series: MLB Players, Fans Rage Over Controversial Interference Call." *USA Today*, October 29, 2019. https://ftw.usatoday.com/2019/10/world-series-interference-call-reaction.

Sens, Josh. "Final Version of New Rules of Golf Include Significant Changes that Affect Everyday Golfers." *Golf.com*, March 11, 2018. http://www.golf.com/tour-news/2018/03/11/usga-unveils-final-version-proposed-rules-golf-main-changes-affecting-everyday-golfer.

Simon, Robert L. "The Ethical Coach: An Interpretive Account of the Ethics of Coaching." In *The Ethics of Coaching Sports*, edited by Robert L. Simon, 41–59. Boulder, CO: Westview Press, 2013.

———. "From Ethnocentrism to Realism: Can Discourse Ethics Bridge the Gap?" *Journal of the Philosophy of Sport* 31, no. 2 (2004): 122–141.

———. "Internalism and Internal Values in Sport." *Journal of the Philosophy of Sport* 27, no. 1 (2000): 1–16.

Simon, Robert L., Cesar R. Torres, and Peter F. Hager. *Fair Play: The Ethics of Sport*. 4th ed. Boulder, CO: Westview Press, 2015.

Solum, Lawrence B. "The Aretaic Turn in Constitutional Theory." *Brooklyn Law Review* 70, no. 2 (2005): 475–532.

———. "Natural Justice: An Aretaic Account of the Virtue of Lawfulness." In *Virtue Jurisprudence*, edited by Colin Farrelly and Lawrence B. Solum, 167–192. London: Palgrave Macmillan, 2008.

———. "A Tournament of Virtue." *Florida State University Law Review* 32, no. 4 (2005): 1365–1400.

———. "Virtue Jurisprudence: A Virtue-Centered Theory of Judging." *Metaphilosophy* 34, no. 1/2 (2003): 178–213.

Spiegel, Jackie. "Stefanos Tsitsipas and Bathroom Breaks: Explaining 2021 US Open's Biggest Controversy." *Sporting News*, September 2, 2021. https://www.sportingnews.com/us/tennis/news/stefanos-tsitsipas-bathroom-breaks-explaining-2021-us-opens-controversy/djk9ak3td65h1wzrunwkp4swt.

Suits, Bernard. "The Elements of Sport." In *The Philosophy of Sport: A Collection of Essays*, edited by Robert Osterhoudt, 48–64. Springfield, IL: Charles C. Thomas, 1973.

———. *The Grasshopper: Games, Life and Utopia*. Peterborough, Ontario: Broadview Press, 2005.

Tamburrini, Claudio. "The 'Hand of God'?" In *The Ethics of Sports*, edited by Mike McNamee, 132–144. London: Routledge, 2010.

Torres, Cesar R. "Furthering Interpretivism's Integrity: Bringing Together Ethics and Aesthetics." *Journal of the Philosophy of Sport* 39, no. 2 (2012): 299–319.

———. "What is Wrong With Playing High?" *Journal of the Philosophy of Sport* 36, no. 1 (2009): 1–21.

Torres, Cesar R., and Peter F. Hager. "Competition, Ethics, and Coaching Youth." In *The Ethics of Coaching Sports*, edited by Robert L. Simon, 167–184. Boulder, CO: Westview Press, 2013.

———. "The Desirability of the Season Long Tournament: A Response to Finn." *Journal of the Philosophy of Sport* 38, no. 1 (2011): 39–54.

United States Golf Association. *Decisions on the Rules of Golf 2012–2013*. The United States Golf Association and The R&A, 2011.

———. *The Rules of Golf for 2019*. R&A Rules Limited and the United States Golf Association, 2018. https://www.usga.org/content/dam/usga/images/rules/rules-modernization/golf-new-rules/Rules%20of%20Golf%20for%202019%20(Final).pdf.

U.S. Congress. Senate. Committee on the Judiciary. *Confirmation Hearing on the Nomination of Hon. Brett M. Kavanaugh to be an Associate Justice of the Supreme Court of the United States*. 115th Cong., 2nd sess., Sept. 4–7 and 27, 2018.

———. *Confirmation Hearing on the Nomination of Hon. Sonia Sotomayor to be an Associate Justice of the Supreme Court of the United States*. 111th Cong., 1st sess., July 13–16, 2009.

———. *Confirmation Hearing on the Nomination of John G. Roberts, Jr. to be Chief Justice of the United States*. 109th Cong., 1st sess., Sept. 12–15, 2005.

Vorstenbosch, Jan. "Doping and Cheating." *Journal of the Philosophy of Sport* 37, no. 2 (2010): 166–181.

Wertz, S. K. "The Varieties of Cheating." *Journal of the Philosophy of Sport* 8, no. 1 (1981): 19–40.

White, G. Edward. *Justice Oliver Wendell Holmes: Law and the Inner Self*. Oxford: Oxford University Press, 1993.

Wilson, Aaron. "Ravens Coach John Harbaugh Tried to Stop Patriots Line's 'Deception' with Penalty." *The Baltimore Sun*, January 11, 2015. https://www.baltimoresun.com/sports/orioles/bal-baltimore-ravens-coach-john-harbaugh-tries-to-stop-new-england-patriots-deception-with-penalty-20150110-story.html.

Zaremby, Justin. *Legal Realism and American Law*. New York: Bloomsbury, 2014.

Index

About the Author

Aaron Harper is associate professor of philosophy at West Liberty University.

www.ingramcontent.com/pod-product-compliance
Ingram Content Group UK Ltd.
Pitfield, Milton Keynes, MK11 3LW, UK
UKHW041838031026
15587UKWH00002B/866

9 781666 920086